D1112139

Real Federalism

Why It Matters,
How It Could Happen

Real Federalism

Why It Matters, How It Could Happen

Michael S. Greve

The AEI Press

Publisher for the American Enterprise Institute

WASHINGTON, D.C.

1999

Available in the United States from the AEI Press, c/o Publisher Resources Inc., 1224 Heil Quaker Blvd., P.O. Box 7001, La Vergne, TN 37086-7001. To order, call toll free 1-800-269-6267. Distributed outside the United States by arrangement with Eurospan, 3 Henrietta Street, London WC2E 8LU, England.

Library of Congress Cataloging-in-Publication Data

Greve, Michael S.
    Real federalism: why it matters, how it could happen /
    Michael S. Greve.
        p.   cm.
    Includes bibliographical references and index.
    ISBN 0-8447-4099-3 (cloth: alk. paper).—ISBN 0-8447-4100-0
(pbk.: alk. paper)
    1. Federal government—United States.   I. Title.
JK311.G825   1999
320.473'049—DC21   99-17225
                                                          CIP

1 3 5 7 9 10 8 6 4 2

The AEI Press
Publisher for the American Enterprise Institute
1150 17th Street, N.W., Washington, D.C. 20036

Printed in the United States of America

Contents

Acknowledgments

As orginally conceived, this book was to provide an analysis of a half-dozen recent Supreme Court decisions on federalism. Much of that analysis found its way into chapters 3, 4, and 5. Curiosity and perhaps a lack of discipline gradually prompted me to pursue a larger question: How, when, and under what circumstances is it possible to reimpose serious constitutional constraints on government?

Scholars have argued for such constraints, and think tanks and advocacy groups are engaged in their pursuit. Nonetheless, and despite the urgency of the task, we have nothing remotely resembling a systematic answer. An inquiry into the necessary conditions of all possible constitutional reconstruction (if it is feasible) is an intellectual project of near-Kantian proportions. This book, while much broader in scope than originally intended, attempts nothing so ambitious. It is a case study: What will it take to reestablish serious federalism constraints on government—now, here, and in light of the small beginnings that have been made? If my preliminary answer to this question induces more learned minds to pursue the larger project, it will have served its purpose.

Candor compels the admission that I direct the Center for Individual Rights (CIR), one among the organizations that pursue the reconstruction of constitutional norms. CIR, a public interest law firm, has served as counsel to the following cases mentioned in the book: *Brzonkala* v. *Virginia Polytechnic Institute et al.*, 132 F.3d 949 (4th Cir. 1997) (discussed on pp. 43–44); *Coalition for Economic Equity* v. *Wil-*

son, 122 F.3d 692 (9th Cir. 1997), *cert. denied,* 118 S. Ct. 17 (1997) (p. 181, n. 18); *Hopwood* v. *State of Texas,* 78 F.3d 932 (5th Cir. 1996), *cert. denied,* 518 U.S. 1033 (1996) (pp. 96, 99); and *Rosenberger* v. *Rector and Board of the University of Virginia,* 515 U.S. 819 (1995) (pp. 98, 99).

My views on these cases and on federalism's virtues and future are my own, not CIR's. Unsurprisingly, however, my perspective coincides with the interests of CIR's clients in those cases, and my remarks concerning pending cases were vetted so as to avoid a possible prejudice to CIR's and its clients' litigation positions. This thankless task was performed by Michael E. Rosman, CIR's general counsel and counsel of record in most of the above-mentioned cases.

Hans Bader, CIR's associate counsel, deserves gratitude for his capable research assistance and credit for steering me through the thicket of Eleventh Amendment law, which he falsely claims not to comprehend. For helpful comments and suggestions I am indebted to Jonathan H. Adler, Roger Clegg, Ann H. Coulter, Douglas Cox, Michael W. McConnell, Robert F. Nagel, Jeremy A. Rabkin (as always), Michael E. Rosman, and Daniel E. Troy. Leonard Leo and Eugene Volokh supplied useful comments on an early abstract of the book.

I am particularly grateful to Louisa Coan for improving me and my book in numerous ways; and to Christopher C. DeMuth for his friendship and his personal enthusiasm and support for the project. The Earhart Foundation provided generous financial support, which I gratefully acknowledge.

Alexandria, Virginia
February 1999

Real Federalism

Why It Matters,
How It Could Happen

1

Real Federalism:
What It Is, Why It Matters

I think that in the dawning centuries of democracy individual independence and local liberties will always be the products of art. Centralized government will be the natural thing.

—ALEXIS DE TOCQUEVILLE, *Democracy in America*

Recent constitutional and political developments suggest a modest federalist renewal. Supreme Court decisions since 1995 have signaled the reemergence of federalism as a constitutional principle, and the U.S. Congress has intermittently transferred federal authority to the states. From these small beginnings, I argue, bigger things may come—and should come. Six decades after federalism fell victim to the nationalist ambitions of the New Deal, it may yet be possible to reestablish decentralized, competitive political institutions and arrangements.[1]

The prospect of a federalist renaissance may seem neither very plausible nor, to ordinary citizens, terribly important. While Americans continue to profess federalist sentiments, they are less dependent on— and certainly less attached to—their state governments than at any time in the country's history. Only six of every ten Americans still live in the state where they were born; 40 percent—well over 100 million citizens—do not.[2] Many citizens relocate more than once in their lifetimes, and those who stay put usually do so for reasons other than a sentimental attachment to their home state and its government. Moral issues once thought to be the province of state or local governments, from gun control to homosexual rights, are now fought over in Washington, D.C. On economic matters, American citizens have long looked to the federal government to address the issues that most concern them.

In a thoroughly integrated national economy, one cannot easily think of a reason why people should look at matters any other way. In fact, the global economy has rendered even the *national* government less important. In November 1997 Virginians elected Governor James Gilmore on his promise of a car tax cut worth (at most) a few hundred dollars per car owner. Meanwhile, more prosperous Virginians worried that a currency crisis in faraway Asian countries might burn a deep hole in their retirement plans. The politicians in Richmond continue to command attention, chiefly because Virginians can vote them in and out of office. On a dollar-for-dollar basis, though, Asian cronyism may be more of a concern.

In this light, federalism may look like a "national neurosis," as the authors of a much-cited, opinionated law review article have put it.[3] There seems to be little point in pleading that American citizens should kindly direct their attention to Richmond or Albany instead of Washington, D.C., or, for that matter, the International Monetary Fund. Against the backdrop of an intense debate over the (perceived or real) loss of *American* sovereignty to global capitalism and international organizations, a concern for the proper role and the dignities and powers of the states seems secondary, if not wholly anachronistic.

These observations are quite sensible. But they miss what I take to be federalism's central point. The federalism I have in mind—*real* federalism—aims to provide citizens with *choices* among different sovereigns, regulatory regimes, and packages of government services. So understood, federalism does not seek to restore some elusive balance between the states and the federal government or to reinvest sovereign states with the glory they may have possessed in Andrew Jackson's days. Federalism is about *competition* among the states. It serves not so much to empower the states but to discipline them. Competitive federalism (in this sense) is not the only plausible federalism conception, and federalism may help to advance values other than choice and competition, such as civic affection or participation. But citizen choice and its salutary effects are federalism's most attractive features—the ones that command it to our attention.[4]

Citizen choice among competing jurisdictions, regulatory regimes, and packages of government services is a familiar phenomenon. It operates at all levels of government and irrespective of whether citizens consume government services as business owners, investors, workers, or for that matter as retirees or welfare recipients. The phenomenon occurs at the international level: Swedish tennis stars renounce their citizenship and establish residences in Monaco not because they prefer sunshine to saunas but because they detest confiscatory tax rates. The same dynamics operate at the national level: given a choice between right-to-work and union states, manufacturers will build plants in Tennessee rather than in Ohio. New York residents who have to pay sales taxes in Manhattan will shop in Jersey City, in turn inducing New York City to provide tax-free shopping days. At a local level, home purchasers buy not simply a building but also a stream of government services and regulations. Property tax rates, school quality, and police protection profoundly affect purchase decisions and local mobility.[5]

The citizens' ability to vote with their feet and to take their talents and assets elsewhere will discipline government in the same way in which consumer choice, in nonmonopolistic markets, disciplines producers. By harnessing competition among jurisdictions, federalism secures in the political arena the advantages of economic markets—consumer choice and satisfaction, innovation, superior products at lower prices. The comparison between private and political markets does not work without fail. For an obvious example, government monopolizes the use of force to procure public goods, precisely because private markets cannot provide them. Figuring out a set of legal and institutional constraints that reliably secure the benefits of government competition is actually difficult, and the actual operation and consequences of federalist structures are the subjects of considerable scholarly disagreement.[6] What matters for present purposes, though, are not the details but the paradigm. Compared with a monopolistic system of uniform rules, jurisdictional choice has several advantages for the consumers of government services.

Consumer Satisfaction. Consumers do not all share the same preferences. A broader range of choices will satisfy the preferences of a larger number of citizen-consumers. At the same time, centralized, uniform rules and regimes invariably produce rigidities and inefficiencies. Even with broad agreement on a given social purpose, tailoring general rules to a vast, diverse country where local circumstances and preferences vary greatly is exceedingly difficult. Federalism gives more citizens more of what they want, more of the time.

For reasons that will emerge in later chapters, it bears emphasis that the advantages of citizen choice extend not only to economic matters but also, and with equal force, to social or lifestyle issues.[7] Some people do not wish to live near homosexual enclaves or in jurisdictions that permit same-sex marriages; others like a tolerant, bohemian environment. Some people (including some smokers) feel good about themselves when banning smoking in public places; to others (including some nonsmokers), such restrictions smack of creeping fascism. Federalism permits the various constituencies to sort themselves and to go their separate ways.

Some matters are so fundamental that we do not permit any jurisdiction to provide a choice. Slavery and Jim Crow laws are obvious examples. Polygamy is another, and one can have a long, difficult debate about whether abortion should fall in that category. But the fact that we declare *some* preferences and choices off-limits should not obscure the basic principle. Jurisdictional choice provides a sensible, tolerant way of sorting out our moral differences.

Innovation. Citizen choice and government competition foster political innovation and, at the other end, tend to obliterate useless government products. To be sure, political markets rarely operate with the efficiency of economic markets, where marginally better products drive out inferior ones and small improvements are promptly imitated. In contrast to private producers of goods and services, political entities generally do not confront the disciplining possibility of a complete wipeout, and the consumers' choices among jurisdictions are not quite so convenient as their choice of a new car. In government competition as in economic markets, however, what counts is the *marginal* effect. Much as a private company will respond to competition long before it loses hordes of customers, no great migration is needed to discipline competing jurisdictions. High exit costs may dull the force of competition, but the principle and the general tendency of the effect are the same.[8]

Discipline and Constraints. Federalism disciplines and constrains government. The free movement of citizens, goods, and capital across jurisdictional boundaries tends to produce smaller government and lower regulatory standards than would a monopolistic, centralized system— not always and invariably, but on average and as a rule. When governments are forced to compete for business, investment, and productive citizens, they can ill afford to sustain costly, inefficient schemes. The exit rights are excessively powerful.

This tendency to provide a check on an unconstrained political process is to my mind federalism's chief attraction. Politically, however, it has been federalism's open flank. Jurisdictional diversity and the states' role as innovative "laboratories of democracies" have been celebrated, even by the most nationalist-minded constituencies in American politics, as federalism's genius. Federalism's competitive, disciplining effects, in contrast, have perennially been denounced as a collective action problem—a "race to the bottom," the bottom being the level of government services provided by the least intervention-minded (or least humanitarian) state. If the world were their oyster, the citizens of jurisdiction A might choose clean air level Z. In a competitive world, the need to attract business and investment may force them to settle for less.

The race-to-the-bottom argument has played a decisive role in eroding federalism. For a conspicuous example, it appears prominently in Supreme Court decisions of the 1930s and 1940s, which, as we shall see, effectively dismantled federalism's constitutional safeguards. The rationale also played an important role in the enactment of modern environmental statutes. In recent years, however, scholars have severely and persuasively criticized the conventional view that the race-to-the-bottom argument constitutes an unanswerable objection to competitive federalism.[9]

Foremost, the metaphor of a "race" conceals that the collective action problems run in several directions at once. The same competitive dynamic that may inhibit public-regarding legislation also inhibits states from legislating extortionate special-interest schemes. Many political scientists—prominently those associated with public choice theory—argue that the vast majority of ostensibly public-spirited enactments are in fact thinly disguised wealth transfers to special interest groups. Such arguments have gained wide currency, owing in part to the prevailing atmosphere of public cynicism about government. But one need not subscribe to an extreme cynicism to suspect that the benefits of forestalling interest group rackets and political redistribution exceed the costs of losing a few public goods in a "race to the bottom."[10]

Moreover, one cannot simply point to expansive, ostensibly public-regarding federal programs (for example, environmental legislation) and adduce the lack of similarly ambitious schemes in the states as evidence of a race to the bottom. This or that (hypothetical) federal scheme may be superior to a (hypothetical) world of state competition, but one cannot take this for granted. If anything, the observed rigidities and inefficiencies of much federal legislation suggest the opposite presumption, and one can in fact show that centralized decisionmaking on local matters virtually guarantees a level of government spending and taxation *in excess* of anybody's preferences.[11]

Nor is it the case that competition produces a political equilibrium only at the libertarian bottom. Some states (such as New Jersey) sport environmental regulations in excess of already demanding federal standards. Other states (such as New York and California) provide more generous remedies for employment discrimination than federal law affords. These things happen because many citizens *like* government. Some citizens welcome and appreciate government practices that strike others as outrageous intrusions. Some take exception to pedantic zoning regulations or to police officers who stop and interrogate unknown pedestrians; to others, that makes the place a neighborhood. And because government on a smaller scale can make it easier for political factions to have their way, collective experiments are often more—not less—likely to be staged and preserved at local levels. Cambridge, Massachusetts, controlled apartment rents until the issue was yanked up to the state level, where rent controls died an ignominious death. New York City's rent control laws are contested and periodically endangered in Albany; left to the city, they would probably exist in perpetuity.

In the economists' parlance, citizens have a differential willingness to pay for public goods. They also have a differential willingness to pay, through government, for someone else's welfare. Federalism inhibits political redistribution and interest groups' schemes, but it is not a prescription for a universal nightwatchman state. Far from making collective experiments impossible, federalism allows citizens to run such experiments—and to run *from* them. Federalism protects the freedom that comes from having choices.

The short of it is that the race-to-the-bottom argument does not owe its historical influence to its merits; they are far too modest. Rather, the argument has played a huge role in federalism's demise because it disguises and rationalizes ideological ambitions and political designs that push toward centralization. Those designs, however, have lost much of their appeal, and the rationalizations have lost much of their plausibility.

Egalitarians and government planners like centralization. They want to put people in their place, whereas federalism encourages them to move about. Interest groups want government to redistribute wealth to their own advantage. As a rule, this purpose is best accomplished at a centralized level of government, because the costs can be distributed over a larger population of losers and because the losers cannot thwart the designers' schemes by voting with their feet. "No exit" is the motto of centralized government. For obvious reasons, the architects and beneficiaries of collective, redistributionist schemes prefer to denounce the rush for the exits as a race to the bottom.

This rhetoric and the underlying push toward centralization appeal to pervasive—and understandable—popular illusions. All of us want the government to execute our particular schemes even while thwarting everyone else's. An unconstrained government accommodates this temptation; federalism inhibits it. Moreover, a federalism that permits citizens to choose in a sense also forces them to do so. Choices come in bundles, the good wrapped up with the bad, and the constant temptation is to try to unbundle those choices. Everyone wants a cheap, high-mileage car that offers the safety and protection of a medium-sized tank. Everyone wants an innovative, efficient, American-style economy with Swedish welfare benefits and German job security. The race-to-the-bottom demagogue plays to the stubborn illusion that politics just might allow us to have the sweet without the bitter. He picks one stick in the governmental bundle (say, stingy unemployment benefits) as proof positive of a "Mississippi effect" and asks why we should not trump that effect with federal rules.

This question, though, has answers. Redistribution has costs as well as benefits. A state that provides low unemployment benefits may have decided to make work and business investment more attractive, and its choice may well be efficient and humane. A central, more remote government cannot avoid the trade-offs that federalism forces us to confront. It can only hide those trade-offs, and it makes matters worse by abolishing our freedom to choose among different packages and trade-offs.

To be sure, such responses seem harsh, especially in contrast to the absurd but tempting promises of a centralized politics. Federalism demands of its citizens a modicum of realism, a certain tolerance for imperfection, and an understanding that we can *not* have the best of all worlds. In this demand lies a certain political weakness. It is not, however, an insurmountable weakness. Much as an unconstrained national government both panders to and encourages the infantile notion that we can have it all (and for free!), even a partially reconstructed federalism not only requires but also *teaches* adult realism and tolerance for imperfection. The debate over international free trade illustrates the dynamic. Protectionism never stops at the border: protect one constituency from trade, and another constituency will demand protection from some other change in the economy. Protectionism has been a losing force in American politics, however. We have come to understand that the benefits of international competition vastly outweigh the costs to selected industries. Once this insight gains hold, *competition* no longer stops at the border: having said no (or sorry) to the victims of free trade makes it easier to say no to the next interest group that demands protection.

In time, this learning process enhances realism. The voters understand that we cannot protect everyone from everything in any event, and they have become increasingly disenchanted with centralized attempts to control a rapidly changing environment—with the rigidities, inefficiencies, and intrusiveness of such schemes; with their lack of transparency and discipline; and with their seeming immunity to democratic controls. Federalism offers an alternative. Instead of centrally designed and enforced regimes, federalism offers choice. Instead of a voice, it offers citizens an exit—and, in due course, better government.

Choice and competition have always been among federalism's chief attractions. But those virtues are now much more attractive than at any time in American history. The modern trends that at first sight seem to weaken the case for federalism—the citizens' mobility, their lack of attachment to their home states—greatly strengthen its appeal. Highly mobile and prosperous citizens will be particularly inclined to vote with their feet and to choose among competing jurisdictions. They will particularly appreciate that option, especially when (and because) they are not terribly sentimental about their place of birth or residence.

The fact that competitive federalism is uniquely suited to modern circumstances does not make its revival inevitable. Powerful interests and ideological demands push in the opposite direction. Much evidence buttresses Tocqueville's characterization of centralization as the "natural" tendency of democratic societies. But while federalism's friends have ample reasons to be realistic, they need not despair. Under the right circumstances, political constituencies and federal judges with sufficient will and "art" can reestablish constitutional constraints on government. This book attempts to show that for the first time in many decades, a federalist revival has become a practical, political possibility.

2

Federalism's Demise— and Renaissance?

Constitutional Intuitions

For much of the twentieth century, the notion of state competition and citizen choice has been denigrated and suppressed. Before the New Deal, however, state competition was central to the constitutional understanding of federalism. This earlier understanding mapped the Founders' elementary intuitions about the nature and the purposes of republican government.

Admittedly, the Founders themselves said little about interstate competition. The *Federalist Papers* emphasize competition between states *and the federal government,* and the competition they discuss is not for business, labor, or capital (which can move between states but not between a state and the United States) but "for the affections of the people." When interstate competition becomes a subject of discussion—prominently, in connection with the power of Congress to regulate commerce among the states—it is "competition" in the form of tariffs, trade barriers, retaliation, and other protectionist measures. The Commerce Clause delegated power over interstate commerce to Congress so as to *suppress* such destructive competition. This concern came to be reflected in the "dormant" Commerce Clause—that is, the notion that federal authority over interstate commerce implies a prohibition on *state* regulation of such commerce.[1] The Founders' silence on beneficial forms of state competition is readily explained, however.

For one thing, the Founders believed that "it is only within a certain sphere that the federal power can, in the nature of things, be advantageously administered."[2] The Founders viewed federal intervention as inherently unsuitable to local affairs, and on this point at least, their adversaries agreed. So long as this shared understanding prevailed (as it did for almost the entire nineteenth century), the alternative between state competition and a flattened world of federal intervention did not distinctly present itself. Then, too, the Founders lived in a world where citizens had strong natural attachments to their states and, moreover, could not vote with their feet without incurring substantial hardships. The Founders did contemplate the possibility of government-induced mobility. For example, they prohibited the federal government from establishing religion while leaving the states free to do so, on the theory that religious dissenters could move. And move they did. It was unrealistic, however, to expect that people would relocate without compelling reasons and embark on a universal shopping spree for better government.

That said, three features of the Founders' federalism point toward the salutary effects of citizen choice and state competition. At the same time, those features distinguish competitive federalism from other, much less attractive conceptions—notably, a federalism that begins and ends with state sovereignty.

First, the Founders' federalism revolves around the welfare and liberty of *individual citizens,* not around the states' sovereignty and independence. The distinction is far from trivial, and the Founders' focus far from natural. Much as France, for instance, is worrying about its sovereignty and autonomy in a Europe run by the Central European Bank, it may seem that the preservation of the states' independent existence under the new Constitution should have been *the* federalism issue of the Founding Era. It was a very big issue. Remarkably, however, the idea of state sovereignty as federalism's object and purpose was *not* a part of the Founders' vision. It was the *anti-Federalists'* idea of federalism, and it drove the Federalists up the wall. Alexander Hamilton inveighed against it at great length, and even the less-nationalist-minded James Madison denounced the concept with unusual impatience:

> Was . . . the American Revolution effected, was the American
> Confederacy formed, was the precious blood of thousands spilt,

and the hard-earned substance of millions lavished, not that the people of America should enjoy peace, liberty, and safety, but that the governments of the individual states, that particular municipal establishments, might enjoy a certain extent of power and be arrayed with certain dignities and attributes of sovereignty?[3]

The point of Madison's rhetorical question is that the perspective of the citizens, not the parochial interests of state governments, must govern the analysis—and the political organization of the republic. State autonomy plays a subordinate, instrumental role. To the extent that state sovereignty is conducive to the "peace, liberty, and safety" of the American people, the states may retain it. To the extent that it is not, the states must give it up. Sincerely, Publius.

A second, closely related feature of the Founders' citizen-centered federalism is a preoccupation with government *outputs* and a corresponding distrust of collective decisionmaking.[4] The somewhat paradoxical idea of investing two sovereigns with (partially overlapping, partially independent) jurisdiction over the same territory and citizens gains plausibility only against this background. To paraphrase Madison: the central problem of government is, in the first instance, to control the governed and, in the second instance, to oblige government to control itself.[5] For the purpose of controlling the governed, one sovereign is quite sufficient, thank you, and may be better than two. The purpose of creating a rival sovereign is to limit government. In the language of the Founders, federalism's purpose is to make ambition counteract ambition, to make multiple sovereigns compete for the affection of the governed, and in that manner to compel government to control itself.

The structure of the Constitution reflects this impulse. The Founders' concern over destructive competition among the states, for example, is conducive to unrestricted state competition: a prohibition on protectionist barriers forces the states to play to their comparative advantages. More fundamentally, federalism's competitive dynamics exemplify the Founders' strategy of creating constitutional mechanisms that will curb the pernicious tendency toward "partial" laws (what we now call special-interest legislation or, in the economists' parlance, rent-seeking). Responding to the concern that such mechanisms may also prevent the enactment of good laws, Alexander Hamilton observed that

this objection will have little weight with those who can properly estimate the mischief of that inconstancy and mutability

in the laws, which form the greatest blemish in the character
and genius of our governments. . . . The injury which may
possibly be done by defeating a few good laws will be amply
compensated by preventing a number of bad ones.[6]

Although the quoted passage discusses the "horizontal" separation of
powers between Congress and the president and, in particular, the
president's veto power, the point applies with equal force to the "verti-
cal" separation of powers between the states and the national government. The Founders expected that private orderings, as a rule, were
best left undisturbed. They did not deny that some social or economic
problems may require a political response. But few such problems require a *federal* response. Moreover, every genuine problem is matched
by a dozen mischievous interest groups' schemes masquerading as a
genuine problem. A Constitution cannot sort the problems from the mischief, case by case. What it can and should do is to create effective (if
somewhat coarse) institutional screening devices. Federalism is just such
a device.[7]

Third, and most important for the purposes at hand, the Founders
recognized that federalism presupposes limits to the federal government's
power and authority and, moreover, independent judicial review. Without constitutional boundaries, the national government would readily
give in to demands to wipe out state competition. In that event, the
states would become mere instruments or administrative subunits of a
central, unitary government.[8]

The constitutional reflection of this recognition is the doctrine of
enumerated powers. *Enumerated powers* means that the federal government, and specifically Congress, possesses all the powers listed in Article I of the Constitution. But Congress possesses *only* those powers
and lacks general, plenary authority either over the states or over private citizens. "The powers delegated by the proposed Constitution to
the federal government are few and defined. Those which are to remain
in the State governments are numerous and indefinite," James Madison
famously wrote during the ratification debates.[9]

The protection of enumerated powers, in turn, presupposes some
form of independent judicial review. Since a federal system will present
conflicts among the member states and between the states and the national government, Madison explained, "some . . . tribunal is clearly
essential to prevent an appeal to the sword and a dissolution of the
compact," and the "decision is to be impartially made, according to the
rules of the Constitution."[10] In other words, the task of safeguarding

federalism's structure must be entrusted, not to the states and, as Professor William Van Alstyne has written, "assuredly not the Congress (what an odd Catch-22 that would be), but rather the courts, in the course of judicial review."[11]

Federalism's purpose is to enhance and protect the citizens' liberty and welfare. To that end, the federal government must be disabled from trumping state competition with monopolistic schemes, and nobody but the courts can provide such restraint. Enumerated powers and the judicial enforcement of the limits they imply are federalism's touchstone. To misappropriate a phrase of Professor G. F. W. Hegel's, they are the shibboleth where federalism's true and false friends part ways.[12]

From Constitutional Limits to "Process Federalism"

Six decades ago, federalism's true friends suffered a loss from which they have yet to recover. Beginning in the Progressive Era, Congress contrived to regulate a wide range of social and economic problems—some (such as antitrust) new in nature, others (such as labor relations) that had formerly been considered the province of state and local governments. The Supreme Court found many such interventions beyond the powers of Congress. In 1937 the tug-of-war culminated in a dramatic confrontation between President Roosevelt and the Supreme Court. The Court lost, and the enumerated powers doctrine and all that went with it were discarded.

The principal constitutional terrain on which the battle over enumerated powers was fought was the Commerce Clause. In an effort to give contours to the power of Congress to regulate commerce "among the several states," the Supreme Court drew distinctions between "interstate commerce" and, on the other hand, state and local matters beyond the reach of Congress. For example, the Court held that Congress may regulate the channels or instrumentalities of interstate commerce (such as railroads) or the shipment of noxious goods (such as prostitutes or lottery tickets) across state lines. But Congress may *not* regulate manufacture, which is not "commerce,"[13] or the trade of goods at the point of sale, which is "commerce" but not "interstate."

This jurisprudence was sharply criticized even at the time. After 1937, it came to be viewed almost uniformly as social Darwinism in legal garb and as a prime example of antidemocratic judicial activism.[14] True, the Supreme Court did not always draw Commerce Clause distinctions with perfect clarity and consistency. Moreover, the technological and organizational changes of the industrial age—interstate rail-roads, national monopolies, the emergence of industrial conglomerates operating across the country, the increasing integration of the national economy—seemed to make nonarbitrary distinctions between local and national matters increasingly difficult.[15] If the Justices nonetheless sought to maintain the distinctions and to protect the constitutional bound-aries, it was from a conviction that anything short of such an effort would soon produce a wholly nationalized government.

That intuition was exactly right, and *both* sides, the Court and Con-gress, understood the stakes perfectly well. While the Court sought to preserve enumerated powers and state competition, Congress sought to trump them, piece by piece, with federal regulation. Congress naturally started where modern politicians bent on expanding national power start—"It's for the children." Long before the New Deal, Congress en-acted a law prohibiting the interstate shipment of goods produced in factories that employed child labor. The Supreme Court, in *Hammer* v. *Dagenhart* (1918), found the law unconstitutional. In defense of the statute, the government invoked the race-to-the-bottom argument: under conditions of competition, no state could legislate suitable child labor laws. The Court responded that Congress did not have the option of

> closing the channels of interstate commerce to manufactur-ers in those states where the local laws do not meet what Congress deems to be the more just standard of other states.
>
> There is no power vested in Congress to require the states to exercise their police power so as to prevent possible unfair competition. Many causes may co-operate to give one state, by reason of local laws or conditions, an unfair advantage over others. The commerce clause was not intended to give Congress a general authority to equalize such conditions.[16]

Hammer did not endorse child labor; in so many words, the Justices said that only a crackpot would defend it. Rather, the Court correctly surmised that there was no race to the bottom. The push for a national child labor law was the final stage in a campaign that, like many other Progressive crusades, had begun and made a great deal of headway in the states. By the time of *Hammer*, all fifty states already had child labor laws, and the only question in the case was whether the federal prohibi-tion on child labor under the age of fourteen should replace North Carolina's age limit of twelve. The federal statute did not attempt to remedy a collective action problem but to "equalize" conditions at the level desired by more intervention-minded states. Moreover, the Court recognized that *Hammer* was only the first step toward a full-scale attack on competitive federalism. The federal elimination of one comparative advantage will promptly produce demands to suppress another and, in the end, all of them.[17] The decision to draw the line in a hard case reflected not an ideological obsession but a profound understanding of the political dynamics that threaten federalism.

The Supreme Court's critics correctly observed that the judicial attempt to preserve federalism's constitutional boundaries implied an assertive role for the Court.[18] In determining the scope of congressional authority, the Supreme Court saw itself as owing little deference to Congress. For reasons noted, however, the presumption of judicial competence is a corollary of federalism's design: no judicial review, no enumerated powers, no federalism, and no state competition. The pre–New Deal Court's claim of primacy in interpreting the Constitution's federalism provisions followed this logic.

The Supreme Court's Commerce Clause distinctions and presumption of competence in deciding federalism questions remained intact until the New Deal. As late as 1935, in the famous case of *A. L. A. Schechter Poultry Corp.* v. *United States*, the Court declared that Congress lacked the authority to impose wage and other employment regulations under the National Industrial Recovery Act on a New York poultry business whose kosher chickens were sold only within the state.[19] Two years later, however, the Supreme Court dramatically changed course. In *National Labor Relations Board* v. *Jones & Laughlin Steel Corp.* and *Steward Machine Co.* v. *Davis*, both written and issued in the shadow of President Roosevelt's threat to "pack" the Court with appointees who could be relied on to sustain federal legislation, the Supreme Court effectively dismantled the distinctions—such as the line between commerce and manufacture—that had informed its Commerce Clause jurisprudence.[20] The Court discarded the premises on which its federalism had rested—the intimate connection between federalism and individual liberty, the notion of enumerated federal powers, and the Court's duty and responsibility to police federalism's constitutional boundaries.

To be sure, the Supreme Court did not put it quite so dramatically. Post–New Deal cases often continued to speak the language of federalism—for instance, in emphasizing the role of states as "laboratories of democracy." Those pronouncements, however, typically came in cases where state and local governments were defending their right to tinker with collectivist schemes without interference *by the Supreme Court*.[21]

The recognition that state experimentation presupposes limits on federal intervention fell by the boards, and federalism's competitive dynamics, once viewed as its central benefit, came to be viewed as a collective action problem—the notorious race to the bottom. Supreme Court opinions progressively stressed the urgency of the national government's purposes and the impossibility of accomplishing them through anything except concerted federal action. In 1941, in *United States v. Darby,* the Supreme Court unanimously overturned *Hammer v. Dagenhart,* relying explicitly on the race-to-the-bottom argument that it had rejected a generation earlier.[22] A year later, in *Wickard v. Filburn,* the Court removed the last remaining federalism constraints and ruled that the Commerce Clause enabled Congress to regulate the production of wheat for private use. The Court accepted Congress's judgment that agricultural production for private consumption might, in the aggregate, reduce demand for products that travel interstate, thereby thwarting the federal government's attempts to control the overhang of agricultural commodities.

Wickard and its progeny turned the notion of enumerated powers on its head. As Justice Thomas has put it, the post–New Deal "case law could be read to reserve to the United States all powers not expressly *prohibited* by the Constitution."[23] The case illustrates, moreover, the post–New Deal Court's extreme deference toward congressional interpretations of federal authority. The pre–New Deal Court had eschewed such deference for the excellent reason that Congress cannot be trusted to define and observe the limits of its own constitutional authority. The post–New Deal Court, in contrast, declared the national economy too complex and interdependent for principled, objective judicial distinctions and, on that basis, ceased to scrutinize congressional finding that local activities "affected" interstate commerce and were therefore subject to federal authority. Eventually, the Court embraced a theory of "process federalism," first propounded by Professor Herbert Wechsler, which maintains that the balance of power between the states and the federal government can safely be left to the self-correcting powers of the political process.[24] As the Court wrote in *Garcia v. San Antonio Metropolitan Transit Authority,* a 1985 decision that proved to be the high-water mark of judicial abdication at the federalism front:

> [T]he Framers chose to rely on a federal system in which special restraints on federal power over the States inhered principally in the workings of the National Government itself,

> rather than in discrete limitations on the objects of federal
> authority. State sovereign interests, then, are more properly
> protected by procedural safeguards inherent in the structure
> of the federal government than by judicially created limita-
> tions on federal power.[25]

Federalism is reduced to the protection of "state sovereign interests"
and thus wholly divorced from concerns about competition and citizen
choice. Judicial restraints on federal power are "judicially *created*," as
opposed to being stated in the constitutional text. Preserving federalism
is no longer the Court's central task; rather, "the Court is on weakest
ground when it opposes its interpretation of the Constitution to that of
the Congress in the interest of the states."[26] "The political process," the
Garcia Court concluded, "ensures that laws that unduly burden the States
will not be promulgated."[27] Ever.

The Supreme Court did not merely abdicate its role in safeguarding the structural norms of the Constitution; it switched sides. Concurrent with the discovery of process federalism, the Supreme Court served
as a principal engine in the nationalization of American politics—sometimes sailing under its own steam, sometimes at the prodding and the
behest of Congress. Beginning in the 1940s, the Court "incorporated"
the provisions of the Bill of Rights (or in any event, the provisions it
liked) into the Fourteenth Amendment. This meant that constitutional
rights that had formerly held good only against the federal government
now also applied to state and local governments. The Court further proclaimed that governmental incursions into such rights would be subject
to exacting judicial scrutiny.[28]

The judicial discovery and aggressive protection of federal rights
against the states contributed mightily to the nationalization of American politics. *Brown* v. *Board of Education* was the beginning of the end
of segregation in the southern states. The Supreme Court's school prayer
decisions declared unconstitutional a practice that had been considered unobjectionable across the country. *Miranda* changed police in-
terrogation procedures in every law enforcement agency in the country.
New York Times v. *Sullivan* swept aside common-law libel laws of all
fifty states. *Roe* v. *Wade* replaced the abortion laws of all states, from the
most liberal to the most restrictive, with what amounted to a federal
right to abortion on demand.[29]

The evisceration of enumerated powers and the concurrent expansion of constitutional rights spelled the death of federalism as a princi-

pal constitutional concern and as a serious constraint on government. For reasons discussed in a later chapter, the states proved unable and, for the most part, unwilling to arrest the displacement of state competition with federal legislation. The "states' rights" opposition to the civil rights movement—the last fundamental challenge to the nationalization of American politics—did not attempt to preserve state competition but rather to defend obnoxious government schemes that denied fundamental rights to an entire class of citizens. The decisive, well-deserved defeat of that movement only hastened the general trend toward nationalization. The civil rights laws of the 1960s federalized vast areas of theretofore private conduct (such as employment) and injected the federal government into functions that had traditionally been thought of as the business of state and local governments, such as elementary education. The civil rights laws, in turn, paved the way for the welfare and entitlement programs of the Great Society and the subsequent wave of comprehensive environmental programs. Congress created countless federal causes of action that enabled private litigants to enforce federal standards against state and local entities. The Supreme Court, in turn, often interpreted those statutes even more broadly than they were written. Throughout the 1960s and 1970s, the two branches cooperated toward a huge expansion of the federal entitlement state—eroding, correspondingly, the authority of state and local governments. Although individual programs and statutes engendered much controversy and litigation, constitutional concerns over federalism played no significant role. They had long been buried.

The Scenario for Federalism's Renaissance

Recent years have witnessed a modest legislative and judicial rediscovery of federalist precepts. Spurred by widespread public discontent with a sprawling, intrusive federal government, Congress has enacted a ban on "unfunded" federal mandates on state and local governments, repealed the federal fifty-five-mile-per-hour speed limit, and entrusted the states with substantial authority to administer welfare programs. At the same time, the Supreme Court has rediscovered federalism as an important constitutional concern. A 1995 decision, *United States* v. *Lopez,* invalidated a federal statute that criminalized the possession of handguns near local schools. For the first time in six decades, the Court found that Congress had exceeded its constitutional authority to regulate interstate commerce. A year later, in *Seminole Tribe* v. *Florida,* the

Supreme Court expanded the states' sovereign immunity from federal impositions.[30]

The Court's 1996–1997 term, widely hailed as the most remarkable in recent memory, confirmed federalism's reemergence as a major theme of constitutional jurisprudence.[31] *Printz* v. *United States* invalidated key provisions of the Brady Act, which compelled local sheriffs to conduct background checks on would-be gun purchasers, as an unconstitutional intrusion on state sovereignty. *City of Boerne* v. *Flores* struck down the Religious Freedom Restoration Act, a federal statute that required state and local government to exempt religious practices from the coverage of many general laws and regulations.[32] Federalism concerns also informed the Justices' decisions in cases that, on their surface, may seem to have little to do with federalism, from doctor-assisted suicide to voting rights.[33]

Casual observation suggests, and later chapters confirm, that congressional "devolution" has been a rather half-hearted affair. And while the Supreme Court has served notice that federalism is entitled to some constitutional respect, the doctrines enunciated in the modern cases are very limited. American history abounds with enthusiastic predictions of a federalist revival; they have all been a loser's gamble. The odds are that federalism's most recent stirrings will likewise prove a mere ripple on a tide of nationalism and political centralization.

Those stirrings may also, however, prove a starting point for a broader return to a much more competitive, decentralized, federalist politics. I do not *predict* such a development. It is possible, however, to sketch a plausible political scenario that would gradually restore competitive federalism to the Constitution and to the political culture.

Such a scenario cannot be based solely on general social trends— on the voters' affection for federalism, for instance, or on their increased tolerance for a more open, competitive politics, or on federalism's compatibility with contemporary economic realities. Diffuse public preferences do not automatically translate into constitutional norms. And while competitive federalism is a functional response to modern conditions, most countries must live with dysfunctional regimes, most of the time. Broad social and economic trends are helpful and indeed crucial to restoring federalism, but they are not enough. A federalist scenario must identify political, institutional pathways and dynamics that will permit the reconstruction of constitutional norms. That, in a nutshell, is the program of this book. I proceed from two general assumptions.

It's the Courts, Stupid! As explained, competitive federalism presupposes enumerated powers. Enumerated powers, in turn, depend on judicial enforcement. The "process federalism" notion that the states will protect themselves is hopelessly at odds with reality and, in Professor Van Alstyne's apt phrase, difficult to understand "as other than a goodhearted joke."[34] Nor will Congress limit itself; barring constitutional constraints, it will suck the states (along with all else) into its impetuous vortex. When it comes to structural constitutional constraints, the federal courts are it. Either the courts constrain Congress, or else federalism is dead and will remain dead.[35]

Chapters 3, 4, and 5 describe the Supreme Court's recent federalism jurisprudence from the perspective of—and with a view to restoring—a robust notion of enumerated powers. Since so much hangs on the Supreme Court's willingness to protect federalism, the case law merits a careful analysis. I have sought to reduce the mind-numbing complexity of constitutional federalism doctrines by limiting the analysis to a handful of legal issues and landmark decisions. I shall have nothing to say on federal preemption, the dormant Commerce Clause, and other doctrines that bear on the topic. Even so, readers with limited patience for legal arcana may wish to turn directly to chapter 6, which summarizes the basic insights and conclusions.

Not by Courts Alone. The Supreme Court cannot restore enumerated powers on its own and simply retrace its steps from *Wickard* v. *Filburn* back to *Schechter* and *Hammer.* Were it to do so, the vast majority of federal statutes, from the Clean Air Act to the Civil Rights Act (in its application to private actors) would go by the boards. In the current political climate, the Justices could not launch such an assault on the federal government, even if they were of a mind to do so (and few of them are). The lesson of 1937 is that the Court cannot enforce constitutional norms against the will of the country and against Congress. As chapters 3–5 show, that lesson hangs over all the modern federalism decisions. Although those decisions represent piecemeal and important steps toward federalism, none has unambiguously resurrected enumerated powers. The Supreme Court has attempted to revitalize federalism values without forcing a constitutional showdown over the scope of congressional authority.

The restoration of more robust, enumerated powers constraints requires a more hospitable political climate. The time must be right,

and that means that some political force must find the constraints sufficiently useful to support their restoration. The Court needs help. Federalism needs a constituency.

That need not mean, though, that the Supreme Court must pas-
sively await a turn in the political climate. Constitutional norms can be
restored, in an incremental fashion, through a pattern of (often implicit)
cooperation between the Supreme Court and constituencies with a strategic interest in competitive federalism. Chapters 7 and 8 develop such
a scenario. The remainder of this chapter sketches its basic premises
and contours.

The Supreme Court, I just noted, cannot unilaterally impose its
will on the country. Still, constitutional law is not a mere reflection of
the reigning interests and ideologies. The late Alexander M. Bickel,
perhaps the most renowned constitutional scholar of his generation, argued that the Supreme Court typically seeks to *anticipate* a social consensus.[36] Supreme Court decisions on fundamental constitutional
questions do not always and immediately settle their political resolution. But such decisions tend to legitimize political constituencies, which
in turn support the Supreme Court as an institution and protect it from
political attacks.

History provides examples. Chief Justice John Marshall's great
Commerce Clause opinions and the expansive constructions of federal
power that they embodied were intensely controversial at the time. They
were a political gamble that the nationalists would defend the Court
against political attacks and, in the long run, carry the day. They did,
even if John Marshall in his old age sometimes despaired of the prospect.[37] In more recent memory, *Brown v. Board of Education* (1954) did
not settle the civil rights issue. But the Supreme Court's unanimous
decision emboldened and legitimized civil rights constituencies, and it
anticipated a broad social consensus on the issue.

The recent federalism decisions obviously lack the drama and the
political saliency of *Brown*. (Everyone knows what *Brown* said. *Seminole
Tribe*, anyone?) As I hope to show, however, the decisions attempt to
reopen a long-suppressed political dialogue on federalism. By *dialogue*
I do not mean that the Supreme Court is inviting a graduate discussion
group or an arid national conversation. I mean that the Supreme Court
is looking for constituencies that will support federalism and provide
the Court with room for greater advances somewhere down the road.

Federalism's great difficulty is that it has no constituency per se—
and that few constituencies will support it as a matter of general dispo-

sition. Economic interests may favor this or that federalist policy, but their general tendency, for reasons mentioned, is to push for centralization. The states, contrary to popular lore, also oppose enumerated powers constraints. They will of course protect their prerogatives—the "dignities and attributes of sovereignty," in Madison's derisive phrase. But the notion that the states will favor competition is approximately as plausible as the expectation that the teachers' unions will support school choice.

The only federalist force in contemporary American politics is what Republican strategist Grover Norquist has called the "Leave-Us-Alone coalition."[38] That coalition is a conglomeration of (loosely speaking) populist, grass-roots constituencies—gun owners, school choice and home schooling groups, the term limits movement, property rights groups, religious advocacy and lay organizations, tax limitation groups, small business owners, and so on. Not all these constituencies wish to be "left alone" in a libertarian sense, and not all of them support federalism all the time and on every issue. All of them, however, are fiercely antinationalist and anti-elitist and, in that elementary sense, federalist. They are the only organized political force that has use for the Supreme Court's federalist advances.

Chapters 7 and 8 describe a political, institutional dynamic between the Supreme Court and Leave-Us-Alone constituencies that may gradually restore federalism. Federalist Supreme Court decisions embolden federalism's constituencies. The constituencies, in turn, support the decisions and the Supreme Court as an institution, thus giving the Court greater leeway for further federalist advances. Meanwhile, changes in the legal environment create legislative opportunities to advance federalism in ways that are consistent with the legislators' tendency toward self-aggrandizement. Over time, this virtuous cycle produces serious constitutional constraints and public support for a more competitive politics.

At first sight, this scenario may seem unlikely, even odd. By institutional design, the Supreme Court is predisposed to distrust populist constituencies and, as we shall see, has often acted accordingly. Moreover, when the Supreme Court looks to the prevailing winds, it looks to elite culture, not the demands of the unwashed. The Leave-Us-Aloners may seem too marginal and too ideological to become plausible partners for the Supreme Court. Conversely, the Leave-Us-Aloners suspect that the Supreme Court—an institutional bulwark of a despised elite culture—can never be their friend. A virtuous cycle for federalism would require each side to overcome its deep distrust of the other.

Trust, however, can be built over time. The parties to the bargain need not actually like each other. They merely have to find each other useful—and, eventually, come to depend on one another. Such a gradual rapprochement does not seem entirely implausible. Despite their occasional stridency, organized Leave-Us-Alone constituencies articulate a much broader discontent with national politics and a desire for more open, decentralized political arrangements. Because the Supreme Court is not unaware of those broader sentiments, and because the Leave-Us-Aloners are in any event the only constituency that would support a serious judicial federalism agenda, the Supreme Court may well cease treating the constituencies as gauche or menacing. Conversely, and in turn, Leave-Us-Aloners may find the Supreme Court quite hospitable to at least *some* populist entreaties that permit a partial reconstruction of constitutional norms.[39] Both sides have more room for cooperation than they think they do, and that room defines the realm of future federalist possibilities.

To repeat: a federalist revival is far from inexorable. The Supreme Court's modest rediscovery of federalism has been the work of five conservative and moderate Justices. Should one of these votes change hands, the new majority would lose little time in nailing federalism's barely revived body back onto the cross of *Garcia.* At a more general level, powerful ideological and economic forces continue to push toward centralization. It would take considerable political will, art, energy, and imagination to counteract those natural tendencies and to sustain the progress that has been made.

It may well turn out that the country and its politicians lack those qualities. The Supreme Court has, however, created an opening for a return to a more diverse, innovative, competitive politics. The offer is sufficiently serious, and its prize is sufficiently large, to merit a serious examination.

3

Enumerated Powers?

Federalism's core is the notion of enumerated powers granted to Congress under Article I of the Constitution. After the constitutional war of 1937, the Supreme Court held, in essence, that neither the Commerce Clause nor any other enumerated power implied limits to federal authority. *United States* v. *Lopez* (1995) breaks with that tradition: for the first time since 1935, the Court found that a federal statute—the Gun Free School Zones Act—exceeded the powers of Congress under the Commerce Clause.

The enumerated powers question arises in substantially the same form under Section 5 of the Fourteenth Amendment, which authorizes Congress to enforce the guarantees of the amendment—due process of law, equal protection, privileges, and immunities—"by appropriate legislation." Here, as in Article I cases, the post–New Deal Court failed to discern or enforce constitutional limits to the powers of Congress. *City of Boerne* v. *Flores*, decided in 1997, is the Section 5 counterpart to *Lopez*. For the first time in many a decade, the Court ruled that a federal statute—the Religious Freedom Restoration Act—exceeded the powers of Congress under the Enforcement Clause.

Neither *Lopez* nor *Flores* revives the enumerated powers doctrine of the pre–New Deal era in full regalia. Rather, both cases attempt to make room for federalism concerns, without at the same time triggering a second constitutional war over enumerated powers. They do so, first, by explaining that Congress has gone far enough and, second, by stressing the constitutional importance of state sovereignty over "traditional" areas of local concern. In ascertaining the limits to federal powers, *Lopez* and *Flores* fall back on the states' protection from federal interference as a distinct, uniquely important federalism concern. Both cases, however, at least start from an assertion of enumerated powers. In future cases, the Supreme Court may well bring federalism back to that starting point.

The Limits of *Lopez*

United States v. *Lopez* arose over the Gun Free School Zones Act of 1990, which criminalized the possession of firearms "at a place the individual knows, or has reasonable cause to believe, is a school zone." Alfonso Lopez, a Texas high school student at the time, was indicted and prosecuted under the statute for carrying a concealed .38 Magnum and five bullets into school. A federal district convicted Lopez on the federal charge and sentenced him to six months' imprisonment and two years' supervised release. The Fifth Circuit Court of Appeals reversed the conviction, finding that the act exceeded the power of Congress to regulate interstate commerce.

The Supreme Court granted *certiorari* and, to the surprise of many observers, affirmed the Fifth Circuit's ruling. The Court was sharply divided. Chief Justice Rehnquist and Justices O'Connor, Scalia, Kennedy, and Thomas formed the majority; Justices Stevens, Souter, Breyer, and Ginsburg dissented. There were two concurrences—one written by Justice Thomas, the other by Justice Kennedy and joined by Justice O'Connor. The former concurrence is memorable for its intellectual integrity and coherence; the latter, for its lack thereof.

After a brief account of the facts and the procedural history of the case, Chief Justice Rehnquist's opinion for the Court begins with what looks like an ostentatious break with post–New Deal Commerce Clause jurisprudence. "We start with first principles," the Chief Justice writes. "The Constitution creates a Federal Government of enumerated powers."[1] There must be *some* limits to national power, *Lopez* says, and the federal courts have *some* role in enforcing those limits. The courts cannot simply rely on congressional assurances to the effect that a given statutory provision falls within the scope of the Commerce Clause; they must make their own, independent assessment.[2]

This language marks the end of "process federalism" and, for precisely this reason, drew strong reactions. The dissenters in *Lopez* sounded dire warnings about the lessons of 1937; legal commentators shrieked that *Lopez* might herald a return to the Articles of Confederation.[3] Such reactions, however, show only that liberal opinion refuses to countenance even the most modest judicial challenge to congressional omnipotence.[4] In fact, *Lopez* is far removed from reconstructing the pre–New Deal regime (to say nothing of preconstitutional arrangements). After its ringing opening, the majority opinion quickly retreats from a robust, principled theory of enumerated powers.

The language of the Commerce Clause and the leading precedents, Chief Justice Rehnquist explains, authorize Congress to regulate the "channels" of interstate commerce (such as waterways), as well as the "instrumentalities" of, and persons or things traveling in, interstate commerce. Quite so. But the Gun Free School Zones Act obviously does not fall into either of those categories. The question then is whether a federal prohibition on the possession of guns in local schools falls into a third permissible category of Commerce Clause legislation—the regulation of activities that "affect" interstate commerce. This, of course, is the battleground of 1937. It was then that the Supreme Court effectively abandoned the distinctions (for example, between commerce and manufacture) that had limited the reach of the Commerce Clause and replaced them with a general congressional authority to regulate activities that have nothing to do with but may "affect" interstate commerce—the production of wheat for home use, for a notorious example.

Significantly, the *Lopez* majority rejects the "formalistic" distinctions of the pre–New Deal era (such as the line between "direct" and "indirect" effects on interstate commerce), and it pointedly refuses to question any of the post–New Deal precedents. Instead, Justice Rehnquist maintains that even under and after those precedents, the commerce power must have an "outer limit." But what is that outer limit? *Lopez* suggests several answers, none of them satisfactory.

First, the majority opinion suggests that even under the modern cases, regulated activities must "substantially affect" interstate commerce to be within Congress's legislative authority. Activities with *trivial* effects would thus appear beyond the reach of the Commerce Clause, and indeed, the *Lopez* majority strains to show that even the post–New Deal case law requires more than simply an "effect." Having made that distinction, though, the majority promptly concedes that Congress may "aggregate" a series of activities with trivial impact into a "substantial" effect on interstate commerce.[5] This concession threatens to render the distinction meaningless.

Probably recognizing as much, the *Lopez* decision moves without a warning or explanation from the scope, scale, or size of the effect to the nature of its cause. To fall within the scope of the Commerce Clause, Chief Justice Rehnquist suggests, the activity that affects interstate commerce must itself be of an economic nature. *That* seems to make the difference between *Wickard* and *Lopez*: wheat production, even for home consumption, is "commerce," whereas the Gun Free School Zones Act "by its terms has nothing to do with 'commerce' or any sort of economic enterprise, however broadly one might define those terms."[6]

Even this distinction, however, turns murky. Rejecting Justice Rehnquist's assertion that one must "pile inference upon inference" to conclude that school violence substantially affects interstate commerce, Justice Breyer's *Lopez* dissent argues that Congress could quite plausibly have made that connection and buttresses this assertion by citing numerous academic studies. The majority responds that "depending on the level of generality, any activity can be looked upon as commercial." It goes on to observe that Justice Breyer's dissent fails to state, and by its terms cannot state, any limits to congressional power.[7] These responses are correct but elliptical. The observation that there has to be *some* limit to congressional power and *some* distinction between commercial and noncommercial activities leads back to the question of where that limit and distinction might be found, and *Lopez* provides no clear answer. All it tells us is that the congressional power to regulate "commercial activities" that "substantially affect interstate commerce" does not extend to noneconomic crimes or to the regulation of "each and every aspect of local schools." So far from turning back the clock to 1937, the Justices merely "decline here to proceed any further" in construing Article I powers.[8]

The distance between this holding and the doctrine of enumerated powers is measured by Justice Thomas's concurring opinion in *Lopez*. Justice Thomas reinvokes the textual distinctions that the majority opinion eschews. He points out that "the term 'commerce' was used [in] contradistinction to productive activities such as manufacturing and agriculture," indicating that Congress's authority to regulate commerce does not imply a further authority, and in fact implies a prohibition, to regulate manufacture.[9] Second, and closer to the holding in *Lopez*, Justice Thomas argues that the Founders would have been perfectly capable of granting Congress a power to regulate activities that "substantially affect" interstate commerce, had that been what they had in mind. Third, he observes that the modern, expansive interpretation of the Commerce

Clause swallows all other powers granted to Congress. If the Commerce Clause were so encompassing as the post–New Deal Court has understood it to be, the Founders need not have granted Congress the powers to raise and support armies, to establish post offices and post roads, or even to make all laws that are "necessary and proper" to the execution of the legislature's enumerated powers. Fourth, Justice Thomas points out that the "aggregation principle," which the *Lopez* majority appears to leave untouched, "has no stopping point" since "one can *always* draw the circle broadly enough to cover an activity that, when taken in isolation, would not have substantial effects on interstate commerce."[10]

Justice Thomas's concurrence sketches the contours of an originalist, enumerated-powers theory of the Commerce Clause. Not one of his brethren, however, joined his opinion. The dissenters argued that the Court's pre–New Deal jurisprudence—the reference point of Justice Thomas's concurrence—was an aberration from an otherwise continuous history of judicial solicitude of national power, only to see that claim, too, demolished by Justice Thomas.[11] The majority, except for a few perfunctory remarks about adherence to precedents, makes no mention of Justice Thomas's opinion—not because it does not require a response, but because there is no good response at the level of constitutional argument. The only response is *political:* to return to a textual theory of enumerated powers is to repeal the New Deal. That the Supreme Court cannot do. All it can do realistically, at least for the time being, is to "decline to proceed any further."

The holding of *Lopez* is not based *explicitly* on this consideration because Supreme Court Justices rarely like to put their political calculations on paper. But the argument has decisive force, as even Justice Thomas is eventually compelled to concede. Thomas claims that his position "does not necessarily require a wholesale abandonment of [the Court's] more recent opinions."[12] There is, however, no way to squeeze *Wickard* or any Commerce Clause case after it into the intellectual framework of enumerated powers. If Congress may aggregate trivial activities into "substantial effects," it may regulate virtually anything; if it may not do so, it is prohibited from regulating most of the things it now regulates. "A wholesale abandonment of more recent opinions"—meaning, all Commerce Clause cases since 1935—is precisely the import of Justice Thomas's opinion. "One Justice down, only four more to go," Richard Epstein, an ardent advocate of pre–New Deal doctrines, has deadpanned in a paean to Justice Thomas's gutsy opinion.[13] He knows, though, that five Justices are not free to *do* what one Justice is free to *say.*[14] Certainly, Justice Thomas knows that, which is why his otherwise compelling opinion ultimately yields to politics and terminates in an unpersuasive plea to "temper" and "modify" the Court's Commerce Clause jurisprudence.

Confronted with the contradiction between constitutional norms and the administrative state, the *Lopez* majority attempts to reclaim *some* ground for federalism. It fails to delineate that ground with any great precision. Both the majority opinion and Justice Kennedy's concurrence do, however, permit certain inferences concerning the contours of the Supreme Court's federalism. Chief among these is that federalism, to the Court's mind, revolves not around state competition and citizen choice but rather around the states' autonomy and prerogatives.

As noted, the *Lopez* majority distinguishes between crime and economic matters. This distinction is more central to the Supreme Court's thinking about federalism than is suggested by the cursory remarks in *Lopez*. While agreeing to hear and decide *Lopez*, the Supreme Court has consistently denied *certiorari* in "economic" cases—involving, for example, environmental regulation and federal criminal statutes regulating economic activities—that would have presented excellent opportunities to reexamine the scope of the Commerce Clause.[15] Plainly, the first case in decades to relimit the scope of the Commerce Clause is a case about (noneconomic) crime—as opposed to commerce—because the Supreme Court wanted it that way.

Limiting federalism principles to a discrete subject matter compartmentalizes federalism, thus confining the challenge to congressional authority. But what principle of distinction removes crime, of all things, from the scope of the Commerce Clause? It cannot be that crime—even crime on school grounds—is peculiarly local and noneconomic. Under the Endangered Species Act, for instance, the federal government protects insects that barely cross county lines, never mind state jurisdictions. The fate of the insects affects interstate commerce no more substantially, and is of no greater economic or commercial interest, than handgun possession. Yet the Supreme Court has consistently taken a pass on environmental Commerce Clause cases.

By way of explaining why the case for federalism may be particularly compelling in the criminal area, the *Lopez* majority suggests that criminal law enforcement, along with family law and education, is an area of "traditional state concern." Justices Kennedy's and O'Connor's concurrence articulates that rationale more explicitly. But the categorization explains nothing. One can plausibly argue that nuisance abatement—the stuff of much federal environmental law, where the Supreme Court has so far allowed Congress free reign—is also a "traditional" state concern. Conversely, after four decades of comprehensive federal legislation, funding, and intervention, it is rather hard to argue that education is somehow the "traditional" prerogative of state and local governments.

Putting aside for a moment the arbitrariness of determining "traditional state concerns," one must wonder what that legal category is doing in a *Commerce Clause* case. From the perspective of enumerated powers—the starting point and the ostensible basis of *Lopez*—Congress either had or did not have the power to legislate under the Commerce Clause. The question whether Congress "merely" exceeded its powers or also intruded into "traditional" state concerns is analytically distinct and secondary at best. A suggestion to the contrary implies that the commerce powers are somehow more enumerated when Congress tramples on state governments and less so when it does not.

So, alas, it would appear. The category of "traditional state concerns" is borrowed from sovereign immunity cases and especially *National League of Cities* v. *Usery* (1976). Those cases, which we encounter in chapter 5, are precisely *not* about enumerated powers. Instead, they read the Tenth Amendment as prohibiting federal legislation that regulates the "States as States" and thereby infringes on (yes) traditional state concerns. *National League of Cities* in particular held that Congress possessed "plenary" authority to regulate commerce and proceeded to carve out an enclave of state sovereignty.[16]

National League of Cities, moreover, was overruled in *Garcia* v. *San Antonio Metropolitan Transit Authority* (1985)—interestingly, on the grounds that a legal rule that relies on the designation of state functions as "traditional" or "integral" is "unsound in principle and unworkable in practice" and "inevitably invites an unelected federal judiciary to make decisions about which state policies it favors and which ones it dislikes."[17] The odd reappearance of that "unsound and unworkable" rule in *Lopez* suggests that *Garcia* may no longer be good law. Conversely, and more ominously, it suggests that state sovereignty and prerogatives, not enumerated powers and state competition, lie at the heart of *Lopez*.

A different analysis buttresses that conclusion. Crime and education, the areas that *Lopez* marks as "traditional" state concerns, have nothing in common and do not materially differ from areas implicitly designated as less "traditional." As already suggested, local flies are no more "commercial" and affect commerce no more directly than crime in schools. In each case, moreover, the problems are local in nature. The difference is this: when the states regulate desirable, productive activities, they run a risk of losing valuable business and good citizens to less meddlesome neighbors. When it comes to crime, in contrast, federalism's competitive dynamics typically work in reverse: if Texas "overregulates" crime relative to its neighbors, it will at the margin induce actual and potential lawbreakers to move to Oklahoma. One can think of exceptions to this generalization. Interstate competition may induce the decriminalization of gambling and other lifestyle crimes. Competition may also prevent states from criminalizing conduct that is closely tied to productive activities, such as pollution. As a rule, however, crime-control federalism induces more, not less, state regulation. The federalism problem (if there is one) is that the states may spend *too much* on crime prevention.

This observation, too clever to be mine,[18] suggests that *Lopez* very nearly inverts the rationale for federalism: the states can be permitted to regulate, and Congress can be enjoined from doing so, not when and where the market constrains the states' behavior but when, where, and because that constraint does *not* operate. Federalism's point is not to discipline state governments but to allow unimpeded regulation in areas where the states' incentives cut in an interventionist direction to begin with. Justices Kennedy's and O'Connor's concurrence comes very close to saying so:

> While it is doubtful that any state, or indeed any reasonable person, would argue that it is wise policy to allow students to carry guns on school premises, considerable disagreement exists about how best to accomplish that goal. *In this circumstance*, the theory and utility of our federalism are revealed, for the States may perform their role as laboratories for experimentation.[19]

The "theory and utility" of "our federalism" are revealed when everyone this side of Charles Manson agrees on a collective goal: *then*, the states may experiment with the means. Consider crime on school grounds, for example. Mr. Lopez was initially indicted and could easily have been convicted under a Texas statute corresponding to the federal Gun Free School Zones Act. That circumstance reassured the *Lopez* Court, as did the fact that "over 40 states already ha[d] criminal laws outlawing the possession of firearms on or near school grounds."[20]

Lopez starts out as an enumerated powers case about the outer limits of federal power. Its central value, however, is the protection of the states' regulatory prerogatives. Even that sort of federalism creates room for state experimentation and innovation and, in that sense, is connected to the values of citizen choice and competition. But the competitive dynamics push toward intervention and regulation, and they extend only to the means, not the ends, of collective action. *Lopez* suggests that the Supreme Court's federalism has a distinctly statist bias. *City of Boerne* v. *Flores* confirms this interpretation.

The Fourteenth Amendment According to *Flores*

Flores is part of an intriguing confrontation between the Supreme Court and Congress that began with the Court's controversial decision in *Employment Division* v. *Smith* (1990).[21] In *Smith*, members of the Native American Church who used peyote for sacramental purposes were denied unemployment benefits under a state statute that criminalized the use of drugs, including peyote. The Supreme Court sustained the denial of benefits. Breaking with precedent, the Court declared that the state may enforce rules of general applicability even if those rules impose incidental burdens on religion. The Free Exercise Clause of the First Amendment, the Court declared, does not entitle religious citizens to claim selective exemptions from otherwise valid laws.

Responding to widespread concerns among religious groups over the impact of *Smith*, Congress in 1996 enacted the Religious Freedom Restoration Act (RFRA, pronounced "riff-rah"). Explicitly designed to override *Smith*, RFRA prohibits any and all government agencies from "substantially burdening" a person's free exercise of religion, even when the burden results from a rule of general applicability, unless the government can demonstrate that the burden "(1) is in furtherance of a compelling governmental interest; and (2) is the least restrictive means of furthering that compelling governmental interest." In purpose and effect, these demanding tests often require the exemption of religious citizens or institutions from generally applicable laws—from prison rules to health and safety regulations to zoning ordinances.

In *Flores*, a Catholic archbishop sought a RFRA exemption from a local historic landmark ordinance that precluded the enlargement of a church. The Fifth Circuit Court of Appeals sustained the claim. The Supreme Court reversed, on the grounds that RFRA's enactment—or at least the application of the statute to state and local governments, as distinct from the federal government itself—was beyond the powers of

Congress. The Court found that Congress had exceeded its authority to "enforce" the Fourteenth Amendment under Section 5 of the Amendment, the so-called Enforcement Clause.

Compared with the substantive, rights-granting guarantees of the Fourteenth Amendment (in particular, the Due Process Clause and the Equal Protection Clause), the affirmative power of Congress "to enforce, by appropriate legislation, the provisions" of the amendment has played a fairly modest role in constitutional law, in the popular imagination, and for federalism. During the Reconstruction Era, federalism concerns produced restrictive judicial interpretations of Section 5, paralleling similarly narrow interpretations of the substantive provisions of the Fourteenth Amendment.[22] Thereafter, the Enforcement Clause essentially disappeared from constitutional sight for some eight decades.

Constitutional concerns over Section 5 and its possible limitations reemerged only in the 1960s, with the enactment of the modern civil rights statutes. In a series of Supreme Court decisions arising over the constitutionality of those statutes and especially the Voting Rights Act, the Enforcement Clause assumed the same limitations as the post–New Deal Commerce Clause—that is to say, virtually none.

The Enforcement Clause contains two enumerated powers constraints. First, the Fourteenth Amendment covers only *state action*; it generally does not permit Congress to legislate directly on private citizens. In other words, private discrimination is beyond the reach of the Fourteenth Amendment. That was the holding of the *Civil Rights Cases* (1883) and other Supreme Court decisions of the Reconstruction Era.[23] During the modern civil rights era, however, the Supreme Court greatly expanded the notion of "state action," thus eviscerating one limitation of the Enforcement Clause.[24] The second limitation concerns the extent to which Congress may impose civil rights constraints on state actors. Since the Religious Freedom Restoration Act regulated government agencies, that question was the principal issue in *Flores*.

The basic framework of analysis was established in *Katzenbach* v. *Morgan* (1966), where the Supreme Court sustained a federal ban on literacy tests that effectively prevented New York residents schooled in Puerto Rico from voting. *Katzenbach* held that federal statutes pass Section 5 muster if they may be viewed as enforcing the Fourteenth Amendment, are adapted to that end, and are consistent with the letter and the spirit of the Constitution.[25] *Katzenbach* and subsequent cases applied these tests with extreme deference. A mention of the Fourteenth Amendment somewhere in the legislative history, for instance, often sufficed to conclude that Congress had the authority to legislate under Section 5.[26] As for the means of legislation, Congress need not make specific findings and tailor its legislation to those factual circumstances. It suffices that Congress *could have* discerned a problem that merits remedial or preventive legislation.[27]

Most important, *Katzenbach* defined permissible Section 5 legislation as a one-way ratchet. Under the decision, the Supreme Court determines the constitutional *minima* of Fourteenth Amendment rights.[28] But judicial interpretations of substantive Fourteenth Amendment rights serve only as a floor for congressional action under Section 5. While Congress may not drop below that floor by defining Fourteenth Amendment rights more narrowly, Congress may exceed the floor and expand judicially defined Fourteenth Amendment rights.[29]

These presumptions have two implications. First, federalism plays essentially no role in constraining Congress; like the pre-*Lopez* Commerce Clause, the Enforcement Clause is all power and no limit. Second, the Religious Freedom Restoration Act appears plainly constitutional. The basic argument is easily stated: The Supreme Court's 1990 decision in *Smith* defines the scope of free exercise rights under the First Amendment. Under *Katzenbach*, however, the holding of *Smith* only establishes the constitutional minimum or floor; notwithstanding the Supreme Court's view that the Free Exercise Clause does not entitle religious citizens to selective exemptions from general laws, Congress retains the power to define free exercise rights more broadly. RFRA can be viewed as a Section 5 enactment, since Congress specifically invoked the Enforcement Clause. And surely, RFRA is "adapted" to the enforcement of Section 5 rights. Critics argued that Congress relied on no more than anecdotal evidence of antireligious bigotry and discrimination in enacting RFRA and, moreover, that the statute was a very dramatic response to those anecdotes. But the pre-*Flores* case law teaches that judges should refrain from second-guessing congressional responses to perceived problems of discrimination, provided that the rights ratchet runs in the right direction.[30]

The *Flores* Court, however, decisively rejected this argument and, along with it, the central premise of modern Section 5 case law. *Smith*, according to *Flores*, is the authoritative constitutional interpretation of the Free Exercise Clause. It is a ceiling as well as a floor, and Congress may not depart from it one way or the other. Amazingly, not a single Justice in *Flores* defended the tenet that Supreme Court precedents are a mere floor for congressional action under the Enforcement Clause—

even though RFRA merely restored what had been the Supreme Court's own view of the Free Exercise Clause for more than two decades before *Smith*.[31] This momentous shift is prompted largely, though not exclusively, by federalism concerns.

The substantive part of Justice Kennedy's opinion for the *Flores* Court begins where the *Lopez* majority began, with a pronouncement that "[u]nder our Constitution, the Federal Government is one of enumerated powers."[32] The Fourteenth Amendment wrought a dramatic shift in the federal balance by conferring on the federal government powers it had not theretofore possessed. Still, the Enforcement Clause cannot be boundless; like every enumerated power, it presupposes a limit. The *Flores* majority finds that limit in a distinction between the *enforcement* of constitutional rights, which Section 5 grants to Congress, and the congressional creation of *new* rights, which *Flores* deems outside the scope of Section 5. RFRA, the majority opinion says, does not "enforce" anything; its stated purpose was to change the First Amendment right to free exercise of religion, as interpreted by the Supreme Court in *Smith*. "Legislation which alters the meaning of the Free Exercise Clause," the *Flores* Court declared, "cannot be said to be enforcing the Clause. Congress does not enforce a constitutional right by changing what the right is."[33]

The distinction between the "enforcement" of constitutional rights and the creation of new rights defines the limits of the Enforcement Clause. It is thus central to the *Flores* opinion—and, upon inspection, alarmingly thin. Chief Judge Posner's observation—expressed in a pre-*Flores* case—that a "new right" is created "[w]henever Congress passes a law under the authority of section 5" may be going too far.[34] The line between the enforcement of rights and the creation of new ones is probably no more elusive than other legal distinctions that can and have been drawn through successive approximation in a series of judicial precedents. In the case of the Enforcement Clause, however, practically no case law exists on which to build. The post–New Deal precedents consistently slight the distinction between remedial and substantive legislation—between the "enforcement" of rights and their creation. Congress plainly changes or creates a constitutional right when, for example, it declares that the right to vote shall henceforth encompass a right against vote "dilution" and against at-large electoral systems that have the effect of preventing the election of minority candidates. The Fourteenth Amendment, the Supreme Court has found, contains no such right. But the Voting Rights Act does—without presenting, to the Court's mind, a Section 5 problem.[35]

Faced with that difficulty, the *Flores* majority shifts ground. It concedes that "the line between measures that remedy or prevent unconstitutional actions and measures that make a substantive change in the governing law is not easy to discern, and [that] Congress must have wide latitude in determining where it lies." "There must," however, "be a congruence and proportionality between the injury to be prevented or remedied and the means adopted to that end. Lacking such a connection, legislation may become substantive in operation and effect."[36] The Religious Freedom Restoration Act, the *Flores* Court maintains, lacks the connection. On the one hand, RFRA's legislative history reveals little evidence of widespread religious bigotry or persecution—in contrast, says Justice Kennedy, to the findings that underpinned or could have underpinned the enactment of the Voting Rights Act.[37] On the other hand, "[t]he reach and scope of RFRA distinguish it from other measures passed under Congress' enforcement power, even in the area of voting rights."[38]

It is at this point that federalism reenters the Fourteenth Amendment equation, and it does so in the fashion of *Lopez*. RFRA's "reach and scope" trouble the Supreme Court on account of the consequences for state and local autonomy. "Requiring a State to demonstrate a compelling interest and show that it has adopted the least restrictive means of achieving that interest is the most demanding test known to constitutional law," Justice Kennedy writes. Thus, RFRA constitutes a "considerable congressional intrusion into the States' traditional prerogatives and general authority to regulate for the health and welfare of their citizens."[39]

Once again, the argument is thin. For instance, how and why does RFRA's "intrusion" differ from the equally "considerable" but constitutionally unproblematic federal intrusions under the Voting Rights Act, which implicate the states' sovereign functions far more centrally and directly? True, RFRA affects a broader range of state government activities. But the states' "general authority to regulate" health and welfare has not been thought to enjoy constitutional protection since the nineteenth century. On its own, the federalism argument cannot fully explain the result in *Flores*. Something else is at work.

That something is a concern over the Supreme Court's own powers, as distinct from those of the states. As noted, RFRA was an explicit attempt to overrule a particular Supreme Court decision by congressional enactment. Faced with that direct challenge, the Court asserted its presumed authority as the ultimate arbiter of the Constitution.

On one interpretation, that is all that there is to *Flores*. While explicitly addressing only "the most far reaching and substantial of RFRA's provisions, *those which impose its requirements on the States*," some passages of Justice Kennedy's majority opinion suggest doubts even about applying RFRA to the federal government itself.[40] If such applications, which obviously implicate no federalism concerns, are unconstitutional along with the rest of the statute, *Flores* has nothing to do with federalism.

This cannot be right, though. The federal RFRA is merely the equivalent of a legislative amendment to federal enactments, past and future, and if the underlying enactments are a valid exercise of congressional authority, then so is the limitation (barring only a violation of other constitutional norms). To escape this logic and to hold that Congress may not limit the enforcement and application of validly enacted federal statutes against the federal government itself would require a truly astounding notion of judicial supremacy.

Even assuming (as I think one should) that RFRA's federal application is still good law, it remains true that the *Flores* Court showed a remarkable lack of deference to Congress on a very close question of constitutional interpretation.[41] The majority's assertion of the Court's ultimate authority to interpret the Constitution smacks of judicial imperialism. It also raises doubts that *Flores* is a genuine federalism case. Two considerations, however, point in the opposite direction.

First, the judicial supremacy claims in *Flores* are tied up with federalism concerns. The point of *Smith* was largely institutional: it was to remove the federal courts from the business of balancing religious freedom and state interests in case after case. Barring antireligious discrimination, the states are free to strike the balance. The Religious Freedom Restoration Act kicked the balancing task back into the courts, and to forestall that transfer of authority the Supreme Court felt compelled to assert its own authority. Admittedly, the Court did so with unusual firmness. The intended result of *Flores*, however, is a kind of religious accommodation federalism. The states must comply with the minimum neutrality requirement of *Smith*. Beyond that, nothing at all prevents them from enacting more generous accommodation provisions along the lines of RFRA. In finding fault, not with religious accommodation but with its federal *imposition*, the Supreme Court effectively declared corresponding state measures constitutionally unproblematic.[42]

Second, the relative significance of federalism arguments in *Flores* is in the end less important than the question of whether the Supreme

Court will run from those arguments in the next Section 5 case, which may present federalism issues in a cleaner fashion than did *Flores.* That, fortunately, seems unlikely. *Flores* is consistent with the Court's general federalism orientation.

Katzenbach was to the Enforcement Clause what *Wickard* v. *Filburn* was to the Commerce Clause—that is, a judicial endorsement of congressional omnipotence. By the same token, *Flores* is a Section 5 counterpart to *Lopez.* While purportedly adhering to a posture of judicial deference, both cases move toward a more demanding scrutiny of congressional enactments—an independent judicial assessment of interstate commerce connections in *Lopez,* a rough "congruence" of legislative means and ends in *Flores.* In both cases the Court declined to overrule a single precedent, while manfully struggling to distinguish cases whose tenor and, quite probably, whose holdings point toward opposite results—*Wickard* v. *Filburn* and its progeny in *Lopez, Katzenbach* and subsequent cases in *Flores.* To that end, both *Lopez* and *Flores* draw lines, albeit without great confidence. Congress may not regulate noneconomic activities that do not substantially affect interstate commerce, says *Lopez,* conceding that such a principle is less than crystal clear. Congress may not create new rights under Section 5, says *Flores,* conceding that the line between the (permissible) legislative enforcement of existing rights and the creation of new ones is blurry. Without those distinctions, however, nothing would be left of federalism. "We decline to go further" is the stated rationale of *Lopez;* it is the unstated rationale of *Flores.*

Most important, *Flores* embodies the same federalism notion as *Lopez*—that is, the idea of federalism not as a limit to congressional authority but as a special protection for states and localities. *Lopez,* as noted, and especially Justice Kennedy's concurrence in the case, skirted the primary question concerning the scope of enumerated Article I powers and strongly suggested that the states' sovereignty over their "traditional" concerns posed a special obstacle to the congressional exercise of those powers. The same is true of *Flores.*

Unlike the Commerce Clause, the Fourteenth Amendment specifically authorizes the federal regulation of the states qua states. The *point* of the amendment was to regulate state action, as distinct from private conduct. From an enumerated-powers perspective, then, federal intrusions into private conduct are *more* problematic under Section 5 than the regulation of the states in their collective, political capacity. The tone of *Flores,* though not its actual holding, indicates that the Supreme Court views the federalism issue quite differently. Suppose Congress had enacted a "private RFRA" prohibiting, for example, otherwise law-ful public accommodation policies that place an incidental burden on religious customers unless the proprietor can show a "compelling need" for the practice. Would the *Flores* Court have considered such a law to be as problematic, federalism-wise, as the actual RFRA?[43] Conceiv-ably, but not likely. Justice Kennedy's incongruous laments about RFRA's unbearable burdens on state and local governments strongly suggest that *Flores*, like *Lopez*, is less concerned with congressional usurpation than with intrusions into state autonomy; less with restoring limits to federal power than with preserving islands of state autonomy in a sea of federal omnipotence.

After *Lopez* and *Flores*

Lopez and *Flores* may remain (or rather become) interesting outliers. The progeny of *Flores* is too limited to permit firm conclusions; that of *Lopez* seems disheartening. With the exception of a handful of—so far, unsuccessful—challenges to federal environmental statutes, the Free-dom of Access to Clinic Entrances Act, and the Violence against Women Act, *Lopez* cases have remained confined to the federal regulation of noncommercial crime.[44] *Lopez* has been read as a narrow exception for federal crime regulation, and even that may be an exaggeration. The precedent may be good for Section 922(q) of volume 18 of the *United States Code* (the Gun Free School Zones Act)—and for nothing else. Appellate courts have routinely upheld the Drug Free School Zones Act, a twin of the Gun Free School Zones Act, in opinions that are charitably described as cursory. Federal criminal prohibitions for the mere posses-sion of machine guns have likewise been upheld against *Lopez* chal-lenges. And so on. The astonishing fact is that to this day, no appellate court has found any federal enactment unconstitutional under *Lopez*.[45]

Closer inspection, however, suggests a more optimistic assessment. Given the consistency with which the modern Supreme Court has in-voked federalism arguments, *Lopez* and *Flores* will probably develop some bite. In that event, it will be difficult to limit federalism to the protection of "traditional" state regulatory autonomy.

Among the encouraging aspects of *Flores* is the majority's implicit attempt to redefine the race and voting rights cases, from *Katzenbach* on, as special rather than paradigmatic for the federalism analysis un-der Section 5. Consider, for instance, the emphasis on the paucity of legislative findings of antireligious bigotry as a way of illustrating the lack of congruence between the ends and the means of the Religious Freedom Restoration Act. As noted earlier, no such congruence has been required in cases dealing with race: there, the Court readily infers that Congress *could* have found discrimination and bigotry, whether or not Congress actually looked for it. Even if RFRA is a mismatch between means and ends, Section 5 race discrimination cases hold that the sweep of congressional enforcement power easily extends to measures that intrude into "legislative spheres of autonomy previously reserved to the states."[46] And, in any event, in matters of race Congress has often exercised and the Supreme Court has often sustained the authority to prohibit discrimination regardless of intent or "bigotry." None of the formal distinctions between the race cases and *Flores* holds water. The tendency of asserting them is to put race and voting rights cases to one side and everything else, beginning with religion, to the other.

This analysis may look silly, since practically all modern Section 5 cases deal with race.[47] *Flores* may merely signal judicial bigotry: only when it comes to *religious* liberty, it appears, do federalism constraints happen to impede the otherwise plenary authority of Congress to protect and expand civil rights. The *Flores* shoe really is on the other foot, however. In distinguishing *Katzenbach* and race away, *Flores* has effectively put all other legislative antidiscrimination laws up for grabs. Statutes prohibiting discrimination based on family status, handicap, and perhaps age are examples.[48]

The underlying concern is articulated more clearly in lower-court opinions than in *Flores* itself. To simplify somewhat: the extension of *Katzenbach* beyond the realm of race and voting rights would leave Congress at liberty to define any undesirable state of affairs as "discrimination." Congress could then proceed under Section 5 to order the states to remedy the situation. Section 5 would have no limit, and nothing would be left of federalism. In an instructive pre-*Flores* ruling, the Sixth Circuit observed that the deferential

> *Katzenbach* factors cannot be kept so permissive as to make them collapse into the "rationally related" test generally used for the enforcement clauses of other constitutional amendments. . . . *The general goal of equal protection of law encompasses every facet of a citizen's interactions with government.* If we were to say that an act is valid if it is rationally related to achieving equal protection of the laws, then §5 becomes a license to Congress to pass any legislation whatsoever.[49]

Following this passage, the Sixth Circuit reaffirmed the broad discretion of Congress to combat racial, ethnic, and gender discrimination. Missing from that list are quasi- or nonsuspect classes, such as the handicapped or families with children.

In the wake of *Flores,* the courts have given widely varying answers as to whether entitlement statutes that designate such groups as statutory beneficiaries can be viewed as enforcing the Fourteenth Amendment. The general answer is in the affirmative, provided that Congress specifically indicates its intent to legislate under the amendment and that the statute under consideration bears some resemblance to generally recognized Fourteenth Amendment concerns. But Section 5 legislation in these areas is now subject not to the deferential *Katzenbach* analysis but to the more demanding standards of *Flores*—a narrower understanding of "enforcement" and a stricter scrutiny of the proportionality—that is, the means and ends—of Section 5 legislation.[50]

To illustrate the possible consequences, some courts have drawn a distinction between congressional demands for nondiscrimination and the creation of special benefits. Relying extensively on *Flores,* two federal district courts have struck down the application of portions of the Americans with Disabilities Act (ADA) to state agencies as beyond the scope of Section 5. While perceiving no constitutional problem with respect to ADA provisions prohibiting discrimination against the disabled, one of the courts observed that "the accommodation provisions of the ADA and the Rehabilitation Act demand unequal treatment for disabled employees. . . . Thus, in enacting the accommodations provisions, Congress created a substantive right to preferential treatment where no such right previously existed under the Equal Protection Clause."[51]

While the ADA cases have gone both ways, they do suggest that some judges are prepared to limit existing Section 5 schemes that have developed intensely interested, well-organized beneficiary groups. In that light, the picture looks bleak for groups seeking to extend traditional antidiscrimination schemes to new classes and in new directions. The much-debated federal ban on partial-birth abortions is one example; the proposed Employment Nondiscrimination Act, which would essentially extend the protections of Title VII of the Civil Rights Act to homosexuals, is another. If enacted, both proposals would be very vulnerable to Section 5 challenges.[52]

Section 5 cases of the type just discussed remain tied to the federalism theme of *Flores*—a "due regard for the autonomy and responsibility of state and local governments" and a concurrent fear that the

Enforcement Clause might "swallow up the remaining powers of state government," as Chief Judge Posner has put it.[53] This focus implies a curiously twisted view of enumerated powers, federalism, and government in general. If anyone should be prohibited from discriminating (for instance, on the basis of handicap), it should probably be the government, not private employers. While *Flores* sometimes permits state governments to escape the impositions of the ADA and similar antidiscrimination statutes, however, Congress can still regulate the living daylights out of private employers by enacting the same statutes under the Commerce Clause.[54]

In short, while *Flores*-style cases are nominally concerned with the scope of congressional power, they create not a limitation on Congress but an exception for the states. The enumerated powers problems lie elsewhere. Specifically, the question is, first, whether the state action limitation of the Fourteenth Amendment will hold and second, whether the Supreme Court's Commerce Clause jurisprudence can be severed from the purpose of protecting state sovereignty, to which it is tied in *Lopez.*

Brzonkala v. *Virginia Polytechnic Institute* illustrates the salience of both points. Pending, at this writing, before the Fourth Circuit Court of Appeals, the case arises over the constitutionality of the Violence against Women Act of 1994 (VAWA). VAWA's core provision creates a private claim for damages and other relief in federal court for "crime[s] of violence motivated by gender," meaning because of or on the basis of gender "and due, at least in part, to an animus based on the victim's gender." A particularly demagogic piece of legislation, VAWA rests on the contention, allegedly buttressed by several years of congressional hearings and "findings," that America is being swept by a tidal wave of violent hate crimes against women. Misogynist crimes—as distinct from ordinary crimes, which VAWA does not reach—are said to have a grave effect on the national economy and on women as a class. The state courts are allegedly unable or unwilling to provide appropriate relief.

The defendants in *Brzonkala* argue that neither the Commerce Clause nor Section 5 of the Fourteenth Amendment provides a warrant for the Violence against Women Act. The Section 5 problem is the state action limitation: even under the broadest construction of "state action," purely private acts of violence—which the states actually prosecute and punish—would appear to lie beyond the scope of Section 5.[55] The Commerce Clause issues are those of *Lopez.* The conduct regulated under VAWA is surely not of an economic nature, "however broadly one may define those terms." And, as in *Lopez*, one must pile "inference upon inference" to reach the conclusion that *domestic* violence or campus date rape—more particularly, the vanishingly small number of such crimes that are committed for misogynist reasons—constitute *interstate commerce*. A U.S. District Court agreed with the *Brzonkala* defendants on both issues. An appellate decision by a panel of the Fourth Circuit Court of Appeals reversing the trial court's ruling has been vacated, pending a resolution by the full Fourth Circuit.

Brzonkala illustrates the difficulty of confining the Supreme Court's federalism jurisprudence to its present contours. On the Section 5 issue, *Flores* points the way: while the state action limitation was not at issue, the decision did affirm that limitation, albeit a bit obliquely.[56] Lo, in *Brzonkala* the limitation promises to develop force as a genuine enumerated powers constraint.

So, too, with the Commerce Clause. The Fourth Circuit panel sustained the Violence against Women Act against a Commerce Clause challenge. As Judge Luttig observed in a harsh dissent, however, the panel could reach that conclusion only by assuming that *Lopez* means nothing outside the context of Section 922(q) (the Gun Free School Zones Act). In the panel's words, "*Lopez* did not alter [the] approach to determining whether a particular statute falls within the scope of Congress's Commerce Clause authority."[57] Unless *Lopez* was a joke, that interpretation must be wrong. And if it *is* wrong—if, in Judge Luttig's words, *Brzonkala* presents the Supreme "Court with the logical next case in its considered revisitation of the Commerce Clause"[58]—a ruling to the effect that VAWA's tort remedy lies outside the bounds of the Commerce Clause implies an extension of *Lopez*. In particular, the *Lopez* limitation to crime and, more broadly, "traditional state functions" turns out to be so vague as to pose no real obstacle to a broader application of Commerce Clause arguments.[59] While the VAWA provision at issue in *Brzonkala* is predicated on acts of violence that are criminal under state law, it is a *civil* remedy provision. Similarly, on the very day that the Fourth Circuit sustained the act, a different panel of the same Circuit relied on *Lopez* arguments in overturning the criminal convictions of defendants charged with filling local wetlands in violation of federal regulations.[60] Such increasingly common federal prosecutions for environmental crimes (such as violations of federal wetlands or endangered species regulations) resemble *Lopez* in that they involve—well, crimes. They differ from *Lopez* in that they involve *environmental* regulation and enforcement—a subject matter that, unlike the Gun Free School

Zones Act, has quite a bit to do with state competition for business and investment.

Judicial refusals to follow *Lopez* effectively render it meaningless. Every application of *Lopez,* on the other hand, will almost surely extend it. This dilemma helps explain why appellate courts have been so reluctant to apply *Lopez* without further guidance from the Supreme Court. The Court itself has so far sidestepped the alternative between extending *Lopez* and dismantling it only a few years after it went on the books. Once the Court confronts the choice, though, it is likely to opt for an extension. Hard cases usually make bad law. The next hard federalism cases are bound to be exceptions to that rule.

4

Federal Commandeering

Twice in the past six years, the Supreme Court has struck down portions of congressional enactments as violating the Tenth Amendment to the Constitution. *New York* v. *United States* (1992) invalidated provisions of an environmental statute that compelled states under certain circumstances to "take title" to nuclear waste generated within their borders. The second, more important case, *Printz* v. *United States* (1997), struck down a portion of the Brady Act, which compelled local law enforcement officers to conduct background checks on would-be gun purchasers.[1]

Unlike *Lopez* and *Flores*, *New York* and *Printz* are *not* enumerated powers cases. Tenth Amendment cases do not contest, and in a sense presuppose, that anything and everything is or may become a proper object of federal legislation. Rather, they hold that Congress lacks the authority to do certain things *to states and localities*. *Lopez* and *Flores* suggest the notion of federalism as a protection of the states' regulatory autonomy; the Supreme Court's Tenth Amendment cases spell it out. Moreover, the Tenth Amendment protects the states only to the extent that Congress may not impose on state and local governments *in a certain fashion*, which the Court, in a word apparently introduced by Justice O'Connor, calls "commandeering."[2] Congress remains free to pursue the same objectives and to impose substantially the same burdens by other means. The constitutional quarrel is not with the ends and the substance but with the means and the form of federal regulation.

From the perspective of enumerated powers, the Tenth Amendment challenge to federal authority seems rather modest and less "activist" than *Lopez* or *Flores*. That impression is correct, but it hides a certain irony. When measured by the constitutional text, the Supreme Court's Tenth Amendment cases are actually much *more* activist than *Lopez* or *Flores*. Whereas enumerated powers have textual limits (even if the Supreme Court, from 1937 to *Lopez*, chose to ignore them), the Tenth Amendment merely states the general principle of enumerated powers: it provides that all powers not granted to the federal government are "reserved to the States respectively, or to the people." This language provides no textual basis for the proposition that Congress may not commandeer states and localities.

The rationale for construing the Tenth Amendment in an extratextual manner lies, paradoxically, in the collapse of the enumerated powers doctrine. Unwilling or unable to contest the premise of congressional omnipotence, the Supreme Court has seized on the Tenth Amendment as a means of salvaging a piece of federalism—state immunity from certain federal impositions. Like *Lopez* and *Flores*, but more clearly, Tenth Amendment cases embrace the states' sovereignty over their traditional affairs as a way of advancing federalism concerns short of revisiting the basic premises of post–New Deal jurisprudence. *New York* is the most important modern example of that stratagem.

Printz compounds the irony of the Tenth Amendment: it provides an aggressive interpretation of the prohibition against federal commandeering and finds the warrant for that interpretation, not in the Tenth Amendment, but in the larger structure of the Constitution. *Printz* is the flip side of *Lopez*. Whereas *Lopez* gravitates from an assertion of enumerated powers to the protection of "traditional" state regulation as federalism's core, *Printz* moves in the opposite direction. It starts from the notion of state immunity and ingeniously reconnects it with the fundamental principle of enumerated powers.

Intergovernmental Immunity

The Tenth Amendment declaration that all powers not granted to the federal government are reserved to the states or to the people has often been called a "tautology" or "truism." This characterization belittles the central importance of the enumerated powers doctrine and has typically served as the starting point of a complete evisceration of that doctrine.[3] Nonetheless, there is some truth to it. Enumerated powers are the cornerstone of the constitutional structure, but the crux of the constitutional inquiry is the scope of the powers that have been delegated to the federal government. Congress possesses the constitutional authority to regulate manufacture under the Commerce Clause or it does not. Either way, the Tenth Amendment adds nothing of substance to the inquiry. It is not an independent constraint on Congress but at best an interpretive help.[4] And in fact, the Supreme Court has never used the Tenth Amendment as free-standing enumerated powers constraint on national power.

What the Supreme Court *has* done is to elevate the Tenth Amendment into an extratextual, judge-made principle of intergovernmental immunity. The amendment, that is to say, has served as a defense of state sovereignty against national impositions, even and especially in areas where Congress is unquestionably competent to legislate. An early, pre–New Deal example is *The Collector* v. *Day*, an intriguing case decided in 1870. Chief Justice Marshall's famous decision in *McCulloch* v. *Maryland* (1819) had held that the states may not tax the instruments of the federal government (in the case at bar, the operations of the Second Bank of the United States). *Day* is *McCulloch* in reverse: it posed the question of whether the federal government could levy a tax on the salary of a state employee. The answer, according to the Supreme Court, was that the Tenth Amendment forbade the federal government from doing so.[5]

The result in *Day* is questionable. As Justice Bradley observed in a forceful dissent, the tax at issue applied to all citizens. While there may be a constitutional problem with a federal attempt to destroy state governments by means of taxation, *Day* created a selective *exemption* of state employees from federal impositions that are otherwise within the powers of Congress. Certainly, the text of the Tenth Amendment compels no such conclusion.

Whatever its merits, *Day* illustrates the constitutional intuition behind the Supreme Court's Tenth Amendment cases: when the Court has perceived a lack of direct constraints on federal power, it has used the amendment as a second-best means of preserving state sovereignty. Decided shortly after the Civil War, *Day* reflects the Supreme Court's nervousness about the national government's newly established powers under the Fourteenth Amendment. Of one piece with the post–Civil War Court's narrow construction of those powers, *Day* attempted to prevent the changes wrought by the amendment from spilling over into the entire universe of state-federal relations.

The Tenth Amendment guarantee of state immunity fell into desuetude soon after *Day* and, for varying reasons, remained there for roughly a century. During the *Lochner* era, the Court's federalist sentiments gave way to a more libertarian impulse to protect individual citizens against deprivations by government at all levels—an agenda that is at odds with broad claims of governmental immunity. Moreover, so long as the Court was prepared to enforce direct, enumerated powers constraints on Congress, the subsidiary question of what Congress could do to the states in particular was not so terribly important. *Day* was rarely invoked; it was effectively distinguished with respect to federal income taxes levied under the newly enacted Sixteenth Amendment.[6] The case could have played a more prominent role after 1937, when the ignoble death of the enumerated powers doctrine lent new urgency to the protection of state sovereignty. The New Deal Court actually overruled *Day*, however.[7] Judicial abdication at the federalism front not only entailed the demise of direct constraints on Congress; it was sufficiently complete to dispose even of the secondary issue of national impositions on state and local governments.

The Tenth Amendment reemerged as a guarantee of state immunity in fits and starts in the near-perennial litigation over the application of the federal Fair Labor Standards Act to state and local employees. The Court sustained the statute against a Tenth Amendment challenge in 1968, struck it down in 1976, and sustained it again in *Garcia v. San Antonio Metropolitan Transit Authority* (1985), the high-water mark of process federalism.[8] The Court returned to the theme in 1992, in *New York v. United States* (1992). The scope of the Tenth Amendment defense of *New York* is very modest. It has, however, proved lasting, and it has provided the basis for the more assertive federalism conception of *Printz*.

New York presented a challenge by the state of New York and two of its counties to portions of the Low-Level Radioactive Waste Policy Amendments Act of 1985. To induce states to dispose of low-level radioactive waste generated within their borders, the statute provided three separate threats (which the act, true to congressional form, called "incentives"): surcharges on noncomplying states and the distribution of those funds to complying states; so-called access incentives, meaning that states that failed to meet statutorily prescribed deadlines could be denied access to disposal sites in other states or regions; and a "take-title" clause, which provided that states that failed to provide for disposal of waste generated within their borders by a certain date must take title to the waste, take possession of it, and bear liability for all damages incurred by a waste generator or owner. New York contested all three provisions as violations of the Tenth Amendment. While sustaining the first two schemes, the Supreme Court declared the take-title provision unconstitutional, reasoning that the provision offered state governments a meaningless "choice" of either accepting ownership of and liability for waste or regulating its disposal according to Congress's instructions. Finding both options—standing alone—to be outside Congress's authority, the Court determined that a choice between them was "no choice at all." "Either way," the Court said, "'the Act commandeers the legislative processes of the States by directly compelling them to enact and enforce a federal regulatory program,' an outcome that has never been understood to lie within the authority conferred upon Congress by the Constitution."[9]

New York is often said to forbid the federal commandeering of state and local governments, subject to certain exceptions. But the truth is that the federal government, as a rule, *may* commandeer, subject only to the narrow exception of *New York.* As the word *commandeering* suggests, the Tenth Amendment limits Congress only in the choice of regulatory means, not with respect to the ends or objects of legislation. And even in that limited regard, the Tenth Amendment of *New York* is not much of a constraint.

First, the prohibition against federal commandeering applies only when and where the federal government regulates the "states as states"— as distinct from displacing their regulatory authority even on matters of peculiarly local concern. Time and again, the Supreme Court has "rejected the suggestion that Congress invades areas reserved to the States by the Tenth Amendment simply because it exercises its authority under the Commerce Clause in a manner that displaces the States' exercise of their police power."[10] By the same token, the federal government may commandeer states and localities so long as it regulates them along with private parties and in the same manner. The basic presumption is that state and local entities—when acting as market participants rather than sovereigns—enjoy no Tenth Amendment exemption from federal fair labor laws, wage controls, or tax schemes.[11] The only commandeering that is prohibited is the regulation of the states alone and in their political capacity.

Second, the prohibition against commandeering the "states as states" applies only to statutes enacted pursuant to some (not all) of

Congress's powers under Article I. The prohibition does not apply with full force when Congress legislates under the Fourteenth Amendment.[12] Nor, more important, is Congress thought to be "commandeering" when it bribes the states into accepting onerous programs or, to put it more charitably, legislates under the Spending Clause of Article I and attaches strings to the receipt of federal funds. That is so even when the federal funding is *de minimis* or more akin to a payment for services rendered than to a grant. The fact that federal funds may amount to less than the state's taxpayers paid into the program to begin with is of no consequence: the courts will examine only the second leg of the transaction and conclude that the federal government may "grant" program funds on conditions that it could not impose directly. The only limitation on congressional commandeering under the Spending Clause is that there must be *some* connection between the purpose of the federal funds and the conditions attached to their receipt. In practice, this proviso has not been much of a restriction, since the courts have been very lenient in construing the nexus requirement.[13]

Finally, the federal government may leave the states a "choice" between regulating on their own and abiding by a federal regulatory scheme. Many environmental statutes work in that fashion. They have consistently been upheld against Tenth Amendment challenges—even when the federal default rules are so expensive as to leave the states no choice but to regulate on their own and even when the states' "choice" of environmental standards and regulatory instruments is so sharply circumscribed as to be no choice at all.[14]

Given this range of constitutionally permissible means of cajoling state and local governments, it comes as no surprise that commandeering challenges remained rare and mostly unsuccessful after *New York*. The decision was followed in only two appellate cases, both involving minor environmental programs. The Fifth Circuit struck down a provision of the Lead Contamination Control Act that required states to assist local education agencies, schools, and day care centers in remedying potential lead contamination in their drinking water systems. And the Ninth Circuit held that a portion of the Forest Resources Conservation and Shortage Relief Act, which required the states to issue regulations restricting the export of lumber harvested from federal lands within their borders, violated the Tenth Amendment.[15] The Supreme Court left the commandeering question alone for some five years. In 1997, however, the Justices revisited the Tenth Amendment, with a startling result.

The Structure of *Printz*

Printz v. *United States,* decided in June 1997, involved a challenge to certain interim provisions of the Brady Handgun Violence Prevention Act, which commanded state and local law enforcement officers to conduct background checks on prospective gun purchasers. Appellate courts were divided as to whether those mandatory background checks constituted impermissible commandeering. The Supreme Court, in an opinion authored by Justice Scalia and joined by Chief Justice Rehnquist and by Justices Kennedy, Thomas, and O'Connor, answered it in the affirmative and struck down the Brady Act. The decision produced a sharp division on the bench. Justice Stevens submitted a fierce and in many respects persuasive dissent, which was joined by Justices Souter, Ginsburg, and Breyer.[16]

Little of substance seems to be at stake here. Like *Lopez*, *Printz* involved a federal anticrime provision of largely symbolic value. Just as most states already prohibited the possession of guns in and around schools, most states already required the background checks mandated by the Brady Act. Moreover, the Brady Act requirements were only an interim measure, scheduled to expire with the establishment of a federal computer system by November 30, 1998. To be sure, gun control tends to produce agitation on all sides, and the *Printz* dissenters expressed their dismay with what they viewed as the majority's cavalier disregard for the important purposes of the statute. In the end, though, the dissenters' chief concern and the source of their fury were not the result but the expansive reasoning of Justice Scalia's opinion.

The legal question in *Printz* is this: Does the *New York* injunction against the federal commandeering of state *legislatures* also apply to the commandeering of state and local *enforcement* officers, such as the provisions contested in *Printz*? Justice Scalia concludes that it does. He portrays the distinction between state legislatures and executive officers—for Tenth Amendment purposes—as a distinction without a difference: commandeering either tends to undermine the exercise of sovereign state power. The dissent objects that a federal order to a state's elected representatives implicates state sovereignty far more centrally than the recruitment—limited, under the Brady Act, both in scope and in duration—of state and local officers into federal law enforcement. Justice Scalia, in turn, replies that the federal diversion of state law enforcement always distorts, and may in the end eviscerate, the state's ability to determine its own policies and priorities—the result found objectionable in *New York.*

Surely, though, this is a matter of degree. While one can think of federal orders to state officials that affect state sovereignty as severely as direct commands to the legislature, the Brady Act probably is not one of those orders.[17] And even if it is (as Justice Scalia suggests), Justice Stevens's point retains considerable force for this reason: The Tenth Amendment, from *Day* on forward, has always been a slender textual basis for state and local immunity of *any* sort. The more expansive the claim of immunity, the more problematic the lack of a textual basis becomes.

The genius of Justice Scalia's *Printz* opinion is to turn the textual weakness into a launching pad for an aggressive reassertion of federalist principles. Scalia concedes the limited relevance of the Tenth Amendment—and locates the principle of intergovernmental immunity elsewhere:

> "[Petitioners] contend that congressional action compelling state officers to execute federal laws is unconstitutional. *Because there is no constitutional text speaking to this precise question*, the answer to the [plaintiffs'] challenge must be sought in historical understanding and practice, in the structure of the Constitution, and in the jurisprudence of this Court."[18]

The bulk of the majority opinion in *Printz* is devoted to a discussion of history and precedents. On both points, however, the dissenters give as good as they get. In the end, the *structural* argument turns out to be the firmest ground and the core of *Printz*.[19]

History. The historical evidence shows that the Founders did not intend Congress to commandeer state legislatures. The Founders' position on the federally mandated enforcement of federal law by state and local magistrates, however, is much murkier. The lamentable experience under the Articles of Confederation had proven that an effective federal government required an ability to legislate directly on the citizens, rather than through the states. The Founders' principal concern was to justify that affirmative power of direct legislation (and especially taxation). As the *Printz* dissenters observe, however, this does not show that the Founders meant to *foreclose* the option of "indirect" federal legislation on the states or to prohibit the state or local enforcement of federal laws.[20] In fact, the *Printz* dissent says, the Founders voiced support for the state and local enforcement of federal laws, at least so long as the states consented to such schemes.

The debate between the Federalists and the anti-Federalists on this point (as on many others) is rife with political posturing—in this case, the Federalists' effort to counter the anti-Federalists' dire warnings that the Constitution would produce an overbearing national government and swarms of obnoxious federal enforcers.[21] Justice Scalia is probably right in arguing that there is no conclusive *proof* that the Founders or the early Congresses meant to "dragoon" state officials into federal law enforcement without the states' consent. Then again, the dissent plausibly maintains that a conclusive proof is too much to demand of any historical argument.[22]

However all that may be, the historical evidence cannot possibly be the basis of *Printz*. The entire debate has an air of unreality, for not in their worst nightmares did the Founders envision a government that would claim the vast powers and responsibilities to which we have become accustomed. Far less did they imagine a *federal* government of boundless authority. Thus, the "historical" inquiry must ask what the Founders *would have* thought about constitutional rules for a hypothetical government that lacks the enumerated powers doctrine on which the regime was actually founded. It is a bit like scouring the *Federalist Papers* for instructions on the governance of Jupiter.[23]

Precedent. Justice Scalia's exposition of "the jurisprudence of this Court" is similarly inconclusive. For one thing, there is not a lot of jurisprudence. Justice Scalia admits as much and tries to make the most of what little there is. "Until very recent years," he writes, there were no clear examples of congressional commandeering.[24] Commandeering (in the relevant sense), Justice Scalia maintains, began only with the environmental legislation of the 1970s, and those statutes immediately produced legal challenges. When faced in *New York* with the first "clear" example of commandeering, Scalia concludes, the Supreme Court promptly invalidated the practice.

This account of the precedents is tendentious. It is true, as Justice Scalia observes, that appellate courts invalidated a few environmental commandeering regulations and, moreover, that the Environmental Protection Agency withdrew other regulations in the expectation that they would fail to pass judicial muster. Still, the Supreme Court uniformly *sustained* the early environmental statutes and regulations against Tenth Amendment challenges, albeit by narrow margins. The first and the only exception to that pattern is *New York*—a precedent for *Printz* but, as noted, one of questionable reach and authority. While one can argue (with some difficulty) that various opinions in the environmental commandeering cases weigh, on balance, in favor of *Printz*, Justice Scalia's averment that the Supreme Court's precedents provide the "most conclusive" support for the holding in *Printz* overstates the case by more than a small margin.[25] Presumably, Justice Scalia—an exceedingly competent jurist—knows that. His ostensible emphasis on the precedents is best read as an attempt to make *Printz* seem unexceptional and to soft-pedal his third and central argument about "the structure of the Constitution."

Structure. Justice Scalia's structural argument, contained in Section III of his opinion, presents three separate claims. First, Justice Scalia explains that the Constitution establishes a system of "dual sovereignty," wherein the states and the national government occupy separate "spheres." The Tenth Amendment is only one of the indicia of federalism so understood.[26] Second, Justice Scalia maintains that the congressional commandeering of state and local officers would undermine the federal executive: by dragooning state and local officers into federal law enforcement, Congress could subvert and circumvent the president's constitutional authority to ensure the faithful execution of the law. Third, Justice Scalia argues that Congress *lacked the constitutional authority* to enact the background check requirements under, of all things, the Necessary and Proper Clause of the Constitution, which empowers Congress to "make all laws which shall be necessary and proper" to the enforcement of its delegated powers. A law that presses state and local officers into federal service, Justice Scalia maintains, cannot be "proper." Each of those three claims points beyond the seemingly limited holding in *Printz*. Each implies a notion of federalism, not as a mere protection of state immunity but as a direct constraint on the federal government.

The first structural argument, concerning "dual sovereignty," is more appropriately described as a statement of constitutional principle. Later in the opinion, however, Justice Scalia draws out the implications of that principle and explains why the state and local enforcement of federal laws damages federalism:

> By forcing state governments to absorb the financial burden
> of implementing a federal regulatory program, Members of
> Congress can take credit for "solving" problems without hav
> ing to ask their constituents to pay for the solutions with higher

federal taxes. And even when the States are not forced to absorb the costs of implementing a federal program, they are still put in the position of taking the blame for its burdensomeness and for its defects.[27]

The observation that federal impositions may diminish political accountability is not unprecedented. It appears, for instance, in Justice Kennedy's *Lopez* concurrence and in Justice O'Connor's majority opinion in *New York*. In both these cases, however, the argument was limited to federal programs that interfere in "traditional" areas of state regulation or "commandeer" the states.[28] As stated in *Printz*, in contrast, the argument applies to a vast range of federal programs, including policies that have nothing to do with "commandeering" or even with federal intervention in areas of traditional state regulation. In that more general form, the argument implies a direct assault on "cooperative," the process-based federalism that was celebrated in *Garcia*.[29]

A random example illustrates the importance of the point at issue. Under cooperative federalism, voters in many states have been confronted with a real possibility of stringent air quality regulations, from lawn-mowing restrictions to onerous and expensive car inspection requirements. When such regulations are challenged (politically or in court), local regulators blame the state, which blames the Ozone Transport Commission, which blames the Environmental Protection Agency, which solemnly swears that it had absolutely nothing to do with the matter and in turn blames state regulators for their failure to administer a sensible program sensibly.[30] The arrangement is profoundly federalist. Various levels of government share power. There is no interference in "traditional" state regulation (we are talking cars and commerce) and no "commandeering" (federal highway grants settle *that* question). The states are fully protected, if only because federal officials need them to take the flak for regulatory projects gone awry. Federalism seems alive and well—so long as the focus is on the relationships between levels of government.

Printz, however, shifts the focus and looks at cooperative federalism from the *citizen's* perspective. And from that vantage point, cooperative federalism is very unattractive. Joe Citizen can no longer finger the culprits for obnoxious government schemes. Were he to try, he would never get around to mowing his lawn. He cannot vote them out of office, since he knows not who they are. And he cannot vote with his feet, since his exit rights have been trumped with federal rules. Cooperative federalism, in other words, creates insurmountable information costs, diffuses responsibility, wipes out choice and competition, and in that manner produces a sprawling, meddlesome government. Cooperative federalism is not simply the opposite of real, competitive federalism; it "threatens the very liberty and accountability that federalism is intended to protect."[31] The diffusion of responsibility and the ensuing potential for blame shifting and credit taking are not unfortunate by-products of cooperative federalism; they are its animating principles. American federalism (unlike, say, Germany's, which Justice Breyer's *Printz* dissent touts as a model) separates the spheres of the federal and state governments precisely because the states and the federal government cannot control one another, and the voters cannot choose or control either when political responsibility disappears in a cesspool of cooperation. In bringing the commandeering question back to this fundamental consideration, Justice Scalia reinvokes federalism's purposes of citizen choice and government competition.

Justice Scalia's second structural argument is that the congressional enlistment of state and local officers undercuts the president's law enforcement authority. That contention reflects a position the Justice Department has held for some time, and it is surely correct: it cannot be true that Congress may carve up executive power and hand the pieces to actors beyond the control of the nation's chief executive. But the argument—endorsed, amazingly, by four other members of the Court—is unprecedented in the Court's modern federalism jurisprudence.[32] Like Justice Scalia's argument concerning cooperative federalism, moreover, his emphatic insistence on the need for a unitary executive (as an organizational principle of federalism) reaches far beyond the commandeering context.

Suppose Congress bribes the states into executing federal schemes or bludgeons them into regulatory programs under threat of wholesale federal preemption or commandeers them under a program that also covers private parties. All these time-tested strategies are plainly constitutional under *New York*. As the *Printz* dissent observes, however, they are no less intrusive into executive authority than the background checks mandated by the Brady Act. Thus, the *Printz* dissent concludes, Justice Scalia's executive power argument casts constitutional doubt on federal statutes and legislative strategies that have heretofore been thought to satisfy federalism concerns. To be sure, the dissent's charge is not the holding of *Printz*. It is instructive (and quite amazing), however, that Justice Scalia says practically nothing to reject or deny the dissenters' expansive reading of his executive power argument.[33]

Justice Scalia's third structural argument, concerning the limitations of the Necessary and Proper Clause, appears casually and almost as an afterthought. It is the last substantive argument in the opinion and appears in response to the dissent. Lo and behold, though, a Tenth Amendment case about the immunity of state and local officers from laws that are otherwise within Congress's constitutional authority has turned into a case about the scope of congressional power. Justice Scalia explicitly describes the prohibition on federal commandeering not as a Tenth Amendment constraint but as *a limitation of the Necessary and Proper Clause itself.*

Once again, the argument is completely unprecedented.[34] Moreover, and putting aside the interesting question of what else (other than federal commandeering) might be "improper," the mere reappearance of the Necessary and Proper Clause raises a very large flag. The Supreme Court has not decided a Necessary and Proper case in eons, for the reason suggested in Justice Thomas's *Lopez* concurrence: the Court supposed that Congress could enact practically any law—necessary or redundant, proper or improper, inane or insane—under the Commerce Clause or under whatever other "enumerated" power might come in handy. If enumerated powers are boundless, there can be no controversy over the Necessary and Proper Clause. The reappearance of the clause signals that the enumerated powers are *not* boundless but, for lack of a better word, enumerated.

The Scope of *Printz*

Standing alone, the preceding interpretation of Justice Scalia's *Printz* opinion as a portent of the second coming of the enumerated powers doctrine may seem overdrawn. But the concurrences and dissents in *Printz* point in the same direction. The first sentence of Justice O'Connor's brief concurrence professes agreement with the majority opinion's disquisition on constitutional history and precedents. Justice O'Connor, however, pointedly *omits* any reference to Justice Scalia's arguments about constitutional structure and instead invokes the Tenth Amendment as an adequate basis for the decision. As illustrated by her majority opinion in *New York* and by her decision to join Justice Kennedy's *Lopez* concurrence, Justice O'Connor is fond of state-sovereignty federalism and less than fully committed to a federalism that might translate into serious constraints on government. Her failure to endorse Justice Scalia's structural arguments while concurring with the more conventional remainder of his opinion suggests that those arguments transcend state-sovereignty federalism.

Justice Thomas also submitted a concurrence in *Printz*, urging a return to the constitutional text and to the doctrine of enumerated powers. Specifically, he suggested that the Commerce Clause provides no warrant for the federal regulation of intrastate gun purchases and, moreover, that the Second Amendment right to bear arms might bar the federal regulation of handguns. At first sight, this looks like a *Lopez* replay—a lone assertion of principled constitutionalism against a half-hearted majority opinion. Justice Thomas's *Printz* opinion, however, is much shorter than his thorough and devastating *Lopez* concurrence, and it has a certain cheekiness.[35] Justice Thomas can afford to indulge himself and dispense with another elaborate explication of federalism, properly understood, because *Printz* already suggests the considerations of enumerated powers that he wishes to push on the Court.

Most clearly, the dissent in *Printz* suggests an expansive interpretation of Justice Scalia's opinion. Thoughtful and almost persuasive in his discussion of the historical record and the precedents, Justice Stevens loses his bearings when confronted with Justice Scalia's structural arguments. He responds to Scalia's invocation of dual sovereignty with a declaration that "[t]he interests of the States are more than sufficiently protected by their participation in the National Government"[36]—an assertion of the process federalism that *Lopez* had presumably laid to rest. Justice Stevens goes on to charge that Justice Scalia's concern over the difficulty of assigning political responsibility for the costs and consequences of "cooperative" policies "reflects a gross lack of confidence in the electorate that is at war with the basic assumptions underlying any democratic government." Leaving aside that a demagogic insistence on "democracy" is at war with Justice Stevens's consistent record of *opposing* democracy (especially in the states), the argument fails even on its own terms.[37] Justice Scalia is entirely correct in observing that the point and effect of "cooperative" federalism are to immunize regulatory schemes against democratic control.[38]

When the Court announced its decision in *Printz*, Justice Stevens took the unusual step of commenting from the bench that the majority opinion reminded him of the free-wheeling jurisprudence of constitutional "penumbras" and "emanations"—associated most prominently, although Justice Stevens did not say so, with the late Justice Brennan and opposed most vociferously by Justice Scalia. That criticism misses the mark. It is true that the intergovernmental immunity version of the Tenth Amendment from *Day* to *New York* is largely an extratextual construct. But as noted, it is the Court's refusal or, as the case may be, its inability to enforce the textual, enumerated powers constraints on Congress that leads to a search for partial substitutes—even if they are indirect and not exactly covered by the text. The complaint about Tenth Amendment "penumbras" ultimately reflects a stubborn adherence to the process federalism of *Garcia*.

It is likewise true that Justice Scalia's *Printz* opinion goes much beyond the text of the Tenth Amendment and the precedents decided thereunder. But the opinion does not purport to be based on the text of the Tenth Amendment or for that matter its penumbras, and the precedents, as noted, play a subordinate role. The decision is explicitly based on the *structure* of the Constitution. There is nothing "activist" or free-wheeling in a structural constitutional argument, so long as it reflects the *actual* structure and not some fanciful spirit or aspiration. The issue is one of substance, not style; and on the substance, Justice Scalia has the better argument. His *Printz* opinion strays well beyond the text and the precedents, but only to reconstruct a piece of the federalist architecture.

For all that, one must concede to Justice Stevens that Justice Scalia's opinion *is* Brennanesque in the following respect: Brennan routinely laced his opinions with pronouncements that were unnecessary to decide the case at hand. His fellow Justices either failed to notice those land mines or neglected to defuse them on the spot, since they seemed so far afield from the constitutional ground the Court was then treading. But the charges often exploded in a later case, when Justice Brennan, who always thought two or three cases ahead of his fellow Justices, would cheerfully invoke his earlier, expansive dicta as well-settled law.

Printz has the same quality. Questionable as a matter of precedent, it is a masterpiece of judicial statesmanship. Its logic and its arguments point far beyond the issue at hand. The bright-line jurisprudence of *Printz* is much more assertive and more capable of an expansive application than the tentative balancing approach of *Lopez*.[39] Similarly, *Printz* differs in tone from the diffident, "we decline to go further" tenor of *Lopez*. Not once does the *Printz* majority attempt to meet the dissenters' objections by limiting its holding; not once does it disclaim the expansive interpretation the dissent places on it. The dissent sounds dire warnings of further challenges to federal commandeering statutes. The majority responds with a cheerful "So what?"—and, while at it, suggests that even Spending Clause statutes, heretofore immune from commandeering analysis, may now be suspect. Discussing various federal regulatory schemes that require state implementation, including "[s]ome . . . connected to federal funding measures," the *Printz* majority declines to address those enactments because "it will be time enough to do so if and when their validity is challenged in a proper case." State and local officials have wasted little time in accepting the invitation.[40]

What comes of the expansive suggestions of *Printz* remains to be seen. Certain environmental provisions that plainly commandeer state officers seem very vulnerable.[41] Quite possibly, *Printz* may also develop force outside the commandeering context. In light of the language just quoted, the decision may well apply, for instance, when and where a small tail of federal funding wags a large dog of substantially unrelated regulatory impositions. The leading precedent on such conditional grants and regulation under the Spending Clause, *South Dakota* v. *Dole*, sustained the federal imposition of a minimum drinking age as a condition of receiving highway funds. While still good law, the case dates back more than a decade and may well be the second most vulnerable federalism precedent on the books.[42] By the same token, and as noted earlier, *Printz* also casts constitutional doubt on (at least, particularly burdensome) conditional preemption statutes—that is, federal laws that present states with a Hobson's choice to construct their own regulatory edifices or else to surrender to a federal *diktat*. Marshaling five votes for extending *Printz* and its logic into the realm of conditional funding and preemption may prove a tough sell. But the groundwork has been laid.

5

From Collusive Nationalism
to Noncooperation

Congressional inroads into matters once left to state and local governments are only one part of the federalism equation. The other, equally important part is the exercise of federal *judicial* power. Every new federal right and every expansion or extension of an existing federal right correspondingly diminishes the authority of state and local governments (and of private parties) to see to their own affairs. Federal rights flatten the differences among the states and replace federalism's competitive dynamics with universal rules, regardless of whether the rights are created by Congress or by the federal judiciary directly under the Constitution.

As suggested in chapter 2, the post–New Deal Court created quite a few new constitutional rights and aggressively extended their application to the states and to local governments. At the same time, the Court assisted Congress in producing a seemingly endless stream of statutory entitlements, principally through generous interpretations of federal statutes. These developments accompanied the Court's wholesale abdication at the federalism front. Process federalism, in other words, did not simply mean that the Supreme Court would stand aside and leave the states to their own devices. It also meant that the Court would impose new individual rights constraints on states and localities and, moreover, cooperate with Congress in expanding federal power.

Over the past decade or so, however, the Court has reversed course. Paralleling its shift from process federalism to a modest revival of federalism doctrines in enumerated powers and Tenth Amendment cases, the Court has shown an increased reluctance to create individual rights under the Constitution and to cooperate with Congress in expanding federal entitlements. I postpone a discussion of the individual rights cases until chapter 7 and devote this chapter to cases dealing with the Court's relationship with Congress. Most of the cases are somewhat obscure, and the doctrines, unfortunately, are confusing even in their broad outlines. The developments in this area of the law, however, affect the core of the federal entitlement state.

From Collusion to Confrontation

The relationship between the Court and Congress during the 1960s and 1970s can fairly be described as "collusive nationalism." Congress put expansive private entitlements on the books, and the Supreme Court provided yet more expansive interpretations. Much like the "cooperative federalism" described and denounced in chapter 4, the collusive production of entitlements owed its attraction in large part to the accompanying potential for institutional blame shifting and credit taking. Congress and the Court could both take credit for the new benefits and entitlements. Each institution could thus cement its good relations with interest groups, while blaming "the other guy" for the attendant costs.

While the precise terms of collusion between Congress and the Supreme Court differed from issue to issue and from statute to statute, the basic dynamics worked across the board. Most major federal entitlement statutes have been shaped and implemented through private litigation. For example, the federal judiciary played a prominent role in determining entitlements and eligibility rules under the Aid to Families with Dependent Children (AFDC) program.[1] The development of race-based affirmative action programs under federal civil rights statutes was in large measure the courts' accomplishment.[2] The Byzantine edifice of sexual harassment law is principally a judicial construct. Private rights to the enforcement of federal environmental standards and regulations were initially a judicial invention, albeit one that Congress endorsed promptly and enthusiastically.[3] Perhaps the most pristine example of the Court's entitlement-friendly jurisprudence is *Maine* v. *Thibotout*. In that 1980 case the Court discovered that Section 1983 of volume 42 of the *United States Code*, enacted in 1871 to provide federal court jurisdiction to enforce constitutional rights against the states, also confers jurisdiction over cases seeking the enforcement of federal *statutory* rights, even and especially where Congress has failed to provide such rights in so many words.[4]

The joint production of federal entitlements is appropriately characterized as collusive *nationalism* because being nice to interest groups meant being mean to state and local governments. Once a federal rule becomes a private entitlement, the state administration of regulatory programs ceases to be a matter of bargaining between state and federal bureaucrats. Instead, private beneficiary groups use the leverage of litigation to insert themselves into the programs and, predictably, to demand their expansion. *Maine* v. *Thibotout* in particular had a huge impact on state-federal relations by effectively converting a vast array of theretofore discretionary federal programs into entitlement statutes. The average governor's or mayor's idea of federal "commandeering" is not at all the direct order to enforce federal statutes (à la *Printz*); it is the private lawsuit under Section 1983.[5]

Roughly since the beginning of the Rehnquist Court in 1986, however, the Supreme Court has arrested and in some respects reversed the creation of new federal rights, and collusive nationalism has given way to a much more contentious relation between the Court and Congress. This trend is connected to concerns that transcend the federalism question, and it has not been uniform and unbroken. Still, the case law shows a clear tendency toward limiting the federal judiciary's role vis-à-vis state and local governments.

The Supreme Court's growing reluctance to serve as an accomplice in the congressional expansion of federal power parallels *Lopez, Flores,* and the Tenth Amendment cases, and it reflects the same solicitude for state sovereignty. But the cases have a somewhat different thrust. Enumerated powers cases tell Congress that it may not do X, Y, or Z. Tenth Amendment cases hold that Congress may not do X, Y, or Z to states and localities in a particular manner. In contrast, the "noncooperation cases" reviewed in this chapter hold that Congress *may* do X, Y, or Z— but that it will have to do so without the assistance of the federal courts.[6]

Noncooperation cases span a wide variety of legal issues, some of which have only incidentally to do with federalism. For example, the Rehnquist Court has moved progressively toward a formalistic "plain-meaning" mode of statutory interpretation. The statutory language, rather than the legislative history or broad statements of congressional intent, forms the focus of judicial interpretation. For various reasons, including the difficulty of reconciling warring interests, Congress has a strong preference for statutory vagueness. Plain-meaning analysis tends to narrow vague language and to deprive the political factions of the option of filling the statutory blanks with an (often manufactured) legislative history, while at the same time allowing federal agencies to fill ambiguous language with any plausible interpretation, including interpretations Congress dislikes. In short, plain-meaning analysis is a form of judicial noncooperation because it drives up the costs of transacting legislative business. While the concerns that have prompted this formalist shift are much broader than the federalism question, the general tendency of plain-meaning analysis is to constrict federal entitlements, to disappoint interest groups and their congressional patrons, and, correspondingly, to leave more room for state and local autonomy.[7]

For another example, and in another break with past practice, the Rehnquist Court has often refused to exercise judicial review in citizen suits brought by environmental interest groups. In the most important of those cases, *Lujan* v. *Defenders of Wildlife* (1992), the Court effectively declared all environmental citizen suit provisions unconstitutional.[8] Although environmental standing cases are not about federalism per se, many environmental citizen suits are brought against states and municipal agencies (such as water authorities). The scope of environmental citizen standing is of sufficient importance to have prompted the Commonwealth of Virginia to challenge the EPA's refusal to accept the state's implementation plan under the Clean Air Act, which restricted citizen standing against the commonwealth to the boundaries of *Defenders of Wildlife* and state common law.[9] And *Defenders of Wildlife* is of one piece with *Printz:* both decisions are based on concerns over the congressional delegation of federal law enforcement to agencies other than the federal executive—local government in *Printz*, private law enforcers in *Defenders of Wildlife*.[10]

In short, interpretive and jurisdictional rules that confine statutory entitlements exemplify judicial doctrines that have important, albeit incidental, implications for federalism. A full account of such doctrines would make for a very long and ambitious book. For the purposes at hand, it seems best to focus on noncooperation cases that involve federalism concerns directly, not merely incidentally. The most significant line of cases in that vein concerns the states' sovereign immunity under the Eleventh Amendment. The Supreme Court's most recent pronouncement on this constitutional issue is its 1996 decision in *Seminole Tribe of Florida* v. *Florida.*

Seminole Tribe: **The Holding**

Seminole Tribe v. *Florida* concerned certain provisions of the Indian Gaming Regulatory Act, which imposed on states a duty to negotiate "in good faith" with Indian tribes toward the formation of a compact concerning the regulation of gambling on Indian lands. The statute authorized tribes to compel performance of that duty by bringing suit in federal court. The Supreme Court held that this provision violated the states' sovereign immunity under the Eleventh Amendment to the U.S. Constitution.

In *New York* and *Printz*, the Tenth Amendment served to create pockets of state sovereignty against federal impositions. *Seminole Tribe* pursues the same objective under the Eleventh Amendment, albeit in a different direction: it asks what Congress may do to the states *through the federal courts* or, to put it differently, what the federal courts may do to the states at the behest of Congress. And, much as *New York* and especially *Printz, Seminole Tribe* rests on a notion of intergovernmental immunity for which the constitutional *text* provides little warrant. The Eleventh Amendment reads as follows:

> The Judicial power of the United States shall not be construed to extend to any suit in law or equity, commenced or prosecuted against one of the United States by Citizens of another State, or by Citizens or Subjects of any Foreign State.

The amendment was passed in response to an early Supreme Court case, *Chisholm* v. *Georgia,* in which the Court allowed the executor of a South Carolina citizen's estate to maintain a federal suit against the state of Georgia for the enforcement of certain war debts owed by the state.[11] The Eleventh Amendment overruled *Chisholm* and barred federal jurisdiction in "diversity" cases—that is, cases brought by citizens of one state against another state—without the state's consent.

Notoriously, however, there are more opinions than there are law professors as to *what else,* if anything, the Eleventh Amendment was intended to do. Does the amendment simply preclude diversity suits, or does it embody a broader principle of sovereign immunity? In particular, was the amendment—despite its reference to suits "by Citizens of *another* State"—also meant to bar citizens from suing their *own* state in federal court? At the time of the amendment's enactment, the issue did not present itself because federal trial courts possessed no federal question jurisdiction—that is, no general jurisdiction over cases arising under federal law. When Congress conferred such jurisdiction in the Judiciary Act of 1875, however, the question of federal court jurisdiction over federal question cases brought by citizens against their own state could no longer be avoided.

In 1890, the Supreme Court provided an answer. *Hans* v. *Louisiana* adopted the broader reading of the Eleventh Amendment and dismissed a lawsuit brought by a citizen of Louisiana against that state under the U.S. Constitution. *Hans* resembles *The Collector* v. *Day*, the Tenth Amendment case briefly described in chapter 4: much as *Day* read into the Tenth Amendment an extratextual principle of intergovernmental immunity, *Hans* is the origin of a line of cases that have "understood the Eleventh Amendment to stand not so much for what it says, but for the presupposition . . . which it confirms," as Chief Justice Rehnquist put it in *Seminole Tribe*.[12] The Eleventh Amendment according to *Hans* embodies a principle of sovereign immunity that is part and parcel of the English common law and, indeed, of the "jurisprudence in all civilized nations."[13]

In two strongly worded dissents in *Seminole Tribe*, Justice Stevens and Justice Souter (joined by Justices Ginsburg and Breyer) challenged the majority's broad, extratextual understanding. Justice Stevens maintained that the Supreme Court's "modern embodiment of the ancient doctrine of sovereign immunity 'has absolutely nothing to do with the limit on judicial power contained in the Eleventh Amendment.'" On an equally uncharitable note, Justice Souter averred that "neither text, precedent, nor history supports the majority's abdication of our responsibility to exercise the jurisdiction entrusted to us."[14] The fierce *Seminole Tribe* dissents are the latest in a long line of opinions that have contested the broad understanding both on historical and textual grounds and as a matter of constitutional principle.

In only one modern case, however, did a narrower, more textual interpretation of the Eleventh Amendment prevail. That case, *Pennsylvania* v. *Union Gas Co.* (1989), involved an extension of the question presented in *Hans* v. *Louisiana*. Since *Hans* arose directly under a provision of the Constitution (the Contracts Clause), it concerned only the states' immunity from suit under the Constitution and did not answer the question of when and to what extent *Congress may abrogate* sovereign immunity. In *Union Gas* a sharply divided Supreme Court held that the federal Comprehensive Environmental Response, Compensation, and Liability Act (better known as "Superfund") permitted private parties to sue state entities for the recovery of waste site cleanup costs that are attributable to the state's pollution activities. The Court found that the statute, which was enacted under the Commerce Clause, had abrogated the states' Eleventh Amendment immunity.

Seminole Tribe overruled *Union Gas*. Reverting to the broader understanding of the Eleventh Amendment as a guarantee of sovereign immunity, the Court provided a two-part answer to the question of congressional intrusions on state sovereignty. First, Congress *may* abrogate the states' sovereign immunity under the Fourteenth Amendment, provided that Congress clearly states its intent to do so. Because fourteen comes after eleven, the constitutional powers granted to Congress under the Fourteenth Amendment trump the constitutionally inferred limitations of the Eleventh Amendment.[15]

That leaves the question of congressional abrogations of sovereign immunity in the exercise of Article I powers: may Congress abrogate sovereign immunity when it legislates, for example, under the Commerce Clause? The general answer, which *Seminole Tribe* states in a needlessly convoluted form, is that Congress may *not* do so. *Federal courts will not entertain private lawsuits against states under federal statutes, except for lawsuits under civil rights statutes that evince a clear congressional intent to abrogate the states' sovereign immunity.* That, in a nutshell, is the teaching of *Seminole Tribe*.

Expansive as this holding may look at first sight, it is not the end of federal commandeering-by-lawsuit. First, *Seminole Tribe* does *not* hold that Congress may not create private causes of action against the states (pursuant to its Article I powers). It merely holds that federal courts may not entertain such claims. *State* courts, in other words, may generally still do so, and their rulings are in turn reviewable by the Supreme Court.[16] Second, the Eleventh Amendment protects states only against *private* enforcement in federal court but not against enforcement by the federal government. Third, *Seminole Tribe* does *not* hold that the states may not be sued in federal court; it merely holds that they may not be so sued *without their consent*. This exception, further discussed below, is not trivial. Many federal programs authorize both the disbursement of federal funds to the states and private lawsuits against them. To the extent that the acceptance of funds establishes a state's "consent" to be sued in federal court, the Spending Clause provides Congress with a partial escape from *Seminole Tribe*.

The fourth, most confusing, and most important exception to *Seminole Tribe* is the so-called *Ex parte Young* doctrine. This doctrine is actually a legal fiction, named after a Supreme Court case decided only a few years after *Hans*. *Hans*, as noted, resembled *The Collector* v. *Day*. Much as intergovernmental immunity under the Tenth Amendment soon gave way to the *Lochner* Court's more libertarian instincts, so the Supreme Court soon subordinated expansive Eleventh Amendment immunity to the protection of individual citizens against abuses at the hands of state governments. *Ex parte Young* held that lawsuits that the Eleventh Amendment would otherwise bar may still be brought against the state's *officers*, acting in their official capacities.[17]

The *Ex parte Young* "exception" turns out to cover a very large class of lawsuits that are brought in effect, though not in name, against state governments. *Ex parte Young*, it has been said, is not an exception to Eleventh Amendment immunity; since it covers most claims—essentially, all claims for remedies other than money damages—it is the rule to which the Eleventh Amendment is the exception.[18]

In a surprising twist, however, *Seminole Tribe* did *not* permit the tribe's lawsuit to go forward. Even though the plaintiffs sought the type of injunctive relief that is generally available under *Ex parte Young*, the Court found that the statute under consideration contained a "detailed remedial scheme" of negotiation between tribes and the governor. That scheme, the Court reasoned, precluded a lawsuit against individual state officials. Having so concluded, the Court dismissed the entire case for lack of jurisdiction.

Seminole Tribe: Its Meaning and Scope

Seminole Tribe makes explicit the federalism conception implicit in *Lopez, Flores, New York,* and *Printz,* which affords state and local governments a selective exemption from otherwise applicable and constitutional federal rules. Like *New York, Seminole Tribe* employs a fanciful construction of a secondary constitutional constraint—the Tenth Amendment there, the Eleventh Amendment here—as a means of salvaging one aspect of federalism, state sovereignty, from the wreckage wrought by the demise of direct, enumerated powers constraints on Congress.

Seminole Tribe has been described as a highly "statist" federalism decision, inasmuch as it aims to prevent individual citizens from holding state government officials to account.[19] This criticism misses the mark, however. The general point of federal entitlements and their private enforcement is to produce more government, not less.[20] From this vantage point, the private enforcement bar of *Seminole Tribe* is more appropriately characterized as *anti*statist.

Seminole Tribe is decidedly antistatist in a second, related respect—namely, by virtue of granting the Supreme Court a role in policing Congress. The *Seminole Tribe* majority's principal objective is to curb the ability of Congress to utilize private enforcement as a means of commandeering the states. Precisely this antinationalist, anticongressional thrust raised the *Seminole Tribe* dissenters' ire. As in *Lopez* and *Printz*, they hearkened back to process federalism and harangued the majority for its failure to rely on "'the effectiveness of the federal political process in preserving the States' interests.'"[21] Process federalism does not become more plausible or appealing by dint of ritualistic incantation. But the dissenters are surely correct in suggesting that *Seminole Tribe* is hostile primarily to Congress and only incidentally to the private litigants who do its bidding.

So much for the message of *Seminole Tribe*. But what of its practical effects? The multiple exemptions to the Eleventh Amendment immunity bar and in particular the broad *Ex parte Young* "exception" suggest an interpretation of *Seminole Tribe* as more smoke than fire—as a symbolic decision without much real reach. But this reading does not seem quite right. The Court granted review in *Seminole Tribe* only to affirm an appellate court ruling. Having done so, the Court bypassed several opportunities to reach the desired outcome in the case without confronting the immunity question. Notably, the statutory provision at issue in *Seminole Tribe* instructed the state's governor to negotiate in good faith. As Professor Henry Paul Monaghan has pointed out, such a duty, imposed on a state's chief executive, is highly discretionary and, absent explicit statutory authorization, can entail no corresponding private right to sue. In legal lingo, the plaintiffs in *Seminole Tribe* had failed to state a claim on which relief can be granted.[22] The conservative Justices who formed the majority in *Seminole Tribe* usually pay attention to such things. Yet they waltzed past the failure-to-state-a-claim question and decided the immunity issue. Neither the majority's reach for the immunity issue nor, for that matter, the shrill tone of Justice Stevens's and Justice Souter's dissents necessarily disproves an interpretation of *Seminole Tribe* as largely symbolic.[23] Still and on balance, those aspects of the decision suggest that something of substance is at stake.

The key to the likely consequences of *Seminole Tribe*—as distinct from its symbolic content—may lie in the "exceptions" to the sovereign immunity rule. The broader the exceptions, the narrower the rule and the impact of *Seminole Tribe*, and vice versa. In that regard, *Seminole Tribe* reflects a more general trend to narrow the escape routes from the general rule of sovereign immunity, and it will likely serve to accelerate that trend. A firmer notion of sovereign immunity has a certain gravitational force, which tends to contract the exceptions to the immunity rule—waivers of sovereign immunity, *Ex parte Young*, and the Fourteenth Amendment.[24]

The judicial construction of state waivers of sovereign immunity provides the most straightforward illustration. If the mere acceptance of federal dollars constituted a waiver, then the enactment of federal statutes under the Spending Clause would provide a convenient path for congressional end runs around *Seminole Tribe*. Congress could subject the states to federal lawsuits by the simple device of conditioning funds on the states' consent to be sued. In contrast, if more than mere acceptance of federal funds is required to establish a state's consent to suit, *Seminole Tribe*'s range of application may prove remarkably broad. Lo, it turns out that the Supreme Court has for some time been reluctant to infer waivers of sovereign immunity. The mere acceptance of federal funds, without more, is usually insufficient to establish a consent to suit: the state must give its consent freely, and it must know to what it is consenting.[25] In other words, the Supreme Court applied a strong presumption against federal waivers even before *Seminole Tribe*, when Congress could still abrogate (albeit with some difficulty) the states' sovereign immunity under Article I statutes. *Seminole Tribe* itself does not speak very directly and explicitly to the waiver question. By strengthening the sovereign immunity defense in general, however, the decision signals that waivers should be inferred even more reluctantly than the pre–*Seminole Tribe* precedents would indicate.[26]

A probably more important but, alas, much murkier question of *Seminole Tribe* is the fate of *Ex parte Young*—that is, the notion that some federal lawsuits against the state that the Eleventh Amendment bars may still be brought against the state's officers (in their official capacity). The viability of such lawsuits depends in part on the nature of the remedy sought by the plaintiff. If the plaintiff wants money, the answer was clear even before *Seminole Tribe*: *Ex parte Young* permits lawsuits against the state's officers only for injunctive relief, *not* for money. What *Seminole Tribe* adds to this rule is to bar many lawsuits (for money or other relief) directly against the state. Thus, *Seminole Tribe* creates a very substantial impediment to cases in which money is the only meaningful remedy. A lawsuit demanding damages for a (nonrecurring) violation of federal statutory rights by state officers is an example.

The remainder of the *Ex parte Young* exception—that is, the option of suing state officers for injunctive relief in federal court even if the state itself is immune—is probably still intact after *Seminole Tribe*. But it is no longer unquestioned. As mentioned, *Seminole Tribe* added another wrinkle to the Supreme Court's convoluted Eleventh Amendment jurisprudence and held that *Ex parte Young* suits for injunctive relief are *not* permitted under federal statutes that create a detailed, nonjudicial remedial scheme for the enforcement of federal rights. The potential significance of this holding is suggested by the fact that *Seminole Tribe* is the first Supreme Court decision since *Ex parte Young* itself to deny injunctive relief against state officers on sovereign immunity grounds. Moreover, and apart from the novelty of the analysis, the statutory text at hand strongly suggested the opposite conclusion.[27]

The unusual treatment of *Ex parte Young* in *Seminole Tribe* may simply stem from a desire to dismiss the case. As noted, however, easier routes would have led to the same result. That circumstance, as well as some of the language in the majority opinion, suggests that *Seminole Tribe* recasts "*Ex parte Young* as an almost doubtful act of judicial usurpation, justified only in 'narrow' circumstances (possibly those involving constitutional violations not the subject of statutory remedies)."[28] In other words, one can read *Seminole Tribe* as a step toward precluding Congress from using private enforcement in federal court as a means of securing state compliance with statutes enacted under Article I. Again, the firmer assertion of the sovereign immunity rule tends to narrow the exception to the rule.

A final illustration of this tendency involves congressional statutes enacted under the Fourteenth Amendment, rather than under Article I powers. Recall the sovereign immunity ground rules: while the Eleventh Amendment trumps or limits the powers of Congress under Article I (because it was passed, obviously, after the Constitution), it does not trump the Fourteenth Amendment (which was passed, obviously, after the Eleventh). The Fourteenth Amendment does not, however, override *all* principles of federalism, and the Eleventh Amendment—more precisely, the constitutional intuition for which its stands—has *some* application. That application takes the form of a so-called plain-statement rule: courts will not readily infer a congressional intent to abrogate state immunity, even under the Fourteenth Amendment, without a plain, "clear and unmistakable" congressional statement of intent. The leading Supreme Court decision on point is *Fitzpatrick* v. *Bitzer* (1976), a civil rights case that the *Seminole Tribe* majority left untouched.[29]

There have been attempts to claim sovereign immunity even under civil rights statutes that prohibit race and sex discrimination. But these attacks on the core of the Fourteenth Amendment—launched, incongruously, by advocates who have traditionally had a high regard for expansive civil rights protections and almost none for federalism—have come to naught.[30] For the time being, *Fitzpatrick* v. *Bitzer* is safe, and a "plain statement" of congressional intent will suffice to abrogate sovereign immunity.

After *Seminole Tribe*, however, the general rule that Congress may breach sovereign immunity under the Fourteenth Amendment by issuing a plain statement to that effect requires two qualifications. Both promise to become increasingly salient in future cases. The first qualification, which arises not from *Seminole Tribe* alone but from its conjunction with *City of Boerne* v. *Flores*, concerns the scope of Congress's powers under the Fourteenth Amendment and the question of whether a given statute was enacted or can be viewed as having been enacted under the Fourteenth Amendment. The second qualification concerns the breadth of the plain-statement rule and the level of judicial scrutiny under that rule.

A common example illustrates the former qualification and its potential significance. Suppose that a black state trooper sues the state (for money) because the state administers a standardized promotion test that has a disparate impact on minorities so that some minorities do worse on the test than whites. The plaintiff's claim is based on Title VII of the Civil Rights Act, which prohibits employment discrimination, was enacted (in its application to government actors) under the Fourteenth Amendment and, according to *Fitzpatrick* v. *Bitzer*, plainly intends to abrogate sovereign immunity. So the case can proceed on the merits.

Or can it? The plaintiff is complaining about an employment practice with a discriminatory impact, as opposed to *intentional* discrimination. While intentional discrimination is prohibited by the Fourteenth Amendment, the very different protection against disparate impact is not. That protection comes from Title VII, or the Supreme Court's prior interpretation thereof. But *Flores* teaches that Congress cannot simply make up new rights under the Fourteenth Amendment. There must, then, be another constitutional basis for the disparate impact rules of Title VII. That basis is the Commerce Clause. Congress cannot, however, breach the states' sovereign immunity through a statute enacted pursuant to its Article I powers. We know that because we have read

Seminole Tribe. It appears, then, that the plaintiff cannot obtain relief under any theory.

In the context of race and sex discrimination, the courts will probably find ways to escape the logic of an argument that has so unpalatable a conclusion.[31] Still, the state trooper hypothetical illustrates the potentially fateful interplay between *Seminole Tribe* and *Flores.* By disabling Congress from abrogating sovereign immunity through Article I legislation, *Seminole Tribe* pushes Congress to recast plain-vanilla commercial enactments as antidiscrimination legislation.[32] At the same time, *Flores* and its progeny vitiate that maneuver. Congress *cannot* simply shout "discrimination" and invoke the Fourteenth Amendment to circumvent sovereign immunity defenses. The Fair Labor Standards Act of *Garcia* fame has for that reason become the first big casualty of *Seminole Tribe.* A federal appeals court found that the act does not permit private lawsuits against state agencies in federal court. The statute, the court held, was enacted under the Commerce Clause, cannot possibly be viewed as a Fourteenth Amendment statute, and is therefore subject to the analysis of *Seminole Tribe.*[33] By that reasoning, the Family Medical Leave Act of 1993, which compels public and private employers to extend unpaid leave for certain medical and family reasons, is likewise unenforceable against the states.[34] As noted in chapter 3, legislative classifications at the perimeters of the Fourteenth Amendment (such as family status, veteran status, and possibly handicap) have also become problematic under *Flores* and *Seminole Tribe.* Outside the area of race and sex—the hard core of the Fourteenth Amendment—the states' immunity from private antidiscrimination lawsuits has expanded substantially and will likely continue to expand.

The same conclusion emerges from an examination of the second aspect of sovereign immunity determinations under the Fourteenth Amendment—that is, congressional abrogations of sovereign immunity by means of a clear and unmistakable statement of legislative intent. This "plain-statement" rule, sometimes called a "federalism canon," arises from Tenth and Eleventh Amendment considerations and has been deployed often and explicitly as a damper or counterweight to the Supreme Court's deferential Commerce Clause jurisprudence.[35] It was developed principally in the context of Commerce Clause legislation. *Seminole Tribe* has rendered those cases academic, since even the clearest statement of congressional intent no longer suffices to breach sovereign immunity under Article I statutes. The cases do, however, illustrate the bite that the plain-statement rule may develop in Fourteenth Amendment cases.

At first impression, a plain-statement rule of interpretation may not sound terribly demanding, since Congress can always meet the requirement by mouthing the appropriate phrases. The rule is not quite so toothless, however. For one thing, the required statement must appear in the text of the statute itself, not merely in the legislative history, and nothing but the most unequivocal statement will suffice. As developed in Article I cases, the plain-statement rule trumps just about any other canon—for instance, the rule that statutes are to be liberally construed in favor of the Indian nations.[36] It even trumps the otherwise very firm presumption that "reasonable" agency interpretations of ambiguous statutes are entitled to great judicial deference.[37] In fact, in only one of numerous plain-statement cases before *Seminole Tribe* did the Supreme Court find that an Article I statute in fact indicated an "unmistakable intent" to abrogate sovereign immunity. That case, *Pennsylvania* v. *Union Gas*, was overruled in *Seminole Tribe*.

Then, too, the Supreme Court has shown a tendency to up the ante on Congress and, by way of tightening the plain-statement requirement, to thwart repeated congressional attempts to abrogate the states' immunity. The Education of the Handicapped Act of 1975 (EHA), for instance, contained a statement indicating the intent of Congress to overcome what was then a general presumption against implied abrogations of state immunity. When the Supreme Court declared that the Rehabilitation Act, a statute very similar to the EHA, did not contain a sufficiently clear statement of congressional intent to permit damage suits against the states, Congress overruled the Court and amended the Rehabilitation Act. At the same time, Congress sought to prevent the EHA from meeting a similar fate by explaining (on the floor of the Senate) that the act did authorize lawsuits against the states and by providing explicitly that "[a] State shall not be immune under the Eleventh Amendment . . . from suit in Federal Court" for a violation of antidiscrimination statutes such as the EHA. Nonetheless, the Supreme Court found that the intent to abrogate sovereign immunity was not made "unmistakably clear" in the *text* of the statute itself and again held that states were immune from damage suits under the EHA.[38] Only in 1990, in the third attempt, did Congress finally accomplish what it thought it had done in 1975.

Sovereign immunity determinations under Fourteenth Amendment statutes may easily end up on a similar trajectory. Even before *Seminole Tribe*, some courts applied a remarkably robust presumption against abrogations of sovereign immunity in Fourteenth Amendment cases not involving race or sex.[39] Now, after the *Seminole Tribe* expansion of sovereign immunity in Article I cases, the Supreme Court could easily tighten the screws on congressional attempts to abrogate immunity under the Fourteenth Amendment, even while continuing to acknowledge that Congress has somewhat wider latitude to do so under the Fourteenth Amendment than under Article I.

Were that to happen, Congress would find it very difficult to commandeer states by means of private lawsuits in federal court. As noted earlier in this chapter, the requirement of clear legislative language tends to inhibit legislative compromise and to enhance the states' bargaining leverage. The states will be on notice as to what, precisely, Congress is about to do to them. And if Congress must legislate with candor and clarity, it will often prefer not to legislate at all.

The Bigger Picture

Eleventh Amendment cases lack the appealing choreography of constitutional panzer battles such as *Lopez, Flores,* or *Printz.* They are part of a thoroughly confusing guerrilla warfare between Congress and the Court. Statutory cases in which the Court refuses to cooperate with Congress lack even the modest symbolic appeal of *Seminole Tribe.*[40] Still, several points of broader significance emerge.

First, over the past decade, the Supreme Court has substantially expanded the states' sovereign immunity from federal impositions. Put differently, the Court has curtailed Congress's ability to rely on private enforcement in federal courts as a means of ensuring state compliance with federal mandates. While the *Ex parte Young* doctrine and legislation under the Spending Clause or the Fourteenth Amendment provide partial escapes from the rigors of *Seminole Tribe,* the Court has shown a clear tendency to narrow those exit routes as well.

Second, the expansion of sovereign immunity partakes of a larger trend toward an increased judicial reluctance to cooperate with Congress in dismantling state and local autonomy. The plain-statement rule, for instance, governs not only the immunity question but also the judicial interpretation of the *scope* of federal statutes. Much as Congress must clearly indicate its intent to abrogate sovereign immunity, so it must unambiguously state its intent to regulate "core state functions" before the Court will give such effect to a statute. Perhaps the clearest example is the Supreme Court's 1991 decision in *Gregory v. Ashcroft*,[41] which held that the ban on mandatory retirement in the federal Age Discrimination in Employment Act (ADEA) did not prevent a state from requiring its appointed judges to retire at age seventy. The Equal Employment Opportunity Commission deemed appointed judges to be covered by the act, and the Court acknowledged that the statutory language was "at least ambiguous" on the issue. Still, relying on the presumption against federal invasion of "core state functions," the Court broadly construed a statutory exemption for "appointee[s] at the policymaking level" to include appointed judges.[42]

When applied to Article I statutes, the list of state functions covered by the plain-statement rule "would seem to run the gamut from everything within the traditional police power to state operation of all its governmental processes to state methods of selecting high officials."[43] The rule may not appear to apply with quite the same force to Fourteenth Amendment statutes. In *Chisom v. Roemer*, a voting rights case decided on the same day as *Gregory*, the Supreme Court found that Section 2 of the Voting Rights Act applied to the election of state judges, despite the fact that the language of the act no more compelled that conclusion than did the ADEA.[44] The majority in *Chisom*—which included Justice O'Connor, the author of *Gregory*—did not even mention *Gregory* or its plain-statement rule. But *Chisom* and cases decided under it are best read as expressions of the same impulse that underlies *Flores:* define cases involving race and perhaps sex as special and make room for federalism in the rest of the legal realm, including Fourteenth Amendment statutes. The *Gregory* Court, for instance, indicated that the plain-statement rule applied regardless of whether Congress passed the ADEA pursuant to the Commerce Clause or Section 5 of the Fourteenth Amendment.

Similarly, in a sharp reversal of its practice of the 1960s, the Supreme Court has narrowly interpreted federal entitlement programs such as AFDC.[45] Section 1983 cases remain the bane of mayors and governors, but the Court has plainly concluded that *Maine v. Thibotout* was a mistake and has moved toward a narrower construction of protected "rights" that may be inferred from federal statutes.[46] The trend has been sufficiently pronounced to embolden state defendants in one recent Supreme Court case to urge that *Maine v. Thibotout* be overruled. The Court did not reach that question, having already found on other grounds that private litigants may not enforce provisions of the Social Security

Act that compel the states to take certain measures for the collection of child support.[47] Still, the handwriting is on the wall. *Seminole Tribe* is the constitutional tip of a sizable iceberg of judicial noncooperation.

Noncooperation cases glaze eyeballs, but they affect federalism's fate every bit as much as do direct constitutional confrontations between the Court and Congress. True, such cases do not "strike down" federal statutes but merely limit their private enforcement in federal court. And Congress can overturn judicial statutory interpretations, whereas it may of course not overturn constitutional precedents. But the practical differences are not nearly so large as these distinctions suggest. Judicial precedents declaring federal statutes unconstitutional are bound to be rare and limited in reach. Judicial refusals to cooperate have been far more common, precisely because they do not involve an ostentatious confrontation with Congress. Similarly, while Congress will frequently find a way around constitutional decisions (since the Supreme Court is generally wise enough not to choke off all avenues), Congress will often find itself handcuffed when the federal courts refuse to enforce entitlement statutes.

It is thus technically accurate but nonetheless highly misleading to describe noncooperation cases as "merely" limiting the private enforcement of federal entitlement statutes against state and local governments. Private enforcement in federal court is Congress's preferred means of getting its way. It is the operational core of every civil rights statute, of every health and welfare statute, of every environmental statute. Once the courts refuse to serve as an omnipotent legislature's handmaiden, Congress has to find other means of getting its way. All those involve the appropriation of money or direct enforcement by federal agencies or both. None of the alternatives is remotely so attractive as commandeering by private lawsuit. If they were, private enforcement provisions would not be such a pervasive feature of the statutory landscape to begin with.

Chapter 7 examines the implications of the Supreme Court's reluctance to cooperate with Congress in greater detail. Suffice it here to observe that collusive nationalism and judicial enthusiasm for federal entitlements had a far more corrosive effect on federalism than the direct commandeering à la *New York* or *Printz*. By that same token, judicial noncooperation is making a substantial contribution to federalism's restoration.

6

The Supreme Court's Federalism

Since a prolonged discussion of Eleventh Amendment esoterica makes even hardened lawyers beg for mercy, this is a good place and time to summarize the major themes of the preceding chapters and to describe the broad contours of the Supreme Court's federalism. Individually, the landmark decisions of recent years—*Lopez, Flores, New York, Printz,* and *Seminole Tribe*—are open to varying interpretations. Viewed in conjunction and side by side, however, the cases yield a reasonably clear picture.

We can view federalism jurisprudence as moving between two poles. One pole is the nationalist, New Deal model of "process federalism"— characterized, as noted in chapter 2, by strong presumptions in favor of congressional omnicompetence, against state competition, and for extreme judicial deference in federalism cases. Four of the current Supreme Court Justices—Breyer, Ginsburg, Souter, and Stevens—continue to adhere to that view, with varying degrees of dogmatic enthusiasm. A slim but rather solid majority of five Justices, however, has decisively rejected it. Barring the replacement of one of those Justices, the Court will not revert to process federalism. It has come too far.

The Court has not, however, migrated all the way to the opposite pole—that is, to the pre–New Deal model of enumerated powers, confidence in the benefits of state competition, and probing judicial review.

No modern federalism case has unambiguously reinstated the enumerated powers doctrine. Three features distinguish the Supreme Court's
federalism from a jurisprudence of enumerated powers.

First, the core of the Supreme Court's federalism is not citizen
choice and state competition but the preservation of state and local sovereignty. The cases only forbid congressional interference with *public*
(state or local) prerogatives. Statutes that regulate public *along with*
private conduct are usually immune against federalism challenges. The
Tenth and Eleventh Amendments have played a prominent role in the
case law; under a robust doctrine of enumerated powers, neither amendment would. Even the enumerated powers cases gravitate back toward
sovereignty issues: commandeering concerns play a large role in *Flores*,
and in the hands of Justices Kennedy and O'Connor even *Lopez* turns
into a Tenth Amendment case in disguise. The Supreme Court has consistently shied away from cases that implicate federalism's competitive
dynamics. Not one case limits federal authority in a way and in an arena
that would force states to compete by means of limiting the regulation of
desirable economic activities.

Second, the Court has circumscribed the *means*, rather than the
ends, of federal regulation. That is the essence of the Tenth and Eleventh Amendment cases: nothing in *New York*, or *Printz*, or *Seminole
Tribe* limits the purposes Congress may pursue. Nothing is beyond the
authority and the responsibility of Congress, provided only that Congress refrain from extending its reach by means of commandeering or
by means of mobilizing the federal courts. Even *Lopez* and *Flores*, the
only enumerated powers cases, are ultimately about means, not ends—
among other reasons because Congress's powers under the Spending
Clause remain intact. Suppose that Congress had conditioned the transfer of a fistful of dollars on the local enforcement of regulations equivalent to, respectively, the Gun Free School Zones Act or the Religious
Freedom Restoration Act. Would there be a constitutional problem? The
answer, most likely, is no. So long as there are no effective limits on the
Spending Clause, judicial federalism must remain confined to a curtail-
ment of legislative means. There can be no effective enumerated powers constraint on the ends or objects of federal legislation because
Congress can always spend its way around constitutional limitations.[1]

Third, instead of drawing the line against Congress, the Supreme
Court has attempted to advance federalism by means of curbing *judicial* power. *Seminole Tribe* and the statutory "plain-statement" cases show
that the courts are no longer willing to serve as the handmaidens of a

supreme federal legislature. Again, however, the Court is not going to stop Congress from pursuing its objectives, so long as it does not enlist federal judges as its foot soldiers.

In all three respects, the Supreme Court's federalism reflects the lesson of 1937. The Supreme Court is pursuing an agenda of promoting federalism *without* triggering a full-scale war over the scope of congressional authority, which means that the Court must steer clear of an unequivocal reassertion of enumerated powers. None of the federalism strategies just mentioned—the protection of state sovereignty, restrictions on legislative means, and judicial noncooperation—poses a direct, inescapable limitation on Congress. That is why the Supreme Court finds them viable and attractive.

Given the obvious constraints that prevent a judicial repeal of the New Deal, the Justices are well advised to proceed in a circumspect fashion. Still, federalism's piecemeal pursuit entails a risk of disconnecting it from concerns with citizen choice, limited government, and state competition. The question is whether the Supreme Court majority will mistake its faux federalism for the real thing or whether it will instead come to think of the current doctrines as a launching pad for further advances that will eventually reconverge on the central front of enumerated powers.

A transition from a functionalist, sovereignty-centered federalism to the real thing would require not simply a piecemeal extension of the precedents but a change in perspective. The state-sovereignty perspective is not a partial view of federalism but an upside-down view. It does not simply slight federalism's competitive dimension but replaces competition with a cartel. States and local governments, in such a view, must retain some of the attributes of sovereignty lest they lose their ability to provide regulatory services.

This perspective misperceives the monopoly problem at hand. In 1937 the judiciary abandoned the rules—enumerated powers—that forced the states to compete with each other and with the federal government. Sure enough, the market collapsed and gave way to what is, to all intents, a federal monopoly. Having deprived the citizens of the benefits of genuine choice and competition, the Supreme Court has now turned around to protect state and local governments. Acting as an intergovernmental antitrust agency of sorts, the Court intervenes every so often to restrain the federal monopolist and to ensure the survival of state and local governments, which serve as kinds of regulatory mom-and-pop stores. In politics as in markets, however, mom-and-pop stores are often uncompetitive operations with inferior service and higher prices, and for all their alleged flexibility and "closeness to the people," the states may be the least responsible, most interest-group-infested, most meddlesome of all government institutions. As Madison feared, the pernicious tendencies of faction are more difficult to control at the state level than at the federal level. This is precisely why competition must check and discipline state governments. The Supreme Court's federalism, however, shuns competition and instead extols the virtues of shopping locally. The Court subordinates consumer preferences to the protection of a producer cartel—and calls that "federalism."

To make the point directly, fifty Gun or Drug Free School Zones Acts may be better than one uniform federal statute. State statutes can be tailored to state circumstances, and only some of them will be as demagogic as the federal enactment. But a Court that celebrates state government *only* when and where the states will surely regulate—and recall, in that context, the *Lopez* concurrence—will soon forget that federalism's point is to *discipline* state governments, not to empower them. Similarly, the Court's Eleventh Amendment jurisprudence tends to immunize public entities from expensive impositions and regulations that private employers are nonetheless made to bear. A "federalism" of that description suggests, fantastically, that the interests of government, not the rights of private citizens, are somehow particularly deserving of judicial concern.

Antitrust theory shifted decades ago from cartels to competition and from producer interests to consumer welfare as its central concern. That shift was not a marginal adjustment but a paradigm change. Similarly, there is no *natural* progression from state-centered to competitive federalism. The transition implies a genuine change in perspective.

To a considerable extent, the transition is a matter of judicial will and votes. Chief Justice Rehnquist, Justice Scalia, and Justice Thomas recognize that state-sovereignty federalism makes sense only as a temporary substitute for enumerated powers federalism.[2] Justices Kennedy and O'Connor, on the other hand, seem to be enamored with state sovereignty and fearful that competitive federalism might rend the seamless web of government regulation. It is unclear how far the three conservative Justices will be able to drag along their two more conflicted colleagues. Three features of the Supreme Court's federalism may, however, enable Justices Scalia and Thomas and Chief Justice Rehnquist to push beyond the preoccupation with state sovereignty and toward a more robust, competitive federalism.

Open-Endedness. The Supreme Court's landmark federalism cases have a certain open-ended quality. None of the cases forecloses, and some actually invite, a return to a more principled federalism. *Lopez* and *Flores* at least mention enumerated powers as federalism's lodestar and, as noted, neither decision is easily confined to the bounds of state sovereignty. Both cases are preoccupied with federal intrusions into "traditional" state concerns, but that category is essentially meaningless. Should the Supreme Court so choose, traditional state regulation could come to encompass what it encompasses in statutory immunity cases— that is, practically everything the states happen to regulate. One must occasionally be grateful for phony legal categories.

Similarly, the Supreme Court's focus on legislative means rather than ends lends itself to a step-by-step approximation of enumerated powers. Restrict the means severely enough, and sooner or later the ends move beyond reach. As chapter 7 shows, Eleventh Amendment limitations have already become a major nuisance for Congress. And even if the commandeering cases do no more than force Congress into legislating under the Spending Clause, that is *something*—especially if Congress should come to recognize that money is scarce and if in future years the Supreme Court were to tighten the constitutional constraints on permissible Spending Clause legislation.

The latter prospect is more likely than the former. As noted, Justice Scalia's majority opinion in *Printz* hinted at the possibility of reconsidering *South Dakota* v. *Dole* (1987), where the Court sustained federal legislation that conditioned the states' receipt of federal highway funds on the adoption of a minimum drinking age. Only two Justices (O'Connor and Brennan) dissented from this ruling. All the Justices agreed, however, that conditions on federal grants may be unconstitutional if they are unrelated "to the federal interest in particular national projects or programs."[3] In other words, there must be some nexus between the federal grant and the conditions attached to it. Loosely applied in *South Dakota* v. *Dole*, the nexus test could easily be tightened, probably even without overruling the specific holding of the case.

Then, too, some of the Court's federalism cases invoke secondary themes that are connected to federalism's concern with choice and competition. *Lopez*, *Flores*, and the plain-statement cases illustrate the Court's irritation at Congress's tendency to meddle with the states, which may well gel into a more general annoyance with federal meddling in general. On other occasions, the Court has shown a concern over the loss of political responsibility entailed by the demise of formal constraints on the federal government. *Printz* in particular reconnects state sovereignty to the concerns of citizen-consumers. The point of dual sovereignty, *Printz* explains, is to enable individual citizens to assign political responsibility. That ability merits constitutional protection because it is a prerequisite for political choice and competition.

Text. The Supreme Court's sovereignty-centered federalism rests on shaky textual foundations. That, too, cuts in favor of a return to more principled judicial rules. The Supreme Court's Tenth and Eleventh Amendment decisions are defensible on the grounds explicitly articulated in some statutory plain-statement cases: once the enumerated powers doctrine has been jettisoned, aggressive interpretations of the Tenth and Eleventh Amendments are the only way of salvaging at least some of federalism's elements. But the Court cannot forever create islands of state sovereignty without a textual basis—and refuse to police the federalism boundaries explicitly stated in the constitutional text. The majority's defenses of its imaginative Tenth and Eleventh Amendment rulings are already wearing thin. Chief Justice Rehnquist's response to the dissents in *Seminole Tribe*, for a prominent example, has an infuriating air of "enough already—we have five votes." A retreat into a textualist Tenth or Eleventh Amendment is now foreclosed by the precedents and would imply a return to process federalism. Hence, the gravitational pull is in the other direction—toward Justice Thomas's *Lopez* opinion, which fully embraces enumerated powers, and toward Justice Scalia's *Printz* opinion, which instructs us to forget the text of the Tenth Amendment and to turn to the structure of the Constitution, including enumerated powers.

The Role of the Court. The Supreme Court's federalism lacks a coherent theory of the role of the judiciary's role in federalism disputes. The enumerated powers doctrine implies that the Court should police federalism's boundaries in the way in which it polices the boundaries of, for example, the First Amendment. Conversely, process federalism counsels complete judicial abdication. But what lies in between? "A lot of deference to the Congress, but not boundless deference," seems to be the formula of *Lopez* and *Flores*. Attempting to explain that federalism merits some (but not too much) judicial protection, Justice Kennedy and O'Connor's *Lopez* concurrence argues that the modern economy is excessively "complex and interdependent" for principled constitutional lines and, moreover, that the Supreme Court lacks full institutional competence to decide federalism questions, which require "political judgment." We are being asked to believe, first, that the pre–New Deal economy was a commercial stone age and, second, that the "political" nature of federalism questions somehow distinguishes them from the rest of the Court's business—as if First Amendment cases involving modern communications technologies or campaign finance laws were somehow free from "political" judgments.[4] To put it gently, the intermediate position lacks a plausible justification.

Viewed in conjunction, the Court's federalism cases suggest a more plausible, *pragmatic* definition of the judicial role: the Supreme Court should police federalism boundaries *to the extent that this is politically possible*. That extent is narrower than the Court's role in protecting individual rights. Whereas federal rights operate mostly against state and local governments, which have no easy way of resisting the impositions of the federal judiciary, the enforcement of structural constitutional constraints (and especially of federalism constraints) involves confrontations with Congress, which possesses both more political authority than state and local governments and the means to assert that authority against the Court. A Court that has a hard time winning direct fights with Congress, should pick them carefully.

The Supreme Court cannot easily articulate this pragmatic rationale without endangering its cherished image as the independent guardian of the Constitution. Both *Lopez* and *Flores*, however, are transparently pragmatic decisions. They try to draw some sort of line where it seems possible to do so without unduly upsetting Congress or, for that matter, the precedents. Justice Scalia's *Printz* opinion cleverly seized a limited, tactical opportunity to reassert the Court's authority, to reintroduce broader constitutional considerations, and to invite further challenges to federal impositions. The Eleventh Amendment and plain-statement cases point in the same direction: judicial noncooperation is an attractive means of advancing federalism because Congress cannot do much about it.

So long as an assertion of modest judicial scrutiny on federalism questions is accompanied by constant reassurances on the need to defer to Congress (as it is, for instance, in the *Lopez* concurrence), such an assertion threatens to lead back to judicial abdication. But while many appellate courts have taken that route, it is plainly not what the Chief Justice and Justices Scalia and Thomas have in mind, and even Justices O'Connor and Kennedy are unlikely to accept so restrictive an interpretation of *Lopez*. Thus, the need to define the judiciary's role in federalism disputes will likely tend toward an expansion of that role.

Judicial pragmatism at the federalism front points toward a broader role for the Supreme Court.

* * * * *

The Supreme Court's federalism protects state sovereignty. It stops at the water's edge—that is, the fundamental question of the scope of enumerated federal powers. Even so, the Supreme Court's federalism at least contains the seeds of a more principled federalism of enumerated powers, citizen choice, and state competition. To an extent, the modern cases reflect judicial intuitions that are inimical to federalism's blossoming—a statist disposition, sentimentality about the "federalist balance" and the "etiquette of federalism," and (as the next chapter shows) an unwarranted fear of more open, indeterminate politics. But the Court's reluctance to approach the enumerated powers issue more directly also reflects the sensible recognition that the reassertion of constitutional constraints requires more than coherent legal theories and five votes on the Court. It requires political support. Much will depend on the profederalist Justices—for example, on their ability to marshal five votes in tough cases and on their imagination in identifying cases and doctrines that would permit a closer approximation of real, competitive federalism without, at the same time, forcing a dramatic return to an enumerated powers doctrine. Primarily, however, federalism's fate depends on developments in the larger political world—not on some amorphous political climate, but on the disposition and the actual decisions of political constituencies that might support a broader revitalization of federalist politics and, in the process, give the Court greater leeway to pursue a federalist agenda. These political dynamics are the subject of the remaining chapters.

7

Federalism's Constituency

There is no constituency for federalism as an abstract principle. Political constituencies have always supported (or opposed) federalism for instrumental reasons and in the hope of advancing substantive objectives. Federalism's architecture has undergone large changes when constituencies with some other agenda managed to overrun the system. Reconstruction, the New Deal, and the civil rights movement are obvious examples. By the same token, a federalist *revival* is possible only in the context of a larger, substantive movement and agenda.

That movement, I suggested at the end of chapter 2, is the "Leave-Us-Alone" coalition, a universe of loosely connected, partially overlapping grass-roots constituencies—property rights advocates, the term limits movement, home school and school choice organizations, right-to-life groups, gun owners, tax limitation initiatives, certain religious denominations and lay organizations, small business owners, and others. Some of these constituencies have a very strident tone and a decidedly ideological agenda. Many of them seem marginal to American politics. As I argue at greater length in a later chapter, however, the Leave-Us-Aloners reflect a much broader public discontent with the national government's rigidities, inefficiency, and meddlesomeness. Organized Leave-Us-Alone constituencies are the leading edge of a widespread, if somewhat diffuse, desire for a more open, competitive, experimental politics. To a large extent, federalism's future hangs on the Supreme Court's recognition of that fact.

The central argument of this book is that the Supreme Court and Leave-Us-Alone constituencies, through a "virtuous cycle" of (often implicit) cooperation, can build momentum and support for federalist institutions and arrangements. Modest judicial advances at the federalism front, the scenario has it, embolden Leave-Us-Aloners to pursue federalist strategies, in turn providing the Court with occasions and room for further federalist advances. Over time, tactical advances and commitments harden into a broader public consensus for a more decentralized, competitive politics—and into constitutional constraints.

The remaining chapters develop this scenario and attempt to show that it is much more plausible than it may appear at first sight. Skeptical readers may wish to suspend judgment for a pragmatic reason: there is no point to thinking about real federalism unless one can imagine *some* scenario that leads from here to there.

The Supreme Court and the Constituency for Federalism

"To some degree," Justice Antonin Scalia once observed, "a constitutional guarantee is like a commercial loan: you can only get it if, at the time, you don't really need it."[1] Five Justices cannot unilaterally impose their will on the country. Constitutional law will in the long run reflect the reigning political interests and social consensus. The pre–New Deal jurisprudence of enumerated powers and expansive constitutional protections for property rights, for example, reflected the dominance of business interests and laissez-faire ideology over American politics. In the post–New Deal era, the Court proved a reliable ally of liberal constituencies on issues ranging from free speech to affirmative action to welfare rights and, not least, process federalism. In both cases the Supreme Court developed a firm and lasting relationship with a political coalition that protected the Court and its agenda. In both cases the dominant constituencies won "their" constitutional rights in the courts by and large because they were winning in *every* political arena. In both cases constitutional jurisprudence shifted when the Court's constituencies lost their grip on American politics—business in the 1930s, liberalism in the 1980s.

These observations may seem to suggest that we shall be stuck without effective constitutional constraints on the federal government, at least barring a sea change in the political climate. But the view of Supreme Court jurisprudence as a mere reflection of the existing consensus and power structure is much at odds with scholarly accounts and with public perceptions of the Court as a very powerful force in American politics. And in fact, as Justice Scalia himself put it, the view just sketched holds true only "to some degree." While the Supreme Court is not a free-wheeling elite institution, it does more than merely register the existing political consensus. Rather, Alexander M. Bickel has argued, the Supreme Court has tended to *anticipate* a social consensus. Supreme Court decisions have set a political tone and agenda and provided a sense of direction for the country. The most famous and successful modern example of such an anticipatory judicial move was *Brown v. Board of Education* (1954). *Brown* did not end school segregation, and the Supreme Court made no effort to hasten the process until 1968— well after the federal government had taken up the fight against Jim Crow. Still, few doubt that the Court's unanimous decision and opinion in *Brown* shaped the civil rights struggle.[2]

In an effort to explain how, why, and under what circumstances the Supreme Court can play such an anticipatory, agenda-setting role, Martin Shapiro has argued that the modern Supreme Court owes its role as a dominant policymaker to its ability to articulate and enforce norms that have "consonance with some widely held but inchoate values of the American people and with ideas whose 'time has come.'"[3] Broad legal principles, enunciated by the Court, "summate" political preferences, both by giving voice and intensity to diffuse attitudes and by uniting political constituencies that pursue widely varying political objectives. Owing to the public perception of the Supreme Court as the guardian of the Constitution and as more than a mere policymaker, the Court's agenda and the constituencies that stand to benefit from it gain legitimacy. The constituencies return the favor by defending the Court as an institution and by helping it accomplish, through political means, what the Court could not accomplish on its own. "Court decisions may call into being, encourage, or greatly strengthen interest groups that will then aid the Court in achieving its policies."[4] These factors, Shapiro argues, and in particular the process of mutual support and encouragement, account for the late Warren Court's ability to play a dominant policymaking role in American politics (despite the unpopularity of some of the Court's policy choices, such as school busing).

For all the differences between Bickel's sobriety and Shapiro's cynicism, both authors focus on the Supreme Court's agenda-setting role. Both, moreover, emphasize the Warren Court's egalitarian agenda (beginning with *Brown*), and both view that agenda as a particularly dramatic example of a general pattern of anticipatory Supreme Court jurisprudence.

No historical pattern or political alignment is ever replayed in precisely the same form. But in terms of the formal dynamics, one can imagine a federalism scenario that conforms to the pattern identified by Bickel and Shapiro. In light of the broad (albeit diffuse and inchoate) public support for federalism values, a judicial federalism agenda might well resonate—more so, perhaps, than the Warren Court's egalitarian agenda. And if the Court's reputation as a constitutional authority could sustain and support the Warren Court's extraconstitutional policy choices, it would surely sustain a federalism agenda.

Quite clearly, the Supreme Court's modern federalism decisions *are* anticipatory and agenda-setting. The decisions bear no comparison to *Brown*: they are less central to American politics, more limited in reach, and less confident. Still, the decisions from *Lopez* on forward are plainly intended to send a message. By announcing in consecutive cases that congressional overreach *is* a problem, that there has to be a line *somewhere*, the Court has reintroduced federalism as an issue of political debate. At the same time, the modern decisions reflect a clear judicial awareness that federalism's judicial restoration requires a political climate that would enable the Court to confront Congress and to impose constitutional constraints. More precisely, a federalism agenda that implies serious constitutional constraints requires a political coalition with sufficient clout to protect and defend the Court and its agenda. This is not to suggest that the federalist Justices are tailoring their decisions to (presumed) interest-group demands. Clearly, however, the Justices are looking for support.

The Leave-Us-Alone coalition is a very plausible addressee of this invitation. To be sure, the coalition members pursue disparate agendas, and they do not consistently favor federalism in the sense in which liberalism consistently agitates for centralized politics. Egalitarian ambitions require central control, which is why environmentalists, feminists, and civil rights advocates have always favored the destruction of federalism and local autonomy. Conservatives and libertarians, in contrast, face conflicts between form and substance. Should one celebrate local monopolies and moral legislation as a wholesome expression of local control and diversity or should one trump such "grass-roots tyranny" with federal, constitutional prohibitions?[5] Should one favor the repeal of federal entitlements that eviscerate local control, or should one trump them with conservative entitlements? How heavily should federalism concerns weigh against a federal ban on partial-birth abortions?

On the whole, though, such dilemmas are less serious than they appear at first inspection. Liberal constituencies also had their disagreements, which rarely got in the way of the common interest in a more expansive and centralized government. In the same way, a broad agenda for a more limited, more decentralized, more federalist government may unite disparate populist constituencies.

Leave-Us-Aloners are uniformly antinationalist on the issues that brought them to politics. They may hold nationalist, redistributionist views on most issues, but not on the issues on which their preferences are most intense. All Leave-Us-Alone constituencies, moreover, share a resentment against the Washington establishment. These sentiments act as a powerful political glue. And certainly, the *objects* of the Leave-Us-Aloners' animosity have been predominantly national in nature and origin. Federal gun controls have produced far more strident opposition than have comparable state and local laws, and whereas even the strictest local land-use controls have rarely prompted organized political responses, the federal Endangered Species Act and wetlands regulation produced a grass-roots movement of intensely ideological property rights groups.[6]

It is true that the national origin of so many impositions has drawn many populist constituencies to Washington, D.C. Having made the investment in establishing a federal presence, some groups have felt compelled to justify it by pressing federal legislation, thus inviting Congress to further strain its authority. Proposals for a constitutional school prayer amendment illustrate the phenomenon. The remarkable fact, however, is not the extent to which Leave-Us-Aloners have succumbed to this pressure but the extent to which they have resisted it. Most Leave-Us-Alone constituencies, from the term limits movement to property rights groups, have retained a strongly federalist organization and orientation.

Leave-Us-Alone constituencies favor federalism—at least as an interim strategy—because they often can win more easily in the states. While the National Rifle Association is playing defense in Washington, D.C., it has prevailed on more than two-thirds of the states to authorize concealed-weapons permits (the NRA's most extreme demand). Right-to-life advocates or (for a less dramatic example) advocates of official colorblindness would be appalled at the suggestion that their substantive demands should be a matter of citizen choice among competing states; the values at stake are too fundamental to be a matter of mere choice and preference. Still, so long as the national government proves unreceptive to their entreaties, those constituencies tend to favor federalism as an attractive fallback. Federalism provides opportunities to organize resistance to national impositions, to keep political issues alive, and to make piecemeal progress.

In short, the Leave-Us-Aloners are a reliable strategic force for federalism. Were the Supreme Court to provide a federalist rallying point for the constituencies, it could—in Shapiro's language—easily "summate" their preferences and legitimize their agenda for a more open, decentralized politics. The Leave-Us-Aloners, in turn, would protect and defend the Supreme Court and its agenda. The huge difficulty in anticipating such a virtuous cycle for federalism lies in the fact that the Leave-Us-Aloners are the Justices' least favorite crowd. The feeling, moreover, is mutual.

The Supreme Court is by design the most nationalist, elitist institution in American politics. It is naturally suspicious of constituencies that agitate for a more open, decentralized politics. The Leave-Us-Aloners seem too strident, ideological, and, by the lights of elite opinion that guide the Justices, too unenlightened to become a suitable coalition partner for the Supreme Court. Conversely, populist constituencies are painfully aware that many of the things against which they rebel, from abortion to prohibitions on school prayer, are the work of the Supreme Court. Rightly or wrongly, antielite opinion attributes many other social maladies, from crime in the streets to pornography, to the Supreme Court's influence.[7] More libertarian advocates and constituencies are exasperated with the Court's unwillingness to protect gun ownership or property rights—or for that matter, the enumerated powers constraints of the Constitution.

Were this mutual hostility to prove permanent, there would be no prospect for a more open, federalist politics. Open hostility may, however, gradually give way to (albeit uneasy) cooperation.

Much as the Supreme Court—more precisely, its centrist members—may wish to reconstruct federalism on nonideological grounds, federalism is about the government's role, not merely its organization. It is not about means but about ends; not about reinventing government but about relimiting it. A federalist reconstruction, if it is to happen, *must* be an ideological affair. It will be pursued only by constituencies whose operation and raison d'être push away from, rather than toward, redistribution—an objective best pursued through centralization. This requirement, as noted, qualifies the Leave-Us-Aloners as a federalist constituency and *dis*qualifies every other interest. Economic interest groups may support this or that federalist policy, and the states will defend their institutional prerogatives. As I show later in this chapter, these predispositions provide some hope for federalism. But neither economic interests nor the states will favor federalist competition consistently and as a matter of strategy and principle. When it comes to federalism, the Leave-Us-Aloners are the only game in town. Between a grudging rapprochement of the Leave-Us-Aloners and a wholesale abandonment of federalist aspirations, the Supreme Court may well choose the former.

That choice, moreover, may become easier over time. The Leave-Us-Aloners' role as federalism's only force ensures that the early rounds of a federalism campaign will be fought over their issues, many of which are very controversial. But federalism need not for that reason remain a sectarian cause. To a large extent, populist constituencies derive their ideological, sectarian impulses from perceived or real judicial impositions; the right-to-life movement springs to mind. Even a tentative judicial retreat at those fronts would relegitimize Leave-Us-Alone constituencies—and calm them down.

In recent years, we have in fact seen signs of a possible convergence. In the most intensely contested areas of Supreme Court jurisprudence (race, sex, and religion), things have by and large gone the Leave-Us-Aloners' way, for reasons that are closely, though not always obviously, related to their federalist predisposition. And for a few months in 1995, the Court's federalism agenda and the Leave-Us-Alone agenda actually seemed in alignment. The events of those months provide a suitable starting point to examine both the potential for and the remaining obstacles to a federalist revival.

Judicial Ambivalence

In the 1994 midterm elections, the GOP campaigned for the House and the Senate on a platform called the Contract with America. The contract played on widespread annoyance with the federal government, and it contained several distinctly federalist elements. Some of these found their way into the Unfunded Mandates Reform Act of 1995, which prohibits certain unfunded federal impositions on state and local governments, and into the 1996 welfare reform, which invested the states with substantial authority over the administration of benefits under the Aid to Families with Dependent Children program.[8]

United States v. *Lopez* was decided in April 1995, at the height of the House Republicans' campaign to limit the federal government's reach. The decision served as a powerful political symbol, for it seemed to suggest that the Supreme Court had blessed the crusade against the Washington establishment. Conservative advocacy groups organized strategy sessions and produced policy papers on *Lopez* and federalism; public interest law groups discussed opportunities for Commerce Clause litigation.

The congressional rebellion collapsed a few months later over the Republican majority's failed attempt to force President Clinton to accept its budget proposals. Of greater interest to the federalism debate, however, was a different event: only two months after *Lopez*, the Supreme Court struck down state-imposed term limits for members of Congress and declared that Congress alone retained control over the qualifications of federal legislators.[9]

That decision, *U.S. Term Limits* v. *Thornton*, had an enormous impact. Grass-roots groups had advanced term limits, principally by means of state referendums and initiatives, to ensure that federal legislators would retain some connection to their constituencies instead of succumbing to the Beltway culture. As Professor Robert F. Nagel has written,

> The terms limits movement . . . , based in the states and springing in part from local experience with the imposition of qualifications for state legislative offices, is evidence that our political community is not yet completely nationalized. Indeed, it demonstrates that people within some states are ready to challenge national political elites both intellectually and politically.[10]

The Supreme Court recognized the challenge—and rudely rejected it. The brief path from *Lopez* to *Term Limits* illustrates three salient points.

First, the episode illustrates the real-world effects of symbolic Supreme Court decisions. *Lopez* prompted a federalism debate not just in the law reviews but on the political ground. By the same token, the *Term Limits* ruling had real, political results: it extinguished the federalist enthusiasm *Lopez* had helped spark. The political culture—or at any rate the Leave-Us-Alone subculture—is very much attuned to, and readily responds to, Supreme Court decisions on federalism.

Second, (judicial) federalism is deeply entangled in much broader, more fundamental issues of democratic governance. Nobody thought that the half-hearted, technocratic federalism of *Lopez* marked a revolution. Disparate Leave-Us-Alone constituencies cheered *Lopez* because it seemed to signal a setback to the national political elites. The constituencies for federalism look to that message, not so much to the actual federalist content or effect of each individual decision.

Third, the *Term Limits* decision differs from *Lopez* in two respects (apart from the different outcome). *Term Limits* was decidedly not merely symbolic, and the national imposition at issue came from the Supreme Court itself rather than from the U.S. Congress. By all means, said *Lopez*, let the federal judiciary protect the powers "reserved to the States": when the states regulate, somebody is still in charge. Not so, said *Term Limits*, with respect to the powers reserved "to the people." Who knows what the people might do with those powers? To the *Term Limits* majority's mind, Professor Nagel has observed, "the trouble with federalism turns out to be the same thing that is the trouble with democracy. Both mean that the Constitution leaves too much unresolved."[11]

If the Supreme Court is to build political support for federalism, it cannot flirt with populist constituencies (à la *Lopez*) and slap them in the face (in the fashion of *Term Limits*) when the breathing gets heavy. Moreover, the Court must be serious not only about reining in Congress but also, and foremost, about reining itself in and about directing its energies toward a jurisprudence that is consistent with a more open, federalist politics.

Term Limits and similar decisions, reviewed below, on intensely controversial issues from abortion to homosexuality to school prayer raise serious doubts about the Court's willingness to steer such a course. Four Justices (Breyer, Ginsburg, Souter, and Stevens) will not countenance even the most modest challenge to nationalist presumptions. Justices Kennedy and O'Connor cherish a technocratic, sovereignty-centered, statist federalism precisely because it does not imply a more open and competitive politics.[12] That leaves only three votes for a sustained judicial effort to revive federalism.

It is possible, however, and I believe it is more plausible, to interpret the landmark decisions of the past decade as a gradual movement toward a more federalist jurisprudence and as a judicial appeasement of populist and federalist constituencies. Decisions such as *Term Limits* are best read as periodic reminders that those constituencies should be somewhat circumspect in pushing their agenda. Recent case law on race, religion, and sex indicates a gradual shift toward more open and competitive politics, marred by periodic lapses into judicial imperiousness and condescension.

Race. On the question of civil rights, the Supreme Court has unmistakably allied itself with (loosely speaking) populist, antiestablishment forces. For a full decade, the Court has methodically curtailed affirmative action programs based on race and ethnicity, with only one false and since corrected step along the way.[13] The Court has maintained this course despite angry attacks in the press, the law reviews, and from the civil rights establishment.

The Supreme Court's increasingly restrictive interpretation of the Equal Protection Clause is in some tension with its federalism agenda, inasmuch as it leaves state and local institutions less room to experiment with racial preference schemes.[14] In two respects, however, the Court's civil rights decisions provide a perfect illustration of a virtuous cycle scenario for federalism. First, the Court has pursued its civil rights agenda against Congress. Second, the Court has emboldened conservative, antinationalist constituencies to mobilize against racial preferences. The former tendency is illustrated by the Supreme Court's 1995 decision in *Adarand Constructors* v. *Pena,* which effectively declared federal racial preferences in government contracting unconstitutional. The tendency of restrictive civil rights decisions to mobilize political constituencies is evidenced by California's Proposition 209.

Approved by popular referendum in November 1996, Proposition 209 prohibits all government agencies in California from administering preferences based on race or sex in public contracting, employment, and education. Judicial decisions played a significant role in the political struggle over that proposition. In a pathbreaking March 1996 decision in *Hopwood* v. *State of Texas,* the Fifth Circuit Court of Appeals ruled that racial preferences in student admissions are virtually always unconstitutional. Three months later, the Supreme Court declined to review the appellate court's decision.[15] *Hopwood* lent credibility and momentum to the then-struggling grass-roots campaign for Proposition 209. Subsequently, liberal interest groups challenged the proposition as unconstitutional and as a racist, misogynist measure that would "not just move minorities and women to the back of the bus [but] boot them off all together [*sic*]."[16] But an appellate court firmly rejected that challenge. The Supreme Court again denied *certiorari,* thus effectively putting its stamp of approval on a state-by-state campaign for the repeal of racial preferences.[17]

The political effects are readily discernible. Although legislative bodies—local, state, or federal—have staunchly resisted efforts to repeal race- and sex-based preferences, conservative activists who agitate for colorblind rules are bullish and confident. Emboldened by the victory in California and the federal courts' solicitude for their efforts, they placed a Proposition 209–style initiative before the voters in Washington State, who in November 1998 approved the measure by a large margin. At the same time, conservative civil rights activists look to the federal courts as a reliable institutional ally—in fact, as the only elite institution to lend legitimacy to their endeavor.

The Supreme Court's readiness to endorse and encourage the colorblindness campaign differs markedly from its distrust and, on occasion, its hostility toward other Leave-Us-Alone causes.[18] The difference may have to do with the fact that the civil rights campaign lacks a harsh populist edge and, in a sense, a constituency. Agitation by a (hypothetical) National Association for the Advancement of Angry White Males—or for that matter the appearance of Proposition 209 in Mississippi rather than in racially diverse, laid-back California—would make civil rights politics look like a populist *jihad,* and that would give the Supreme Court pause. In fact, though, Proposition 209 was invented by two professors and promoted by a credible black spokesman (Ward Connerly), and "reverse discrimination" litigation is largely the work of a few small law firms without a membership base. So the Court thinks of civil rights politics not as a crusade but as a healthy (if hard-fought) debate over an important constitutional principle.

These suppositions suggest that the Court's tolerance may not carry over into policy arenas where Leave-Us-Aloners are more organized and perhaps more strident. Later analysis will confirm the Court's pronounced desire to dampen and channel populist passions. Nonetheless, civil rights law illustrates the hugely important point that the relationship between the Supreme Court and Leave-Us-Aloners can change, in less than a decade, from bitter hostility to mutual (if guarded) trust and reliance.

Religion. The Supreme Court's decisions under the Free Exercise and the Establishment Clauses of the First Amendment provide another, albeit more contestable example of a gradual rapprochement between the Court and important segments of the Leave-Us-Alone coalition. In the 1960s and 1970s, the Court interpreted the Establishment Clause as prohibiting many forms of government assistance to religion, even when the state provided such assistance under otherwise neutral programs that benefited secular groups or institutions. During the 1980s and 1990s, however, the Court gradually moved from such selective disenfranchisement toward a baseline of nondiscrimination. In a series of cases, the Court ruled that religious citizens may benefit from government programs (such as tax exemptions or the use of public facilities) on the same terms as everyone else, provided that the program at issue is neutral in purpose and effect and does not selectively favor religious activities. The culmination of this trend (for the time being) was *Rosenberger* v. *Rector and Board* (1995), which held that the First Amendment precluded the University of Virginia from denying a religious student newspaper access to financial subsidies that were otherwise available to student groups of all viewpoints and persuasions. For the first time in many decades, a majority of Justices sanctioned direct financial aid to a religious organization.[19]

Many religious advocacy groups consider the neutrality stance inadequate, if not insulting. They point with some justice to the Supreme Court's continued hostility toward the public accommodation of religion (for example, in the "interior decorating" cases concerning religious invocations at public ceremonies or the public display of creches and menorahs).[20] They also point out that formally neutral laws often burden religious practices, and they maintain that the Court's decision in *Smith* v. *Employment Division*, which declared such impositions unproblematic, reflects a disregard for constitutionally protected religious liberties. This sentiment, of course, provided the impetus for the Religious Freedom Restoration Act. Predictably, many of the constituencies that had helped to enact RFRA perceived *Flores* v. *City of Boerne*, which invalidated the statute, as a slap in the face.

On the whole, however, the response to *Flores* was remarkably restrained. While RFRA constituencies urged Congress to reenact a more limited version of the statute under the Commerce Clause and the Spending Clause, little enthusiasm for that endeavor is apparent—certainly in comparison with the campaign for the original enactment. Several reasons explain this muted reaction. Demoralization among RFRA's advocates is perhaps a contributing factor, as is a disappointment with RFRA's results. With distressing frequency, prison inmates invoked the statute to demand official accommodation of their "religious" dietary or living requirements. Many other cases also involved religious liberties and practices only tangentially; the zoning dispute that gave rise to *Flores* is arguably an example.[21]

More important, however, is the fact that many Leave-Us-Alone constituencies like *Flores*. The Supreme Court strengthened federalism, and it slapped Congress—results that Leave-Us-Aloners are predisposed to cheer.[22] Naturally, religious advocates wonder why the Supreme Court chose "their" case to invoke the enumerated powers doctrines that it ignores in many other contexts. But religious advocates seem to recognize that neither *Flores* nor for that matter *Smith* signals simply an antireligious judicial reflex.[23] As shown in chapter 3, *Flores* sustained RFRA's application to the federal government, and its prohibition on a federal *imposition* of religious accommodation implies a corollary endorsement of efforts to secure such accommodation in the states. In a tangible sense, then, *Flores* provides religious constituencies with political avenues for relief.[24] In a larger, symbolic sense, the baseline of government neutrality—combined with a kind of religious federalism— views religious citizens as equal and legitimate participants in the political debate. Compared with the 1960s and 1970s, when the Supreme Court attempted to cabin religion in houses of worship, this posture is considerable progress.

The Court's posture may, moreover, be enough to win the truly big battles—including the biggest of them all, the inclusion of parochial schools in school choice and voucher programs. Full-blown school choice is a quintessentially federalist, Leave-Us-Alone objective: it would deal a severe setback to a powerful public sector union, substitute competition for one of the largest remaining government monopolies, and further diminish citizens' dependence on public institutions. Like racial preferences, moreover, school choice is a defining issue in American politics, and it has begun to move on a parallel judicial trajectory. In a 1998 decision that relied extensively on *Rosenberger* and similar Supreme Court decisions, the Wisconsin Supreme Court sustained a school voucher scheme that included religious schools. A few months later, the U.S. Supreme Court declined to hear the case.[25] Leave-Us-Alone constituencies, from libertarians to religious conservatives, responded with more enthusiasm than a single state court decision or a mere denial of *certiorari* would seem to warrant. But the judicial rulings in the Wisconsin case have done for school choice what *Hopwood* and the Proposition 209 case did for official colorblindness: the courts have implicitly sanctioned a local or state-by-state campaign for school choice. That implicit endorsement may well suffice to produce a gradual rapprochement between the Supreme Court and Leave-Us-Alone constituencies.

Sex. The area with the least convergence between the Supreme Court and the constituencies for more open, federalist politics is sexual intercourse and anything having to do with it. *Roe* v. *Wade* (1973) stood for more than a constitutional right to "privacy" that encompasses an effectively unlimited right to abortion. It also stood—and stands—for the proposition that decisions pertaining to sexual intercourse and its consequences cannot be left to the voters in the various states but must be forced into the federal courts and, in the process, onto the national level.

The Supreme Court has since reasserted the nationalist, judge-centered presumptions of *Roe*. *Planned Parenthood* v. *Casey* (1992), an abortion case that had been expected to overrule *Roe* v. *Wade*, instead redefined the privacy right of *Roe* as an even broader right to "define one's own concept of existence, of meaning, of the universe, and of the mystery of human life."[26] Four years later, in *Romer* v. *Evans* (1996), the Supreme Court struck down a statewide constitutional referendum, enacted by the voters of Colorado, that prohibited local jurisdictions from enacting homosexual rights ordinances. Justice Kennedy's opinion for the majority declared that the voters' decision could only be attributable to a wholly irrational and impermissible "animus."[27]

It is difficult to think of a plausible excuse for *Casey* and *Romer*. Both decisions are virtually devoid of legal reasoning; both exemplify an obnoxious judicial distrust of the democratic process and a shameless catering to elite opinion.[28] A closer examination, however, suggests that the message of *Romer* and *Casey* is somewhat more ambiguous than just suggested.

The key to interpreting *Romer* lies in the majority's failure to make any mention of *Bowers* v. *Hardwick* (1986). *Bowers*, the Supreme Court's lone precedent on homosexual rights, had sustained a Georgia criminal sodomy statute on the grounds that the privacy rights inferred from the Bill of Rights do not encompass a right to homosexual conduct. Criminal sodomy statutes would appear to be a far clearer example of an "animus" against homosexuals than the referendum at issue in *Romer*, which merely denied homosexuals the civil rights protections available to some other constituencies.[29] But even while invalidating the Colorado referendum, the *Romer* Court did not overrule *Bowers*. Such a ruling would have required a determination that homosexuality enjoys constitutional protection. Lacking the nerve to take that step, the *Romer* majority simply ignored *Bowers* and instead based its decision on the notion that it was somehow impermissible to repeal local ordinances by statewide referendum (more precisely, with the form in which the Colorado referendum sought to achieve that objective). The contorted reasoning suggests a judicial reticence in affording constitutional protection to homosexuality. Consistent with this interpretation, the *Romer* Court left open the possibility that popular repeals of homosexual rights ordinances might pass judicial muster in some other form. The Supreme Court has since tolerated one citywide referendum against homosexual rights,[30] and the voters of one state (Maine) have availed themselves of the opening left by *Romer.*

Similarly, the rhetoric of *Casey* actually masked a modest retreat from *Roe.* Replacing the trimester framework of *Roe, Casey* sanctioned state restrictions on previability abortions so long as such restrictions do not impose an "undue burden" on women seeking an abortion. Regarding postviability abortions, *Casey* conceded that *Roe* "in practice . . . undervalues the State's interest in the potential life within the woman" and on those grounds authorized state abortion bans except when "necessary, in appropriate medical judgment, for the preservation of the life or health of the mother."[31]

That language may be deeply disingenuous, and lower courts have so read it. By the lights of *Casey* itself, previability abortion restrictions impose an unconstitutional "undue burden" when they "operate as a substantial obstacle to a woman's choice to undergo an abortion" in a "large fraction" of cases. In other words, abortion restrictions are constitutional so long as they do not restrict what they are supposed to restrict. Postviability abortion regulations, meanwhile, have become a game of "gotcha." Following the invitation extended in *Casey*, twenty-eight states have enacted bans on partial-birth abortions. Not one of these laws has passed judicial muster. When presented with an opportunity to review a judicial injunction against a partial-birth abortion ban, the Supreme Court declined.[32]

For all that, *Casey* signals a partial retreat from *Roe. Casey* sustained some of the state abortion restrictions at issue in the case, and it spurred a new round of state enactments regulating abortions. And while the Justices are reluctant to legitimize those enactments, they will almost certainly do so when the issue can no longer be avoided—for instance, in the likely event of a split among the appellate courts on the constitutionality of postviability partial-birth abortion bans in the states. The lower courts' hostility to such enactments has increased the already substantial political pressure for a federal ban. Although such legislation can be passed only over the president's veto and by a two-thirds majority in both houses of Congress, it has come closer to enactment with each passing year. To think that the Supreme Court would risk a confrontation with Congress over this issue implies that the Justices are not simply disingenuous (as the lower courts have so far supposed); it presumes that they are obtuse. The Justices are much more likely to defuse the issue by permitting the states to regulate partial-birth abortions.

One cannot take this result for granted. Taken at face value, *Casey* and *Romer* lend themselves to practically anything.[33] But decisions that entail anything also entail nothing, since it is far easier to retreat from absurd opinions than from reasoned ones. If the principle of *Romer* were generally applicable, the Supreme Court would have extended it to California's Proposition 209. There, as in *Romer*, a statewide democratic majority dismantled minority protections enacted by subordinate local entities. And yet, the Supreme Court let stand a strongly worded appellate opinion sustaining Proposition 209. A similar fate has befallen *Casey*. Presumably, a liberty to obtain a physician's help in killing something that at some point becomes someone else should entail a right to medical assistance in killing oneself. In 1997, however, the Supreme Court rejected the notion of a constitutional right to enlist a doctor's assistance in ending one's life. Instead, the Justices declared that questions of life and death other than abortion are best resolved by the voters in the states.[34]

The Supreme Court's residual commitment to sexual nationalism ultimately reflects its inability to find a graceful retreat from *Roe* v. *Wade*. *Roe* was intended as the *Brown* v. *Board of Education* of the 1970s—a beacon of social liberation, a harbinger of a social consensus, the Supreme Court's ticket to new heights of power and prestige. An exasperated Alexander M. Bickel criticized *Roe* as a fateful failure to heed his earlier warnings against excessive judicial confidence in fashionable, egalitarian notions of progress.[35] Even some firm supporters of abortion rights have since come to acknowledge that *Roe* was a major mistake. In a much-noted speech, for example, Justice (then Judge) Ruth Bader Ginsburg argued that *Roe* short-circuited a political debate that should probably have been left to the democratic process and state-by-state decisionmaking.[36] Having staked its institutional prestige on *Roe*, though, the Supreme Court cannot bring itself to acknowledge its mistake. The explicit rationale of *Casey* is that the Court cannot, must not, overrule *Roe* because such a reversal would be seen as a capitulation to political pressure.[37]

Casey and *Romer* constitute lasting obstacles to a closer relation between the Supreme Court and the Leave-Us-Alone constituencies for federalism. Both decisions, however, also signal an implicit concession that the constitutional "privacy" enterprise is intellectually and politically bankrupt. A return to the presumptions of *Roe* is out of the question. The Supreme Court seems to have settled for a gradualist message: give the voters somewhat more leeway—and exhort them to be circumspect. For all the elitist condescension of that message, there lies hope in the fact that even in the area of sex, where the Justices are at their absolute worst, the Supreme Court may have begun to develop some tolerance for a more open politics.

States and Interests

The virtuous federalism cycle, as developed so far and hereinafter, assigns no constructive role to the states or to conventional interest groups because both are forces not for federalist choice and competition but for centralization.[38] One may, however, hope that centralizing forces will not prove so strong as to overwhelm all countervailing tendencies and initiatives. Not all states and all interests favor centralization all the time. Enhanced opportunities to use federalist arrangements to their own tactical advantage may induce those constituencies to tolerate a gradual movement toward state competition.

States. The notion of the states as a centralizing force is at odds with popular folklore and with the current Supreme Court's view of the matter. State and (to a lesser extent) local governments in their political, collective capacities are the principal beneficiaries of the Supreme Court's sovereignty-centered federalism. It is they who benefit from Eleventh Amendment exemptions, from Tenth Amendment protections of "states as states," and from the judicial efforts to fence off areas of "traditional" state regulation from federal interference. The focus on state sovereignty reflects a judicial expectation that states and localities are particularly likely to emerge as a federalist constituency.

The idea of federalism as something the states favor and defend against an overbearing federal government has a long progeny, going back to the Founders' checks-and-balances rhetoric. The Federalists wrote that the great danger to the constitutional scheme lay not in federal usurpations—which the states would easily defeat—but rather in federalism's centrifugal tendencies and in attempts by the states to deprive the federal government of its requisite authority. The Founders were less persuaded of the point than they let on, however, and to the extent that they were so persuaded, they have since been proven wrong.[39]

The states' emasculation stems largely from constitutional changes that the Founders could not have foreseen—the Civil War Amendments, for example, and the Seventeenth Amendment, which initiated the direct election of the Senate and thus deprived the states of representation in their collective capacities. But these changes only illustrate that the states are not an effective check on nationalist tendencies. If they were, enumerated powers would be alive and well.

Perhaps the single most important factor in breaking the states' resistance to nationalist tendencies was the enormous expansion of the federal taxing and spending powers, brought about by the creation of a federal income tax through the Sixteenth Amendment.[40] The federal government's access to heretofore unimagined revenues enabled it to induce state compliance with its schemes. Competition among the states gradually turned into a race for federal dollars. Of course, the states continued to resist uncompensated burdens on their internal operations— that is, what we now call unfunded federal mandates. Enumerated powers constraints, however, became a nuisance for the states. Such constraints entail competition and discipline, and they prevent the states from acceding to popular demands for government benefits or regulatory schemes. Hence, there was no "states' rights" opposition to the nationalist policies of the Progressive Era and the New Deal.[41] In the twentieth century at least, the battle cry of "states' rights" has consistently sounded in the defense of statist, majoritarian schemes (most notoriously, Jim Crow) and never in the defense of a federalism of limited government.

Still, the states' disposition to defend their parochial, institutional prerogatives represents at least a necessary step toward support for a federal government of enumerated powers. One cannot have competition without competitors, and the Supreme Court's federalism has resurrected the states as potential competitors. It has given them a sense that they are more than mere subdivisions of the federal government and more than mere supplicants.[42] During the 1990s, state and local governments have been celebrating a renaissance. They have become more confident, more assertive, more resistant to federal micromanagement, and more vocal in demanding authority and flexibility in administering federal programs. While one cannot prove that the Supreme Court's federalism decisions account for this trend, it stands to reason that the enhanced judicial protection of state sovereignty has done something to stiffen the states' spine. It makes a difference whether a governor must plead with federal bureaucrats or congressional aides who hold the purse strings, or whether he can instead instruct his attorney general to reach for the Eleventh Amendment.

Greater state clout does not automatically translate into support for limiting the powers of Congress. It may easily prompt increased demands for federal pork barrel projects and for state autonomy in distributing the proceeds. Nonetheless, judicial protections of state sovereignty are not easily divorced from a trend toward competitive federalism. For example, judicial determinations that states and their agencies may not be sued under the Fair Labor Standards Act, the Rehabilitation Act, or the Family and Medical Leave Act merely exempt states from obligations to which private employers or landlords are still subject. Such decisions, however, also signal that the authority of Congress has limits, and they raise doubts about the wisdom of paving the country with federal entitlements. Similarly, Supreme Court restrictions on nonbudgetary forms of securing state compliance—private enforcement and commandeering—may seem to do no more for federalism than to force Congress into Spending Clause legislation and to increase the states' bargaining leverage.[43] But budgetary constraints have made it more difficult—compared with, say, the 1970s—for Congress to bribe states and localities into accepting federal mandates, and as federal policies become more stick and less carrot, states and municipalities are bound to resist more frequently.

At the same time, the states' enhanced professionalism, competence, and creativity are giving lie to the race-to-the-bottom notion that only federal intervention will prevent the entire country from becoming one vast Mississippi. As the plausibility of that paradigm diminishes, states that have gained the confidence to resist federal meddling may gain the confidence to subject themselves to economic competition. They will certainly not gain the latter without the former. Such a transition may occur, for instance, because state or local governments tend to oppose federal laws that inflict a disproportionate burden not just on their internal operations but on their citizens or industries.

To be sure, the states' general strategy is not to oppose federal laws that burden their economies but to demand compensating impositions on other jurisdictions. The congressional debates preceding the 1990 Clean Air Act Amendments, for example, showed substantial support for acid rain controls that made little environmental sense and that imposed disproportionate costs on utilities and factories in agricultural states in the Midwest. Legislators from those states responded, not by fighting the acid rain provisions but by demanding statutory mandates for the use of ethanol fuels—which, though making even less environmental sense than the acid rain controls, subsidize Midwestern corn producers.[44] Since Congress usually has the means of cobbling together a coalition just broad enough to ensure enactment, the states know in advance that they will get rolled. Resistance looks impossible, and compensation is the only way to go.

Preemptive surrender, however, has a price. Under the 1990 Clean Air Act Amendments, the Environmental Protection Agency soon sought to impose very irksome and intrusive vehicle inspection programs and permitting requirements. The states noisily protested those programs, not only because the regulations imposed an inordinate burden on state administrators but also because they prompted an extremely hostile reaction from business and car owners.[45] The 1990 amendments also instructed the EPA to require the states to tell employers in eight metropolitan areas that their employees had to establish and maintain car pools. Although this splendid example of cooperative federalism was carefully designed to obscure federal responsibility, Congress itself rescinded the requirement in 1995, after a firestorm of protests from states, employers, and affected citizens. A sufficient number of such regulatory train wrecks may in the future induce coalitions of business interests, labor unions (on suitable occasions), and more confident states to choose a path of resistance or, alternatively, to drive up their demands for legislative compensation to the point where a deal becomes impossible.

A final, often unnoticed or underestimated force in federalism's favor is that Congress is in the end incapable of suppressing state competition for business and capital. When Congress trumps competition with uniform federal statutes (on its own volition, or pursuant to the states' request), it does not abolish competition but pushes it into new venues—prominent among them, the states' coffers. States and cities routinely seek to attract investors by offering tax exemptions, infrastructure improvements, and the like. A portion of those fiscal incentives represent, so to speak, the cash value of lost comparative advantages: a state whose comparatively favorable regulatory landscape is flattened by federal legislation will have to compensate prospective investors for the lost advantage.[46] The displacement of regulatory with fiscal incentives is highly inefficient, both because the value of the lost advantage is hard to calculate and because every such calculation is made in an intensely politicized environment. The transactions tear big holes in the states' budgets. They occur for no better reason than that Congress cannot commandeer the states' fiscal policies with the same ease with which it displaces their regulatory autonomy.

It has occurred to scholars and, naturally, to Congress to suppress even this form of competition through federal legislation or through the courts, under a breathtakingly expansive interpretation of the dormant Commerce Clause.[47] Their questionable legal merits aside, however, such measures would merely shift competition into yet a different venue, accompanied by further distortions, inefficiencies, and political shenanigans. In that light, one may hope that the states may take a step back and begin to contest the federal impositions that compel the displacement of regulatory with fiscal competition.

None of this means that the states will become cheerful advocates of a limited federal government. States do not want competition; they want a cartel. As a general matter, they would be stupid to want anything else. It may be possible, however, to split the states as a constituency and to induce more states to favor competition on a larger number of occasions. Let a few states exploit such cracks, and others may begin to look for different, larger openings. Such a development might in turn give the Supreme Court some confidence that federalism's intended beneficiaries at least do not oppose federalist competition and may even support it on appropriate occasions.

Interests. Like the states, economic interest groups and, in particular, corporate interests tend to favor centralization.[48] Some members of the business community may come to rediscover federalism for tactical purposes, however, and a few successful maneuvers of that kind may trigger further, bolder attempts to instrumentalize federalist doctrines.

Until the victory of the New Deal, corporate interests generally pursued an antinationalist strategy, both in Congress and in the courts. Unlike the modern federalism cases, for example, which are chiefly the province of state and local governments or of the criminal defense bar, the big federalism cases of the Progressive Era and the New Deal—the antitrust cases, *Carter* v. *Carter Coal Co.*, *Steward Machine Co.* v. *NLRB*, *NLRB* v. *Jones & Laughlin Steel*—were brought by large private companies. From the beginning of the twentieth century and into the 1940s, business associations masterminded and bankrolled many of the lawsuits against federal legislation that the nominal plaintiffs—such as Mr. Dagenhart or the Schechter Brothers—could not have pursued on their own. That posture stemmed largely from a straightforward calculation: so long as corporate America could hold the line against national intervention, federalism's antiregulatory, competitive dynamics worked to its advantage.

Much as the federal government's tax-and-spend authority changed the states' disposition toward federalism, however, so the victory of the New Deal and, legally speaking, the collapse of the enumerated powers doctrine after 1937 dramatically changed the business community's calculation. Once the dam had broken, federalism quickly became a tactical concern. Individual firms, trade organizations, or industry sectors are for or against it, depending on the stakes. The drift is toward Washington, D.C., which offers the advantages of uniform regulation, lower transaction costs, and enhanced opportunities to expropriate a larger number of competitors on a grander scale. While business as a whole and in the long run retains a stake in restoring structural limits on government power, collective action problems crowd out long-term strategies. The costs of creating a united front are prohibitive, and few firms will volunteer for a crusade for limited government at the cost of permitting everyone else a free ride—and at the risk of incurring the wrath of federal regulators, who always have a way to get even.

Even so, some business sectors will sometimes oppose federal legislation and favor state-by-state regulation or, as the case may be, no regulation at all.[49] A few old industries—for example, insurance—have never been subject to federal regulation and have managed to resist it to this day. By the same token, some areas of corporate governance and lines of business remain subject to intense state competition, to salutary effect.[50] Industry sectors cannot be cartelized and fenced off from each other quite so easily as the New Dealers imagined, and at least on occasion sectoral competition has led to deregulation. Despite New Deal restrictions on banks (such as prohibitions on interstate banking and on certain financial instruments), the bank of the future eventually arrived. Its name was Merrill Lynch—a brokerage house. The emergence of superior financial services in the less-regulated brokerage industry in turn induced more enterprising banks to diversify into the securities business and to push for deregulation, with a substantial measure of success.[51]

Then, too, the American economy has been sufficiently dynamic to produce new and therefore unsupervised industries. Day care is a mundane example; the computer industry is a high-tech one. Given the presumptions on which the federal government controls old industries, it should also rein in the new ones. For example, federal law has long required drug companies to demonstrate that their products are "safe and effective," on the ostensible theory that consumers do not fully understand the potentially harmful products. That theory also applies to computers. The average consumer knows about computers what he knows about drugs—that is, barely enough to use them (with some professional guidance). And while computers are rarely fatal, they do spread viruses. Still, there is no groundswell for a Federal Computer Commission, and so far from mandating federal premarketing "effectiveness" studies for software products, we seem to be comfortable with the idea of allowing high school and college dropouts to run a vital industry.[52] The fierce efficiency and innovative capacity of unregulated industries stand as a constant challenge to the wisdom of centralized intervention and as an invitation to more efficient producers in regulated markets to push for the relaxation of federal laws.

Much as states often fail to oppose federal mandates—and instead seek to obtain offsetting mandates on competing states—on the assumption that federal regulation is a foregone conclusion, so business typically pursues a strategy of preemptive surrender to proposed federal regulation, in the hope of making it less onerous. Again, though, the plausibility of that strategy depends on the certain expectation of getting beaten. Once someone, somewhere can mobilize federalism constraints (and live to tell the tale), business resistance to new federal impositions may stiffen. For instance, property owners' successful resistance to federal wetlands regulations, briefly discussed in chapter 3, suggests that federal environmental laws do, after all, have some federalism limits, which other firms and their attorneys may come to invoke. With a little help from the federal courts, federalism's structural constraints could begin to move on a trajectory similar to the development of the Fifth Amendment protection against government "takings" of private property. Widely viewed as a big joke only a decade ago, the amendment has since been invoked with some success—usually by desperate plaintiffs who had no other choice. As a result, the Takings Clause is now regarded as a somewhat smaller joke.[53]

In a world without enumerated powers, business's default position will always be a demand for federal regulation. A gradual return to more federalist legal rules may, however, produce federalist tactics among some segments of the business constituency some of the time. That should be enough to permit more substantial federalist advances in political arenas somewhat removed from economic concerns.

Obstacles and Opportunities

Judicial symbols gain political force when the Supreme Court legitimizes a constituency that has use for the symbols, and when that constituency in turn comes to think of the Court as an institutional ally. The notion that such a dynamic between the Supreme Court and the Leave-Us-Aloners might produce federalist constraints—while states and interest groups sit on the sidelines—may seem far-fetched. So many conjectures. So many ifs and buts. There is, however, no shortcut to a federalist revival. The Supreme Court cannot unilaterally repeal the New Deal, and interest group politics will push toward further centralization. One must either accept the futility of the federalist project or else search for a somewhat more circuitous path at the periphery of ordinary interest group politics.

The path just charted presumes that the Supreme Court and the populist constituencies for federalism can overcome their mutual distrust. This hope may prove unwarranted. The Court's statist federalism reflects a deep ambivalence about more open politics, and its sexual nationalism continues to give credence to Leave-Us-Aloners' complaints about the Supreme Court as an instrument of a corrupt elite culture. When told by the Supreme Court that they cannot be entrusted with decisions on matters of profound importance, populist constituencies are unlikely to look to the Court for signals to assert their democratic rights on trucking regulation or municipal waste management.

On the whole, however, the Supreme Court has tended to approach, appease, and encourage Leave-Us-Alone constituencies. Civil rights law is a clear example; religion, a more contestable one. Sex remains the major sticking point. *Lopez* and *Printz* signal that federal legislation is not automatically beyond reproach merely because it involves guns. Outside the areas discussed in this chapter, the Supreme Court has shown a similar inclination to send encouraging signals to Leave-Us-Aloners. *Lucas* v. *South Carolina Coastal Commission* (1994), for example, reasserted the constitutional significance of property rights, in language that encouraged property rights advocates to a far greater extent than the actual holding in the case would have warranted.[54] The federalism message is often ambiguous; enhanced constitutional protections for property rights primarily restrain state and local governments, as do civil rights decisions that curb affirmative action. More important than the legal aspects of those decisions, however, is their symbolic content and their tendency to embolden constituencies that will, on the whole and in the long run, mobilize for a more limited government and more decentralized, federalist politics.

If anything is to come of a federalist alliance between the Court and its (prospective) constituencies, the Justices will have to stay this course. One can easily think of Supreme Court decisions that would grind the process to a halt. A holding to the effect that *Lopez* meant nothing may be one. More obviously and dramatically, a decision sustaining racial preferences in education or employment would sour populist constituencies on the Supreme Court for the foreseeable future. So would the invalidation of school voucher programs that include parochial schools.

Even in its current composition, the Supreme Court may commit such blunders. Moreover, the four nationalist Justices clearly intend to position the Court for a sharp reversal, as is indicated by their drearily predictable, vociferous dissents in every federalism, religion, and civil rights case. All that is needed, it appears, is one more vote. But a judicial about-face is no longer so easy. The case law of the past decade now impedes a retreat—not just because the accumulated precedents are difficult to reverse, but also, and more important, because the Supreme Court has set in motion a political dynamic that has arrested, and perhaps reversed, the centralizing tendencies of the Court's earlier, expansive individual rights jurisprudence and its abdication at the federalism front.

From a political vantage point, the purpose of judicializing and nationalizing salient, defining issues in American politics was to delegitimize and, eventually, to rout Leave-Us-Alone constituencies. Abortion, especially *Casey*, is the most dramatic example; the term limits question is another. In both cases, however, and in several others (such as the place of religion in public life), it has become obvious that the targeted constituencies refuse to slink off. That being so, the Supreme Court has tended to give the Leave-Us-Aloners an "out" and at least a grudging endorsement. The Court will tolerate experiments with school choice and life-and-death regulation in the states, even if it is reluctant to sanction them explicitly.

Greater judicial tolerance has proven sufficient both to embolden *and to calm* Leave-Us-Alone constituencies. Campaigns for term limits, school vouchers, partial-birth abortion laws, colorblind civil rights laws, restrictions on political expenditures by trade unions, and the abolition of bilingual education are alive and doing well—in the states. The Supreme Court's federalism jurisprudence is not the only or even the pri-

mary source of this enthusiasm. Political deadlock at the federal level—
more precisely, the Clinton administration's resistance to the designs
just mentioned, coupled with the Republican majority's reluctance to
advance them—has played a more immediate role.[55] But the Supreme
Court's restraint in creating new federal impositions has reduced the
hydraulic pressure toward nationalization and in fact generated some
momentum in the opposite direction.

A more decentralized politics is a calmer, more responsible politics. The Leave-Us-Aloners' campaigns often turned shrill and ideological because national policy elites and institutions had decided to
nationalize the issue (think gun control), to stamp out local experiments
(think school choice), or to prohibit any state experimentation (think
abortion). Greater judicial tolerance for federalist solutions has relieved
those frustrations. It demonstrates to the Leave-Us-Aloners that the Court
need not be their implacable enemy. In turn, responsible (if hard-fought)
Leave-Us-Alone campaigns in the states demonstrate to the Supreme
Court that populist constituencies can after all be trusted.

Civil rights law, as noted, provides an example of this two-way
street. The Supreme Court trusts the constituencies for colorblindness
because they lack a shrill, populist edge. The constituencies lack that
edge in large part because the federal judiciary has legitimized their
cause. This process of growing mutual reliance may have advanced too
far to be easily reversible. Congress has so far resisted demands for a
federal version of California's Proposition 209 because it is easier to let
the Supreme Court do the dirty work of restoring official colorblindness.
But the Court's decisions have helped to build public support for racial
neutrality—so much so that judicial turnaround at the civil rights front
might well prompt Congress to reverse the Court and to write official
colorblindness into federal law. Conversely, and although the proposition has yet to be tested, the Supreme Court is probably looking to conservative activists and legislators for help and support in the event of a
congressional assault on its civil rights jurisprudence.[56] For reasons explained in this chapter, similar dynamics appear to be unfolding in other
policy arenas that are central both to Leave-Us-Alone constituencies
and to the federalist project.

It remains true that a greater judicial tolerance for democratic constituencies to run experiments in the states does not address federalism's
institutional problem of reining in Congress. But these matters are not
so easily separated. For one thing, constituencies that have been "sum-
mated" and legitimized (*pace* Shapiro) to agitate at the state level will

make their weight felt inside the Beltway. For another thing, and as shown in earlier chapters, the judicial legitimation of the constituencies for a more open politics has been accompanied by a *de*legitimation of nationalist schemes. The Supreme Court has been reticent in confronting Congress, but it has at least opened the door for federal legislative moves toward a more robust federalism. A successful use of those opportunities may in turn give the Supreme Court greater leeway and greater confidence to take further steps toward a federalist jurisprudence.

To sustain that virtuous cycle, federalism's friends—those on the bench and those in the political trenches—will have to invest political energy and take care in picking their targets. Chapter 8 provides some suggestions.

8

The Court and Congress

In August 1996, sixteen months after the U.S. Supreme Court's *Lopez* decision, Congress reenacted the Gun Free School Zones Act, having made cosmetic changes in an attempt to insulate the statute against further constitutional challenges. The reenactment was supported by many conservative senators who have often and loudly proclaimed their support for federalism and the rights of the states, and it occurred in the midst of a legislative term otherwise marked by much cheerful enthusiasm over the "devolution" of federal power to state and local governments.[1] No powerful interests lobbied for the reenactment, and the public and the media had given little attention to the matter. The statute was reenacted because few legislators were willing to run the risk of casting a vote "for guns in schools."

The aftermath of *Lopez* illustrates (yet again) the difficulty of reimposing constitutional constraints on an unconstrained political process. Not only will Congress, left to its own devices, fail to restrain itself; given half a chance, Congress will also seek to circumvent or override judicially imposed restraints. Grandiose federal schemes (health care legislation during the first Clinton administration, tobacco legislation during the second) may collapse under the weight of interest group demands and public skepticism. Proposals for further extensions of federal authority may on occasion prompt opposition; the Clinton administration's designs for national educational standards are an example. But a failure to utilize the full panoply of federal power in this or that case—and mostly for reasons unrelated to federalism—is not a constraint. Few such failures even establish a precedent for exercising restraint in the next, similar case. And yet, one need not draw the demoralizing conclusion that federalism is doomed.

The reason for a guarded optimism lies in the existence of plausible political strategies that would facilitate federalism despite and against the powerful tendencies toward centralization and congressional self-aggrandizement. The first half of this chapter sketches ways in which the Supreme Court can advance federalism and, eventually, make enumerated powers constraints "stick" in Congress. The second half describes legislative strategies through which legislators and political constituencies, under the right circumstances, can advance federalism despite the countervailing political incentives and dynamics.

The chapter does not purport to present a complete inventory of federalism strategies. Nor do I recommend or predict the enactment of any particular piece of legislation. For the purposes of the argument, it is enough to sketch some openings and opportunities for further federalist advances and, in this manner, to show that the Supreme Court and federalist constituencies do not face a hopeless task.

Making Federalism Stick

Earlier chapters identified two judicial strategies of advancing federalism without risking a head-to-head confrontation with Congress that might endanger the Supreme Court's hard-won federalism gain. The first option, which the Court has pursued for the past several years, is to assert federalism doctrines that fall somewhat short of—but point toward—full-fledged enumerated powers constraints. Most of the modern Supreme Court's federalism doctrines—the emphasis on legislative means rather than ends, on state sovereignty, and on judicial noncooperation—fit this pattern. While the doctrines leave Congress with escape hatches and opportunities for end runs around constitutional constraints, they provide stepping stones for further advances and, for the time being, clutter the federal government's path with obstacles.

The second viable strategy is to curtail the federal judiciary's intrusions into state and local affairs. The noncooperation cases reviewed in chapter 5 fall in this category, as do the Supreme Court's constitutional rights decisions that permit more latitude for policy decisions in the states. In terms of building further political support for federalism, judicial tolerance for state experiments is particularly crucial because, as noted, most of those experiments, from school vouchers to civil rights initiatives to abortion restrictions, are the Leave-Us-Aloners' experiments. Lapses into judicial imperialism in the mode of *Casey, Romer,* and *Term Limits* threaten to cut federalism's constituencies off at the ankles. Increased judicial tolerance for state experiments will embolden those constituencies and facilitate further federalist advances at all fronts.

Both strategies just mentioned help to sustain the momentum for federalism. Eventually, though, the Supreme Court must confront the shibboleth of enumerated powers, stare down Congress, and make serious federalism doctrines stick. The modern Supreme Court's federalism cases, and the political responses to those decisions, suggest that two types of federal legislation make for plausible targets. First, enumerated powers doctrines can be deployed against legislation that extends congressional authority to new and often highly symbolic issues. Second, enumerated powers constraints are likely to stick when federalism is an attractive second-best option for the supporters of statutes that are found to exceed congressional authority.

New, Symbolic Issues. To the extent that the modern Supreme Court has confronted Congress on federalism, it has tended to do so when Congress has contrived to extend its already broad authority into areas it had not previously thought of regulating. *Lopez* and *Printz* fit this mold. *Flores,* too, can be viewed as a judicial attempt to confine the exercise of congressional authority under the Fourteenth Amendment to the core issues of race and sex discrimination and to forestall a further extension of that authority to new constituencies and issue areas.

The pattern is neither new nor surprising, as Federalism has generally tended to produce constitutional litigation when Congress addressed new issues in new ways.[2] The New Deal and the civil rights era are the most obvious examples. The difference between the contemporary federalism issues and the historical analogies is that judicial efforts to contain congressional power were futile then but are likely to work now.

The New Deal and the civil rights laws were prompted by manifest crises, and they were backed by an urgent public demand and by powerful political coalitions. When legal challenges to those expansions arrived at the Supreme Court, the sense of crisis and the political demands for action had lost none of their force. The dislocations of corporate capitalism lent urgency to the New Dealers' demands to enhance the federal government's authority, and those demands—and the political constituencies that backed them—were in full force when, in 1937, the Supreme Court saw itself confronted with an all-or-nothing choice between constitutional norms and plenary congressional authority. The remnants of the old order were swept aside by World War II: *Wickard* v. *Filburn* was decided in 1942, when the Supreme Court was understandably reluctant to curtail presidential authority. In the 1960s, when Congress trumped "states' rights" and Jim Crow laws with federal civil rights guarantees, the Supreme Court would have been unable to confine the federal government's new powers even if it had been of a mind to make the attempt (which it was not).

In contrast, modern enactments that further strain congressional authority involve nothing remotely resembling the crisis of capitalism, or World War II, or segregation. Few of those statutes respond to a recognizable crisis or to a credible political demand.[3] When Congress enacted the laws that were struck down in *Lopez* and *Printz*, state and local governments were already regulating the possession of guns on school grounds, and most states were requiring background checks for would-be gun purchasers. Federal statutes at the intersection of crime and civil rights are often passed in response to transient or fabricated "crises." In 1994, when Congress enacted the Violence against Women Act, nobody in his right mind believed that American women were facing a wave of "hate crimes" comparable to the fate of blacks during Reconstruction. In 1996, in response to media reports of a wave of racially motivated church burnings, Congress unanimously enacted a federal church arson statute. By the time of the enactment, the reported incidents had been proven to be neither a wave nor, for the most part, racially motivated, and there was no indication that state and local law enforcement agencies were failing to investigate and prosecute the incidents.[4]

Civil libertarians have denounced recent extensions of federal authority as assaults on individual freedom.[5] That criticism is justified in some instances and respects, especially the growing federalization of crime. But the general theme of modern statutes is not creeping authoritarianism. It is a postmodern politics of empty gestures.

If Congress seriously intended to protect female college students (whose alleged safety concerns played a prominent role in the enactment of the Violence against Women Act) from gender-based violence, it could withhold federal funds from schools that fail to refer sexual offenders for criminal prosecutions. If Congress had any real desire to claim authority and responsibility for controlling guns in local schools, it could withhold federal funds from school districts that fail to expel gun-wielding students and to refer them for criminal prosecution.[6] Although such reforms would put the statutes at issue well beyond constitutional challenges, Congress did not contemplate them in enacting VAWA or in reviving the Gun Free School Zones Act. For the most part, contemporary statutes that stretch congressional authority do not seek to exert control. Nor do they respond to powerful interest group demands. Congress enacts those statutes for the same reason that prompts a dog to lick its testicles: it does it because it can.

Symbolic legislation entails costs. It tends to confirm that anyone's pain, anywhere, is the business of the U.S. Congress. Moreover, symbolic commitments may harden into regulatory programs.[7] On the upside, though, the profusion of symbolic legislation provides the Supreme Court with opportunities to reestablish federalism norms. Judicial interventions are unlikely to be perceived as obtuseness to an imminent crisis, since there was and is no crisis. The Justices face little risk of incurring the wrath of potent political constituencies, since the statutes at issue have no such constituencies. The Court need not thwart federal regulatory commitments, since the statutes embody no such commitments.

Of course, Congress will resent judicial constraints. Witness the congressional response to *Lopez*. But such resistance does not amount to very much. *Lopez* is a constitutional symbol; Congress's embarrassed, cowardly response is not. The Supreme Court can establish federalist precedents without coming within shouting distance of arenas where enumerated powers constraints would produce a serious backlash. Between *Lopez* and a frontal assault on the Clean Air Act or the National Labor Relations Board lie miles of constitutional territory.[8]

Federalism as a Second-Best. Not all successful judicial advances have been directed against marginal and poorly defended positions. The Religious Freedom Restoration Act was backed by a very broad political coalition, dealt with an important political issue, and was enacted with much fanfare and near unanimity. Nonetheless, the Supreme Court struck down the act, and it looks as if the Court will get away with it. As noted earlier, the RFRA constituencies' response to *Flores* has been quite muted, in large measure because many of those constituencies view the federalism solution as a very good second-best. This experience holds an important lesson for the Supreme Court: it illustrates that the Justices can enforce federalism constraints even at the price of disappointing a large and potent political constituency—and live to tell the tale. Specifically, *Flores* suggests that enumerated powers constraints are likely to stick when the "losers" are the Leave-Us-Aloners who like federalism as a general principle, if not exactly in the case at hand.

This lesson may give the Court greater confidence to insist on constitutional constraints in future cases. Perhaps the starkest example of a prospective case that could easily follow the pattern of *Flores* involves the proposed federal partial-birth abortion ban. A constitutional challenge to a federal ban has three possible outcomes. The first of these, a Supreme Court ruling to the effect that even Congress may not interfere with judicially created abortion rights, is almost out of the question. Even if the Court were eager to reassert its preeminent authority over sexual matters (which it is not), it will surely find more suitable occasions than to invalidate a prohibition, enacted by a two-thirds majority in both houses of Congress, on a truly horrid procedure. The two remaining options are to sustain a federal ban or else to invalidate it on the federalist theory that neither the Commerce Clause nor Section 5 of the Fourteenth Amendment provides Congress with the constitutional authority to regulate (privately performed) abortions. See *Lopez,* and see *Flores.*[9]

While right-to-life constituencies obviously prefer the former outcome, the latter is not a total defeat but a second-best. Much as *Flores* effectively sanctioned state RFRAs, the invalidation of the federal statute would carry with it an implication that the states *may* ban partial-birth abortions.[10] Naturally, right-to-life constituencies would be dismayed that even the most modest restrictions on abortions cannot find favor with the Supreme Court. But the premise of the proposed partial-birth abortion ban is that abortion need not be restricted all at once. Having accepted that premise, right-to-life constituencies would probably be amenable to a federalist solution. They would do what RFRA's constituencies have done after *Flores*—fight for the restoration of constitutionally permissible federal restrictions (for instance, a ban on partial-birth abortions performed in interstate commerce) and continue to advance their cause state by state.

At the same time, liberal constituencies and advocates, heretofore fiercely nationalist in orientation, may come to accept the federalist solution because it holds out the prospect of preserving access to late-term abortions in at least some states.[11] Federalism, in short, may force both sides into a standoff along state lines. While both sides would be reluctant to accept this compromise indefinitely, both may prefer a somewhat defused and diversified conflict to a continued deadlock at the national level (all the more so because both sides are accustomed to the state-by-state trench warfare that already accompanies the debate at the national level).

Federal legislators would likewise be prepared to abide by a judicial ruling that, although constituting a setback to congressional ambitions, would get an awkward and risky issue off the table. Few politicians like dealing with such issues. In 1996, for example, in response to fears that judicial endorsements of homosexual marriages in some states might compel other states to recognize such unions, Congress enacted the Defense of Marriage Act, which declared that no such recognition is required. Ignoring the objections of advocacy groups at both ends of the ideological spectrum, Congress enacted a federalist solution that had the intended—and considerable—advantage of diffusing a contentious debate that carries great political risks and almost no rewards.[12] Congress cannot denationalize the abortion debate in this fashion because the Supreme Court has so thoroughly nationalized it.[13] But few legislators would be truly chagrined at a judicial ruling that declares many abortion issues beyond the reach of Congress.

Federalism is rarely anyone's first choice. Very often, however, it is a very strong second choice for a lot of constituencies. Such situations provide the Supreme Court with openings to reassert enumerated powers constraints.

Federalism in Congress

In the wake of the 1994 elections, the Republican majority in Congress pursued the "devolution" agenda announced in the party's Contract with America, with a modicum of success. One crown jewel of the devolution campaign is the 1995 Unfunded Mandates Reform Act, which establishes procedural requirements on Congress and federal agencies to inhibit the imposition of unfunded federal mandates on states and local governments. A second accomplishment is the 1996 welfare reform, which replaced the federal Aid to Families with Dependent Children program, a set of very stringent, "categorical" federal requirements, with block grants to the states. Within general federal guidelines, the states are permitted to design and implement their own welfare programs.

While the devolution enthusiasm has since abated, it suggests that Congress can at times play a role in revitalizing federalism. In this light, my earlier account of Congress as constitutionally incapable of restraining itself may seem overdrawn. But while ostensibly self-restraining, "devolutionist" measures are not entirely worthless, they tend to produce only marginal (and often short-lived) benefits for federalism. The real legislative opportunities for advancing federalism, and the next plausible steps in a "virtuous cycle" scenario, lie in restraining private litigants and federal judges. The federal judiciary's increasingly federalist jurisprudence has greatly facilitated such steps, and Congress has in fact taken some of them.

Devolution and Its Discontents. The Unfunded Mandates Reform Act just mentioned provides a perfect example of a widely touted but illusory federalism initiative. On the surface, curbing unfunded federal mandates is not a bad idea. Assuming that the federal government will find it difficult to raise the requisite funds to induce compliance, an injunction against federal mandates might mark a genuine advance for federalism. But the statute Congress actually enacted applies only to mandates on government agencies, as distinct from private employers or landlords or educators. In other words, it is not a limitation on federal power but a selective protection for subordinate government entities. Moreover, even in that limited domain, the Unfunded Mandates Reform Act is carefully circumscribed so as to prevent any actual interference with nationalist aspirations. The act exempts all existing federal mandates, thus leaving the entire national regulatory state untouched. It exempts all mandates pertaining to antidiscrimination and the enforcement of constitutional rights, along with mandates that advance national security, provide emergency relief, relate to Social Security, or are designated by the president as emergency legislation. And even in the case of new mandates in covered areas, Congress can easily waive the requirements of the act by a simple majority vote. In short, the Unfunded Mandates Reform Act is riddled with so many exceptions and qualifications as to render it utterly ineffective.[14]

The 1996 welfare reform, technically entitled the Personal Responsibility and Work Opportunity Reconciliation Act, merits a more nuanced assessment. By replacing federal, categorical requirements with block grants, the Personal Responsibility Act provides the states with enhanced flexibility in designing their own welfare programs (which are now called "Temporary Assistance to Needy Families" programs). The block grant strategy has facilitated considerable policy experimentation, and it has permitted the states to tailor eligibility requirements, welfare-to-work programs, and other welfare policies to their widely varying welfare populations.[15]

Those advantages are not insubstantial. The states' ability to experiment, to adjust their programs with ease, and to imitate the policies of other, more successful states may have contributed to an astonishing reduction of the welfare rolls (although the roaring economy probably deserves more credit for drawing former welfare recipients into the labor force).[16] Moreover, welfare reform has been widely hailed as a great policy success, inviting similar reforms in other policy arenas—for instance, in 1998, the consolidation of some sixty federal job-training programs into three block grant programs administered by the states.

But block grant federalism implies neither a real limit on federal authority nor, ultimately, genuine state competition. Block grants are, so to speak, unfunded mandates in reverse. Both are versions of a "cooperative federalism" that undermines political accountability—unfunded mandates, because Congress gets to mandate what it does not pay for; block grants, because the states get to dispense favors or to run regulatory programs with money they have not raised. The Personal Responsibility Act declares that responsibility for welfare rests with the federal government (which raises and distributes the money) and, in the next breath, that the responsibility rests with the states (which for that reason get to run the programs). Block grants imply a limitless notion of congressional authority and a resolute refusal to decide what is and is not a federal responsibility.

The problem is not merely theoretical. The states' continued reliance on federal funds acts as a centripetal force. Moreover, the continued presumption that the program in question serves a national purpose (why else fund it?) implies a congressional responsibility to ensure that the funds will be spent as intended, and the much-heralded flexibility of block grants undermines that responsibility. For these reasons, earlier block grant experiments—for example, the Nixon administration's—proved temporary. Sooner rather than later, the programs were recategorized.[17]

Such experiences account for the periodic appearance of proposals for cleaner, more explicitly federalist reforms. For example, the Reagan administration briefly considered a revenue-neutral welfare "swap," which called for an end to all federal AFDC (now Personal Responsibility Act) payments and obligations in return for the federal government's assumption of states' financial contributions to the Medicaid program. This sensible proposal would have wiped out unfunded (or partially funded) mandates, aligned political with fiscal responsibility, and created genuine welfare policy competition among the states. Precisely for these reasons, however, the swap went absolutely nowhere when the Reagan administration floated it. The swap still has adherents, chiefly among centrist Democrats. But welfare rights groups and, more important, the states will have none of it. Even and especially the most entrepreneurial governors—such as Governor Thompson of Wisconsin, who led the fight for greater state flexibility on welfare policy—resist genuine state competition. They want the protocompetition of the Personal Responsibility Act, combined with more federal money—lots of it, with even fewer strings.[18]

Because Congress operates on ambition, ostensibly self-restraining federalism initiatives, while not entirely without value, will always remain very limited. One can, however, identify strategies that are broadly consistent with legislators' incentives to centralize control. First, Congress can advance federalism by curbing not its own impositions but the courts'. Second, Congress can advance federalism by circumscribing federal entitlements. Third, congressional factions—even minority factions—can advance federalism surreptitiously by inducing an institutional "failure" to specify federal impositions with sufficient clarity and precision. Recent legislation provides examples of each of these strategies. Jointly and separately, the strategies undermine the infrastructure of the federal entitlement state. All three strategies build on the judiciary's federalism advances. All three help to sustain a virtuous cycle toward federalism.

Curbing the Federal Courts. Virtually all federal politicians pay lip service to federalism. To be sure, the legislators' proffered commitment to federalism is very weak and easily overcome by seemingly more pressing concerns. Even so, federalist sentiments have enough resonance to persuade legislators that they ought to do something, somewhere, somehow, for federalism. Curbing the "imperial judiciary" is an attractive option because it enables legislators who cannot restrain themselves to vote for restraint. The current emperors, in turn, will welcome many legislative restrictions.

The clearest example of a successful congressional effort to curb federal court jurisdiction is the 1996 Prison Litigation Reform Act, which sharply curtailed the federal courts' remedial authority in litigation over state prison systems. The core provision of the statute in essence terminates pending lawsuits over prison conditions without a judicial finding, within thirty days, of a constitutional violation. Something of a political stealth bomber, the Prison Litigation Reform Act emerged without much outside prompting from the office of Senator Spencer Abraham (R-Michigan) and went largely unnoticed by the public and the media.

Even anticrime groups paid little attention and actually had to be mobilized to support the legislation. The act has, however, enabled several states to escape the clutches of federal judges. Other judges refused to relinquish jurisdiction, with the result that Congress, in 1997, toughened the statute and created additional mechanisms to terminate prison lawsuits.[19]

While prison administration may seem far removed from competitive federalism, the issue has been quite salient in states (such as Arizona and Michigan) that have long operated under judicial prison reform orders. The benefits of terminating judicial supervision are obvious and tangible for the citizens of cities such as Philadelphia, which has been beset by a crime wave caused in no small part by violent convicts who were released pursuant to a judicial order.[20] State and local jurisdictions will be somewhat better at administering prisons than are federal judges. Prison expenditures will reflect local preferences instead of imagined constitutional demands, and citizens will at long last be able to hold administrators accountable for their performance.

Moreover, the Prison Litigation Reform Act can serve as a precedent for legislation concerning issues that involve more central concerns. If Congress can stop federal courts from micromanaging prisons, why can it not stop them from micromanaging school districts under decades-old desegregation orders? To be sure, a "school litigation reform act" would trigger ferocious opposition from teachers' unions and civil rights groups—far more formidable forces than the prison administrators who lobbied against the Prison Litigation Reform Act.[21] By that same token, however, far more potent forces would lobby *for* such an enactment. Moreover, Congress could limit judicial remedies in school desegregation in a piecemeal fashion—for instance, by enabling states and municipalities to prohibit busing for purposes of racial balancing or by providing that federal judges may not prohibit the establishment of public charter schools on the grounds that they might upset the racial balance in the school district.[22]

The federal courts are unlikely to resent jurisdiction-limiting statutes and may even welcome them. A recent statute limiting the habeas corpus jurisdiction of federal courts, for instance, was enacted at the persistent urging of Chief Justice Rehnquist. The Prison Litigation Reform Act has been challenged as unconstitutional (with widely varying results), but in the end the Supreme Court will probably sustain the statute.[23] A hypothetical school litigation reform act need only provide legislative mechanisms for enforcing standards concerning the scope and duration of judicial remedial powers that the Supreme Court has already articulated but that it cannot enforce in any systematic fashion. The Court is unlikely to find fault with such a measure.[24] Congress has ample room to advance federalism by "depriving" the federal courts of jurisdiction that they—or at least a majority of Supreme Court Justices—no longer desire.

Entitlements and Welfare Reform. The Personal Responsibility Act, earlier described as a decidedly mixed bag, produced one real change, which has been widely overlooked in the enthusiasm over the states' newfound flexibility. Section 601(b) of the act, entitled "No Individual Entitlement," provides that the law "shall not be interpreted to entitle any individual or family to assistance under any State program funded under [the Act]."

This explicit repeal of individual program entitlements effectively restores AFDC to its original 1935 design as an entitlement program *for the states* (whose receipts under the program were to be determined by legal rules instead of discretionary appropriations). The creation of *private* entitlements was principally the result of Supreme Court decisions handed down in the late 1960s and early 1970s. These decisions and the ensuing wave of welfare rights litigation drove the expansion of the AFDC program and, in a real sense, modern welfare politics.[25] The Personal Responsibility Act has reversed this development. As the Welfare Law Center has put it, the act "wiped out federal statutory and regulatory protections that had provided the basis for significant welfare reform litigation over the past 25 years."[26]

That is a bit of an overstatement. On the one hand, the demise of entitlements in the Personal Responsibility Act was foreshadowed—and facilitated—by successive rulings of the Rehnquist Court that had substantially curtailed statutory and quasi-constitutional entitlements.[27] On the other hand, the Personal Responsibility Act has not ended all programmatic litigation aimed at shaping—more to the point, at derailing—the states' implementation of the statute. Some state constitutions, for instance, have been read to contain welfare guarantees broader than the federal minimums, and judicial rulings of decades past continue to prohibit states from imposing residency requirements for welfare recipients.[28]

On the whole, though, the "wipe-out" characterization is accurate. The Personal Responsibility Act has terminated litigation as a means of ensuring official compliance with welfare mandates. It has also cut off certain constitutional requirements that apply to entitlement statutes (such as the AFDC program of lore) but not to discretionary programs.[29] With rare exceptions, welfare rights litigation now revolves around peripheral issues and administrative errors in individual cases.[30]

The transition from private entitlements to administrative discretion has several political effects. The most obvious effect is to cut statutory beneficiaries and welfare rights groups from the political equation.[31] When "see you in federal court" ceases to be a viable threat, advocacy groups lose much of their clout. At the same time, constituencies for fiscal and regulatory restraint can compete on a level playing field, instead of having their concerns trumped by a federal "right" of one sort or another.

More broadly, limitations on federal jurisdiction crack the coalitions that grow up around entitlement programs. Entitlements cement coalitions among advocacy groups, local welfare bureaucrats, federal bureaucrats, and congressional committees, all of whom have an incentive to expand a policy regime under the guise and the political cover of legal "rights." In the heyday of welfare rights, congressional committees funded welfare rights organizations. Federal bureaucrats wrote expansive regulations, which the courts would cite as compelling authority for a further expansion. When political obstacles (such as resistance among members of the appropriations committees) precluded that strategy, the courts often took the lead in creating new entitlements. As one legal scholar put it, "Reform could thus proceed in an ever-ascending spiral with no single participant in the process having the capacity to block progressive development."[32]

That game is now over. Abolish the entitlements, and welfare rights advocates can no longer get into court. The dynamics of political struggles over the shape, scope, and funding levels of welfare programs change from legal enforcement (and expansion) to intergovernmental negotiation. Distributional coalitions must seek to ensure state compliance through persuasion, administrative oversight, and budgetary means— measures that are far less effective and far less conducive to a program expansion than litigation. As a last resort, statutes that lack private enforcement mechanisms often permit or even require the federal program administrator to withhold funds from noncomplying states. But that is usually an empty threat since neither the advocacy groups nor Congress will permit its application.[33] By virtue of these changed dynamics, the entitlement repeal has played a substantial role in allowing the states to retain flexibility in designing welfare and workfare programs under the Personal Responsibility Act—instead of being hit by a wave a lawsuits insisting that this or that federal statutory provision actually entailed an entitlement.

Much like the Prison Litigation Reform Act, the termination of private entitlements in the Personal Responsibility Act can easily serve as a precedent, especially once its salutary effects on federalism become more obvious. The act itself, in fact, repealed not only what used to be AFDC benefits but also the federal judicial enforcement of other entitlements, such as Medicaid benefits. Outside the welfare context, programs that provide private entitlements to federally assisted housing or education are obvious candidates for conversion into discretionary programs.

It may seem odd that a Congress that is institutionally predisposed to extend federal control should yet be willing to curtail federal entitlements. But the form of federal control matters a great deal, as does the fact that the Republican Party took control of Congress in 1994. The expansion of federal authority by means of creating private entitlements presupposes a congruity between the objectives of the congressional majority and the interests of statutory beneficiaries—in other words, between private advocacy groups and their congressional patrons, who put the entitlements in the books. In real life, welfare rights mean that the Children's Defense Fund will do Senator Kennedy's bidding. Environmental rights mean that the Natural Resources Defense Council will do Congressman Waxman's bidding. And so on to women's rights and civil rights.

That is not a plausible strategy for a moderately conservative, Republican Congress. On the one hand, sustaining entitlements for what are, after all, Democratic constituencies would foil rather than advance congressional control over reform projects. While this elementary insight has at times eluded the congressional leadership (for example, in the Violence against Women Act, which is in essence an entitlement program for feminist advocacy groups), it has generally registered. Witness the much-underrated "no entitlement" provision of the Personal Responsibility Act, a very explicit and, as just seen, successful effort to protect a conservative reform project. On the other hand, a strategy of expanding "conservative" entitlements is foreclosed by several considerations—among them, the lack of an interest group infrastructure to enforce such entitlements and their fateful tendency to redound to the benefit of groups other than the intended beneficiaries.[34] Under these circumstances, a "no entitlement" strategy for federalism is wholly consistent with congressional ambition.

Two Cheers for Institutional "Failure." Earlier chapters described the rise of judicially enforced federal entitlements during the 1960s and 1970s and the subsequent erosion of this "collusive nationalism." The repercussions of those legal developments in the legislative arena merit a few additional remarks, for they buttress the lesson of the "no entitlement" strategy just mentioned. To advance federalism, Congress need not affirmatively abolish federal entitlements. It need merely fall down on the job of creating them. This is not a lot to ask for, and the courts have greatly alleviated the burden.

When first confronted with the rise of judicial formalism, Congress made strenuous efforts to stem the erosion of judicial cooperation in the expansion of federal mandates and entitlements. In a thorough (though not entirely undisputed) study of congressional overrides of the Supreme Court's statutory interpretation cases between 1967 and 1990, Professor William N. Eskridge, Jr., found that the frequency of such overrides increased substantially in the period from 1975 onward, when a somewhat more conservative Supreme Court clashed with a comparatively liberal Congress that continued to follow its institutional incentive of expanding the rights of statutory beneficiaries. The pattern continued throughout the Reagan and Bush administrations.[35]

The Republican takeover of Congress in 1994 has, however, produced a shift toward a less contentious relationship between Congress and the Court. The Supreme Court has remained persistent in steering a course of judicial forbearance and noncooperation. Occasionally, Congress has still felt compelled to override narrow judicial interpretations of statutory entitlements. For a particularly exasperating example, Congress reversed in 1997 an appellate decision to the effect that school districts need not provide special educational services to violent students whose misconduct is unrelated to a learning disability.[36] On the whole, though, the Republican majority seems much more willing than its Democratic predecessors to accede to narrow judicial interpretations of statutory entitlements.

Civil rights law illustrates the point. In the late 1980s the Supreme Court undertook a modest effort, consisting of a dozen decisions of limited import, to curb civil rights entitlements. In cutting back on civil rights laws, the Justices probably thought they were doing no more (and perhaps less) than was expected of them by the Republican presidents who had put them on the bench. Instead, one of those presidents— George Bush—joined a campaign against the Court to "restore" civil rights law. The result was the 1991 Civil Rights Act, which not only reversed the Supreme Court's decisions but greatly expanded antidiscrimination rights and remedies.[37]

Far from being discouraged by this backlash, however, the Supreme Court went back to business at the civil rights front. For example, the Court sharply limited the creation of racially gerrymandered, "safe" minority districts under the Voting Rights Act. For another, more dramatic example, the Supreme Court's 1995 decision in *Adarand Constructors* v. *Pena* held that race-based set-asides in federal contracting must satisfy "strict" judicial scrutiny, meaning that such programs are almost always unconstitutional.[38] The Court's persistence is beginning to show results: in contrast to the experience of 1991, Congress has made no serious move to stage an end run around *Adarand* or around the voting rights cases, even though the decisions sweep much more broadly across the federal affirmative action landscape than all the pre-1991 civil rights cases combined. While constitutional decisions such as *Adarand* are harder to circumvent than the statutory cases that the 1991 Civil Rights Act overturned, a Congress that can resurrect the Gun Free School Zones Act after *Lopez* could presumably find a way around *Adarand* if it put its collective mind to it. Congress has not, however, done so.[39]

Environmental citizen suit provisions illustrate the same point. In 1987 the Supreme Court held that the citizen suit provision of the Clean Water Act permitted private enforcement actions only over continuing or recurring violations of the Act but not over wholly past ones. Although that very modest ruling did virtually nothing to hinder environmental citizen suits, Congress reversed the decision.[40] As in the civil rights area, though, the Supreme Court responded by erecting more serious obstacles to environmental citizen suits. The most important of these cases, *Lujan* v. *Defenders of Wildlife* (1994), effectively declared all citizen suit provisions unconstitutional. Private enforcement is an essential tool of environmental regulation, and there has been no shortage of suggestions as to how Congress might circumvent the Supreme Court's decisions.[41] None of these suggestions, however, has received serious congressional consideration.

The logic of this trend lies in the fact that judicial formalism makes it more difficult to create new entitlements. The plain-statement rule—that is, the rule that Congress cannot impose mandates without an absolutely clear statement of intent—provides a good illustration. Its principal effect is to drive up legislative transaction costs: when ambiguous language means no new entitlement, Congress finds it much harder to reconcile conflicting interests and, hence, to legislate.[42] The opponents of new entitlements can afford to hold out or pretend to compromise, while their proponents must stamp their feet and insist on crystal-clear language. Correspondingly, the plain-statement rule reduces the legislators' costs of failing to cooperate in the expansion of federal power. Congress need no longer say no to insistent interest groups; to thwart their designs, Congress merely needs to mumble. When the courts deny legal redress under statutes that mumble, Congress can tell the interests that, regrettably, not much can be done about the recalcitrant courts. Conversely, the Supreme Court need not confront the interest groups directly; it need merely direct them to obtain a clear statement from Congress. Both institutions may well expect that the other will fail to accommodate the claimants. But what looks like botched communication between Congress and the Court is a protection for federalism.

The federalism that results from institutional noncooperation is still a step removed from real, competitive federalism. Instead of erecting principled, constitutional limits to federal power, it merely cracks the distributional coalitions that protect and expand federal programs. That, however, is a very big *merely*. Whereas judicial solicitude for federal entitlements gave the upper hand to proponents of national authority, formalism gives the upper hand to legislative factions—even minority factions—who resist such expansions. Where entitlement jurisprudence multiplied access points, formalism creates veto points. Cooperative federalism created an institutional framework that ratcheted nationalism up; judicial noncooperation creates institutional dynamics and incentives that ratchet it down. Judicial noncooperation and its legislative use come very close to a truly constitutional, competitive federalism.

For precisely this reason, legal scholars have complained that the Supreme Court is accomplishing through institutional noncooperation what it dares not attempt directly—that is, to limit congressional ambitions. The Supreme Court's formalist jurisprudence is said to thwart democracy—in demanding plain statements, for instance, or in interpreting old entitlement statutes as written, as opposed to updating them in light of the current legislature's likely intentions.[43] The diagnosis is precisely correct; its normative thrust, profoundly mistaken. We are not exactly blessed with viable means of thwarting interest groups' schemes. Moreover, even and especially on the highly problematic assumption that interests' group bargains and their judicial enforcement somehow deserve the honorific attribute "democratic," we hardly suffer from a deficit of democracy. We suffer from a lack of restraints and responsibility, and it is the courts' business to supply those goods. Courts are *supposed* to be ornery, not "democratic."

The insistence on a cooperative federal judiciary ultimately presupposes the legitimacy of an entirely nationalized politics. The Supreme Court has rejected that position. In offering its noncooperation, it has facilitated low-cost legislative strategies that would further federalist advances. Bilateral noncooperation deserves all the cooperation it can get.

* * * * *

The judicial and legislative strategies described in this chapter may seem too limited to sustain any real momentum toward federalism and too contrived and policy-wonkish to sustain the interest of federalism's Leave-Us-Alone constituency. Federalist beachheads in the form of judicial invalidations of symbolic congressional enactments may be too small and out-of-the-way to launch a full-scale assault on the nationalist ramparts. Indeed, a personnel change on the Court could turn them into federalist Dunkirks. Selective judicial invalidations of federal statutes that happen to help otherwise federalist constituencies may exasperate those constituencies, rather than encourage them. Congressional enactments that disenfranchise nationalist constituencies do not, by virtue of that fact alone, embolden federalist Leave-Us-Alone constituencies.

Each objection along these lines, however, can be met with an equally good argument on the other side. Every judicial beachhead may lend itself to further advances. The fact that explicit judicial constraints on Congress may operate at one remove from—or, in particular cases, even against—the Leave-Us-Aloners' concerns makes the imposition of such constraints more likely, for it enables the Court to advance federalism while keeping a certain distance from the populist constituencies it distrusts. Congressional "court curbing" and disenfranchisement of nationalist constituencies provide Leave-Us-Alone constituencies with much more room to run their own experiments in the states, including experiments that are central to their larger project. After the Prison Litigation Reform Act, one can envision prison administration without American Civil Liberties Union vetoes, and the Personal Responsibility Act has greatly weakened the welfare rights movement. Imagine an education policy with a comparable effect on the National Education Association: at that point, surely, the disenfranchisement of nationalist constituencies and the Leave-Us-Aloners' agenda converge.

The scenario envisions no decisive breakthrough for competitive federalism. But a man's got to know his limitations, and that goes for constitutional reformers, too. A project of constitutional reconstruction cannot rely on the hope for a unilateral judicial assertion of enumerated powers constraints or on an even more illusory hope for congressional self-restraint; it must account for institutional incentives and limitations, the dictates of political economy, and the observed behavior of interest groups. The virtuous cycle scenario meets this test, and it holds out the promise of incremental changes that may over time harden into constitutional constraints. That may not seem much, or even enough. But it is far superior to a futile search for silver bullets.

9

Federalism's Possibilities

Federalism's chief virtue, I have argued, is citizen choice and state competition. So understood, federalism is a structural constraint on government. It presupposes reliable, judicially enforced constitutional norms that protect competition and thwart monopolistic tendencies—enumerated powers and a corresponding realm of state autonomy.

For the past six decades, American government has lacked federalism constraints. Their reconstruction is a matter of considerable interest—and difficulty. Seemingly irresistible forces pull in the opposite, centralizing direction. Impatient citizens demand protections and benefits that only the national government can promise and, occasionally, deliver. Insatiable interests and distributional coalitions are firmly entrenched at the national level. Egalitarian forces persist in demanding uniformity. These forces are endemic to democracy. Tocqueville's "natural" tendency toward centralization operates not only in the United States but also in transnational organizations such as the European Community.

In America and even in Europe, centralization has been accompanied by increased popular discontent with a meddlesome, interest-group-ridden government. This sentiment provides a basis for a federalist revival. But public discontent and cynicism do not automatically translate into public support for constitutional constraints. Far less do they entail the actual restoration of such constraints. Federalism's reconstruction requires institutional pathways and political dynamics that can produce federalism despite and against—or at least around—the natural, centralizing tendencies of democratic government.

The virtuous cycle described in this book is an attempt to identify such pathways and dynamics. Through (often tacit) cooperation and in anticipation of a broader consensus for more open, competitive political arrangements, a federalism-minded Supreme Court and Leave-Us-Alone constituencies with a strategic, long-term interest in federalism can gradually reestablish federalism constraints. In some policy arenas (among them, civil rights and federal entitlement programs), a virtuous cycle seems well underway.

Experience suggests that the scenario may prove a mirage. The Supreme Court has indicated before that federal power has its limits; it did so in 1976, when it decided *National League of Cities*. Both the first Nixon administration and the first Reagan administration produced "new federalism" initiatives. In substance and in even in form, the most recent wavelet of devolution resembles those initiatives. Block grants were a favored policy instrument of the Nixon administration. The Unfunded Mandates Reform Act resembles the imposition of "federalism impact statements" under President Reagan. But the earlier federalist stirrings proved a mere ripple on a tidal wave of nationalist politics. Block grants were soon recategorized. None but a few students of public administration remember the executive federalism measures.[1] The Supreme Court overruled *National League of Cities*.

The federalism initiatives of the past few years may meet with an equally ignominious demise. The Supreme Court may not pursue the logic suggested by its federalism decisions, and the loss of a single profederalism vote on the Court would reverse the current majority's modest but hard-won gains. A few tendentious public opinion polls or focus group findings may produce a spate of new federal entitlements. Still, I remain persuaded that the constellation of forces and the scenario described in this book offer a viable path toward competitive federalism. Compared with the 1970s and 1980s, two crucial variables have changed.

First, the U.S. Supreme Court has become much less nationalist. *National League of Cities* was a lone outlier; the modern decisions mark a trend. Second, the federalism debate of the 1990s is being played out against a more libertarian background in that the voters have become quite skeptical of ambitious government schemes and of further extensions of federal authority. The political environment is not conducive to a showdown of constitutional proportions over the scope of the federal government. It is, however, quite hospitable to incremental policy changes that, in the aggregate, produce more federalism and less government.

Law and Politics

Federalism's future, I have argued, hangs on a pattern of cooperation between the Supreme Court and political constituencies. This picture will strike some as an unsuitably crass and political account of an institution that ought to be beyond politics. But the picture is congruent in its broad contours with the best extant accounts of the Supreme Court's role in American politics. It reflects the elementary insight that the Supreme Court's ability to preserve—or rather, to reestablish—constitutional norms is constrained by the political environment. The Justices can shape that environment, but only up to a point.

The picture reflects the modern Supreme Court's federalism predicament. A majority of Justices has concluded that "process federalism"—that is, the notion that the Constitution contains *no* judicially enforceable limits to federal power—has got to be wrong. This recognition provides the legal impulse for the Court's endeavor to reestablish some federalism doctrines—at long last, some six decades after their demise. The constitutional project, though, must be sustained against the U.S. Congress, against (or at least without) the states, and against political constituencies with enormous stakes in the preservation of an unlimited national government. The task is hopeless unless there is some political force to support a return to constitutional constraints— and some reasonable prospect that those constraints will in the long run enjoy broad public support.

The question, then, is not whether the Supreme Court must, in attempting a federalist restoration, consider the larger political environment. Of course it must. The question is whether the Supreme Court can cooperate (in the sense explained) with the particular, Leave-Us-Alone constituencies that happen to be the only existing force of federalism—and vice versa. Earlier chapters have examined both the Supreme Court's jurisprudence and Leave-Us-Alone politics with an eye toward a gradual rapprochement between the Court and the constituencies. But since so much depends on the answer, the question merits another look from a somewhat broader perspective.

The reason for the Supreme Court's reluctance to make common cause with Leave-Us-Alone constituencies—reflected, for instance, in the Court's continued adherence to a technocratic, statist, sovereignty-centered federalism and in periodic reassertions of judicial supremacy—is *not* that those constituencies are too marginal or sectarian to sustain a federalist dynamic. Constituencies that facilitate constitutional revolutions have often been marginal. In 1938, when the Supreme Court threw in the towel on safeguarding the structural constraints of the Constitution, it simultaneously declared its intention to play a far more aggressive role in protecting the constitutional rights of "discrete and insular minorities." This dual standard, which became the cornerstone of five decades of constitutional jurisprudence, was obviously not targeted at dominant political forces. Its intended beneficiaries were—well, discrete and insular. In 1954, when the Supreme Court effectively ended the "separate but equal" regime of *Plessy* v. *Ferguson,* civil rights organizations were a marginal political force, and few blacks in the South could even vote. In the 1960s, when the Supreme Court constructed a "wall of separation" between church and state, the advocates of strict separation were political oddballs. If in later decades these groups came to look far less marginal, they did so in large part because the Supreme Court had legitimized their agenda and provided them with political credibility, which the groups then leveraged in other political arenas. The modern Supreme Court could easily legitimize federalism's constituencies in the same fashion.

Earlier chapters have suggested reasons other than the Leave-Us-Aloners' presumed marginality for the Supreme Court's evident reluctance to pursue this course. The Justices' endorsement of civil rights or separationist constituencies was consistent with the Supreme Court's inherently nationalist disposition; the endorsement of a federalist agenda and constituency is not. An expansive constitutional rights jurisprudence implies a judicial campaign against state and local governments; a federalist agenda implied a much tougher confrontation with Congress. Unlike the Supreme Court's former, liberal constituencies, the Leave-Us-Aloners do not have national elite opinion on their side, and so the Court treats them as gauche. Four considerations, however, give reason to hope that the Supreme Court's nationalist, elitist disposition will in the long run give way to a more accommodating posture toward federalism and its constituencies.

The Constitution. The first and perhaps most obvious reason is the Constitution, whose structure and text happen to be federalist. Rediscovering federalism is not like constructing a "wall of separation" from a Thomas Jefferson letter, or like discerning mystery rights in the penumbras and emanations of the Bill of Rights. Federalism is right there in the Constitution. It is true that federalism's constitutional contours aren't chiseled in stone. It is also true that a federalist jurisprudence will look quite "activist," both because it has to be superimposed on six decades worth of nationalist jurisprudence and because it requires the Court to confront Congress. Still, the countervailing intuition that process federalism and judicial abdication cannot be the last word on federalism has considerable force. It is, as noted, the intuition that underlies *Lopez*. The notion that "there has to be a line somewhere" is not a constitutional theory or principle; it is more like a constitutional grunt. But it is testimony to the powerful gravitational pull of a written Constitution.

Arms-Length Cooperation. A judicial federalism agenda would require only a mutual (grudging) acceptance between the Court and the Leave-Us-Aloners, instead of the close, symbiotic relationship between the post–New Deal Court and its liberal constituencies. The post–New Deal agenda was principally a matter of coining new constitutional rights, and it was always clear who wanted those rights and on whose behalf they were created and enforced. Blacks wanted and obtained civil rights. Abortion rights were a principal item on the feminist agenda, and the Supreme Court could not create those rights without explicitly embracing the feminist constituency and its agenda. Correspondingly, new rights disenfranchise opposing constituencies. The constitutional right to a secular public environment, for example, implied a disenfranchisement of religious constituencies.

Both effects, the constituency identification and the disenfranchisement, are much less direct with respect to *structural* constitutional constraints, such as federalism. While the reestablishment of such constraints must be in somebody's interest (or else it would not happen), federalism norms are much closer to neutral rules of the road than are constitutional rights, which always have an identifiable owner. The impulse for federalism must come from constituencies whose substantive demands often go against the Justices' grain, but the Supreme Court need not do the constituencies' bidding. For the most part, the Court merely needs to endorse rules that allow the groups to operate in a more open and competitive environment. To sustain momentum toward federalism, the Court need not endorse the Religious Freedom Restoration Act; it need only let RFRA's constituencies lobby for state RFRAs. It need not declare racial preferences per se unconstitutional; it need only

move in that direction, while permitting the voters in the states to decide whether they wish to maintain affirmative action policies. The Court
need not declare abortion unconstitutional; it need only permit restrictions at the state level. It need not endorse school vouchers; it need only
find that there are no constitutional obstacles to the practice. Conversely,
none of those commitments implies disenfranchisements comparable to
those worked by ironclad federal rights. Interest groups against school
vouchers or religious accommodation may still have their way. They will
simply have to protect their turf without the judiciary's assistance.

Constituency Shifts. Even constitutional constraints that are originally
tied to an identifiable constituency typically develop broader support
and a life of their own. For example, the Supreme Court's aggressive
free speech jurisprudence of the 1960s was designed to protect the
speech of institutions that would advance egalitarian values and the
interests of the Court's "discrete and insular minorities"—newspapers,
civil rights groups, academics.[2] To an extent, the First Amendment still
reflects this orientation. The organizers of civil rights or labor boycotts,
for instance, enjoy more constitutional protection than do political campaign contributors, broadcasters, or commercial enterprises. Still, the
Supreme Court's expansive First Amendment doctrines became integral to American political culture, and over the past decade *conservatives* have invoked those doctrines in defense against hate speech laws,
sexual harassment regulations, and other impositions that are now being propagated by the egalitarians who used to favor expansive speech
protections.

Less closely tied to constituency demands to begin with, federalism constraints would soon cease to map partisan-political divisions.
On the one hand, Leave-Us-Alone constituencies may have to accommodate themselves to the federalist arrangements that they are now inclined to favor only as a second-best solution. Conversely, while liberal
constituencies are predisposed to favor centralized, federal regimes,
they may yet come to favor federalism as one line where they can fight
their foes to a standoff. In lawsuits demanding an end to racial preferences, state institutions and their attorneys are now invoking federalism
concerns against the imposition of federal civil rights laws on state uni-
versities. To be sure, an opportunistic litigation posture need not herald
a larger political realignment. But the ready invocation of federalism
arguments despite their lack of merit and despite their ugly "states'
rights" connotations illustrates that liberalism's substantive commitments

may, in important contexts, come to trump its commitment to centralization. Civil rights have been liberalism's chief argument against federalism; now, liberalism seems open to the option of invoking federalism to preserve pockets of its version of civil rights at the state level. And between a federal prohibition on partial-birth abortions and a ban in some states (but not others), which is it to be?

The Leave-Us-Alone agenda for federalism has a fiercely ideological, partisan edge that impedes the Supreme Court's endorsement of that agenda. But tactical commitments may harden into constitutional constraints, and constitutional constraints often attract new and surprising allies. That process should reinforce the Justices' ability and desire to reestablish constitutional norms.

The Libertarian Background. The Supreme Court's endorsement of political constituencies is in effect a bet that their agenda will, over time, come to be sustained by a broad social consensus. The judicial legitimation of constituency agendas is a two-way street: while the Court can legitimize agendas that become consensual, agendas that remain deeply controversial have the opposite effect of delegitimizing the Supreme Court and its jurisprudence. In *Brown* v. *Board of Education*, the Court succeeded spectacularly in anticipating a political consensus. *Roe* v. *Wade* was an equally spectacular failure. A judicial attempt to reestablish federalism constraints is a bet that the Leave-Us-Alone agenda will eventually gel into a consensus—not on every issue or in every particular, but in the sense of a general recognition that we are better off with a more decentralized, more open, more competitive politics.

The odds on this bet are very attractive, and the Supreme Court knows it. Therein lies federalism's irony—and its great hope. When the Supreme Court slapped Leave-Us-Alone constituencies in *Romer*, it did not do so in a belief that those constituencies will never prevail over elite opinion; it slapped them because in enacting the Colorado referendum, they had in fact prevailed. In deciding *Casey*, the Court did not think that an endorsement of the Leave-Us-Aloners' agenda might embroil it in a lasting, national confrontation in the fashion of *Roe* v. *Wade;* rather, the Court reasserted its presumed right to control the terms of that confrontation. In short, the reason for the Supreme Court's reticence is not an expectation that the Leave-Us-Aloners will surely lose but rather an expectation that they will win.

As noted earlier, one can read *Romer* and *Casey* as an arrogant insistence that the Leave-Us-Aloners must not win. But one can also and more plausibly read those decisions as part of a judicial effort to take the ideological edge off a broader sentiment for a more open and federalist politics. The judicial construction of constitutional norms by means of legitimizing political constituencies can take more than one form, depending on the context. Marginal constituencies may require an explicit embrace (as in the case of *Brown*). Winners require only an implicit endorsement, combined with an exhortation to exercise some care, lest the quest for a more open politics become an oppressive populist crusade.

Put differently, there are different judicial ways of legitimizing constituencies whose demands, while heralding a social consensus, look—and sometimes are—somewhat shrill and ideological. Toning down the insistent demands of organized constituencies that reflect broader social trends is one way of doing so. If that is in fact what the Supreme Court is up to, federalism may face a bright future.

Public Norms, Private Choices

Democratic government tends toward centralization. But it also carries with it forces that push in the other direction. Centralized government thrives on promises of organizing society in a coherent fashion. But it will in the end fail to deliver. It will thus disappoint its partisans and "enervate" government. The citizens of a democracy will be enamored with power that can ensure equality and uniformity, but they will always be "inclined to scorn and hate those who wield that power." Citizens will become more compliant and less ambitious, but they will also become more ornery and "impatient in putting up with any regulation." On those countervailing forces, on men's "natural taste for freedom," Tocqueville placed his hope that democratic societies might yet be free.[3] Hindsight provides ample evidence of Tocqueville's prescience, while also allowing us to be more precise.

Contemporary American government is marked by lofty public aspirations—and by a deep-seated skepticism that the federal government can make good on any of them. President Clinton has reliably informed the country that the era of big government—a federal government that does big, ambitious things—is over. We still have the era of government that does many meddlesome little things. Such a government, however, confuses governing with doing favors for an endless array of interest groups. Since it lacks the confidence to actually govern, it fails to inspire affection and allegiance. Instead, it produces cynicism and disengagement.

The widespread resentment against federal meddling suggests that the organized constituencies of the Leave-Us-Alone coalition can build on a large reservoir of latent support. The voters may think that property rights advocates are insufficiently sensitive to environmental needs, but they also believe that the environment can and should be protected without persecuting innocent farmers and well-meaning property owners. The voters are not clamoring to abolish the Department of Education and may in fact resist such dramatic gestures. But they favor local control over education and would be happy to be free of arcane federal rules and regulations. Increasing numbers have come to believe that public education should be open to private competition. When given half a chance, the voters will vote for term limits. There is no doubt at all that the voters are against teenage smoking, for racial integration, and for universal, affordable health care. But they do not want even such common-sensical objectives to be pursued in an overly centralized, organized fashion, because they doubt the federal government's ability to pursue *any* objective in a coherent, sensible fashion.

The growing distaste for centralized bureaucracies and top-down government does not automatically translate into public support for federalism. One can even argue that it actually undermines federalism's prospects. National political institutions have for decades been trapped in a vicious cycle of rising public expectations, ensuing disappointment, greater promises, and even more inflated, sure-to-be-disappointed expectations. On the whole, however, the voters' realism seems to be winning out over democratic temptations, and the democratic taste for uniformity is giving way to a tolerance for variegated local arrangements, for the uncontrollable, and for the less-than-perfect. Two reasons account for this phenomenon.

First, it has become possible to chart institutional pathways out of the vicious cycle of increasing centralization and rising cynicism. For instance, and at the risk of regurgitating a long-digested argument: the cooperative nationalism of the 1960s and 1970s (that is, the strategy of Congress and the Court to create and to take credit for ever-larger entitlement programs) presupposed a general consensus that federally ordained benefits—for the poor, the elderly, consumers, the handicapped, the ozone layer—would always outweigh the economic costs. Now that consensus no longer exists, and political institutions face the task of preventing the creation of entitlements without telling their constituencies, in so many words, to take a hike. As explained in chapters 7 and 8, the Supreme Court's noncooperation strategy is perfectly tailored to those circumstances.

Second, and probably more important, public disengagement from national politics now transcends mere cynicism. It has assumed more constructive forms, which have to do with very tangible social and economic developments. As Charles Murray has observed, our private lives have less and less to do with the government.[4] To an extent unimaginable only a generation ago, citizens have escaped the strictures of the state. They communicate through the Internet, fax machines, and Federal Express. Parents send their children to private or parochial schools or school them at home. Growing numbers of people live in gated communities or in neighborhoods policed by private security forces. Upper-middle-class citizens have given up on Social Security as a principal source of retirement income and instead rely on 401(k) plans. While many of these amenities are so far available only to well-off citizens, democratic societies have always extended to the many what used to be the privileges of the few. This is why full-blown school choice and Social Security privatization (in one form or another) are less than a decade away.

These examples illustrate the already alluded to and hugely important point that the organized Leave-Us-Aloners' projects resonate for altogether nonideological reasons. The private conservation of endangered species is an ideological project for Beltway libertarians; it is a reality for Ted Turner, who practices it on his ranches in the West, adjacent to people who lose sleep over black helicopters. School choice, originally a libertarian project, is being pushed by black inner-city parents. Few home schoolers fit the stereotype of fundamentalist crazies; many are liberals who would entrust the government with positively everything except their children (and who lack the money to send their kids to Sidwell Friends). The near-universal use of alternatives to the Postal Service is no vast right-wing conspiracy. Rather, citizens across America are learning that their private world *works*—and that the government does not.

These dynamics, too, may work against rather than for federalism. If our world is becoming more private, why worry about government organization? The rationale for federalism and the reason why it may hold considerable political appeal lie in the fact that the sharp alternative between centralized political arrangements and entirely private ones does not exhaust the realm of possible, practicable, and desirable means of ordering our affairs. Federalism often offers a good second choice and an attractive third way—a system of government that mimics the competitive dynamics of private markets.

For all the intriguing promises of a more open and more private world, we still have a very large and meddlesome federal government in desperate need of discipline and restraint. We also have an electorate that is vaguely uncomfortable with radical plans to dismantle government. Federalism reintroduces discipline to an otherwise unconstrained political process, and it is especially attractive when the voters resist a dramatic, all-or-nothing choice between unworkable national policies and the brutal discipline of markets. "Abolish welfare" would have been a losing proposition. "Return welfare to the states" was a political winner, and for all its shortcomings and half-heartedness, welfare reform has been a policy success and, perhaps more important, a political learning experience. Welfare reform worked, and on the next issue, there may be support for policy reforms that embody a more robust, competitive federalism. From welfare to education to environmental policy, there are lots of policy arenas where federalism is an attractive alternative.

One may dismiss such advances as merely tactical steps toward a second-best. But federalism is inherently a second-best system. For public purposes, we need and want government—the protection from force, fraud, and aggression, for instance. We also want government to procure services (such as roads) and address common pool and collective action problems that are not easily amenable to wholly private solutions. Indeed, many environmental problems fall in this category. A country composed entirely of libertarians could not privatize all commons. That being so, it is best to carve a very large commons into somewhat smaller commons. Competition among the commons introduces discipline, while accommodating widely varying preferences for public goods.

Even with respect to government schemes that involve redistribution rather than public goods, there are reasons for embracing federalism as a path between markets and political centralization. Centralized political schemes flatten the world and cut off private exit routes. In some measure, though, the same is true of centralized, universal rights that structure the private world. The post–New Deal Court's notorious double standard—wholesale abdication at the federalism front, combined with heightened judicial protection of minority rights—was not so contradictory as it looks from a theoretical, constitutional perspective. Process federalism means unconstrained, centralized political authority, and when political power has been nationalized, one might as well nationalize the rights. In fact, when government ceases to operate under structural constraints, rights become the citizens' last and only line of defense.

The universal character of rights—their ability to trump political schemes and impositions—is what we like about rights. We insist on some realm of private autonomy where no government authority may intrude. Still, expansively defined rights entail costs. Much like uniform, centralized political regimes, universal rights can produce rigidities and restrict the range of available social choices. Rights rarely produce the same rigidities, on the same scale. Universal property rights, for example, are less rigid than dirigistic, centralized land use controls. They permit owners to build condominiums—or to use the same plot of land as a bird sanctuary. Private parties can bargain with their neighbors toward a wide variety of mutually acceptable arrangements—some less environment-friendly than a uniform federal mandate, others more so. Still, when national rights hold good against state and local governments, they suppress collective choices. Santa Monica may have to make do without rent controls. Suburban communities may have to put up with porn shops whose owners trumpet their First Amendment rights. All else being equal, expansive, uniform rights will produce less diversity and fewer choices among communities and jurisdictions.[5]

Hard-boiled libertarians tend to cheer the limiting quality of rights. If the citizens of Santa Monica want to house members of their community at below-market rents, they should pursue their goal by more acceptable means than the expropriation of a minority of landlords. One may agree, as I happen to agree, with this argument, in this instance. Still, many people often experience and think about public life quite differently. For example, citizens' efforts to "do something" about the porn shop down the street rarely signal a rising tide of totalitarian oppression. Most citizens would let the pornographer go about his trade— just not in their neck of the woods. They are trying to preserve or restore a certain moral environment (whether for feminist or more traditional reasons). When such efforts come to naught because the porn peddler plays his First Amendment trump, citizens feel that a piece of freedom has been lost.

One should not give in too easily to this line of reasoning, lest it become a warrant for "grass-roots tyranny."[6] But the argument has an undeniable force, and the libertarian insistence on rights and markets as wholly consistent with community standards seems somewhat beside the point. Given a choice, many citizens may well sort themselves into a jurisdiction that provides broad room for collective action—knowing full well that they may wind up at the losing end of this or that particular collective choice. It seems counterproductive to ignore or suppress such preferences and to insist on private rights and markets as the sole alternative to a dysfunctional, centralized government.

It is often much wiser to offer citizens a choice among jurisdictions and to force the jurisdictions to compete by protecting the private right that matters—the right to exit. Sometimes, exit rights are an acceptable, second-best alternative to property rights; in other instances, they may be genuinely superior. Citizen choice and exit rights will not always and everywhere produce the same results as would libertarian property rights, and as just seen, federalism and private markets coexist in a certain tension. Both, however, follow the same general objective of constraining an otherwise boundless political process.

It is true that a federalist environment will confront citizens with bundles of choices, thus thwarting the democratic urge for uniformity, predictability, and the desire to have the sweet without the bitter. In an increasingly private world, however, everyone comes to understand that the bitter comes with the sweet. No consumer can make heads or tails of airline ticket pricing, yet few hanker for a return to federal airline regulation. Instead of yearning for Ma Bell's return, we switch telephone services every other month or upon receipt of a $100 voucher from one of several competing service providers. With any luck, we shall soon purchase electricity in the same manner. Even when much more is at stake, we choose and exit readily: unlike the lifetime employees of old, wage earners now switch jobs several times in the course of a career.

The skills and habits learned in the private arena translate into the public world. In many instances we have actually traded the questionable comforts of government cartels for the more confusing world of private markets. And in any event, people do not neatly segment their lives into public and private. Eventually, they go with what works. Against a backdrop of positive experiences with government, civic pragmatism tends to translate into demands for more centralized government and inflated expectations. If we can win World War II, why can we not lick racism? Against a background of persistent government failure and private success, in contrast, pragmatism tends to favor decentralization. More mobile and prosperous than any other people on earth, American citizens respond readily to economic incentives, and every one of their trade-offs is made in full awareness that any choice will entail costs as well as benefits. Why should they want or have to put up with a government monopoly without exits?

Complexity

Citizens need not put up with government monopoly, says the federalist (me)—provided we can figure out a way to restore the rules that protect political choice and competition. Citizens will have to live with political centralization—more so than ever before, says the nationalist. In light of the increased complexity and interdependence of the American economy and indeed of the world economy, his argument runs, federalism is hopelessly obsolete and dysfunctional. The most the argument of this book can prove is the desirability and perhaps the viability of federalism in areas removed from economic competition. Maybe there will be federalist solutions to the dilemmas of school choice and homosexual rights. But what about the economy? What about *Wickard* v. *Filburn*?

A good question. As befits a question the author chooses to pose at the end of a long book, however, it has several excellent answers. The readiest response is that a federalist consensus on hotly contested social issues would be very much worth having, even if we have to leave garbage regulation for another day. In fact, though, federalism constraints are unlikely to remain so limited. Constitutional doctrines established in one arena spill over into another: invalidate the Violence against Women Act and wetlands regulations are next to go. Social issues are not so easily disentangled from economic ones: is education a social issue or an economic one?

All that to one side, the complexity argument fails even on its own terms. The premise of increased economic complexity and interdependence is certainly correct, as is the observation of a constant and powerful temptation to trump increased complexity with ever-more centralized political schemes. The New Deal (and, before it, the Progressives) responded to the perceived ravages of corporate capitalism with national legislation. Today, nation-states attempt to discipline global markets and to cure their perceived defects through multinational agreements on labor conditions, environmental protection, and discrimination against women and minorities of various descriptions. Powerful interest groups push for centralization, as does the general sense that we cannot let capitalism spin out of control.

These forces cut against federalism, if by "federalism" we mean a system built on local affection for the states or a desire to govern in isolation from the larger world. If, however, we understand *federalism* to mean jurisdictional competition and citizen choice, the complexity question becomes—well, more complex. Consider television, a crystal-clear example of increased complexity and interdependence. The world has become a global village. We can all watch the same pictures. We do not actually do so, however, because we have progressed from three networks to 100-plus cable stations.[7] In some ways, we have become less connected, and the world has become more competitive and less political and centralized. The increased complexity of the communications industry has eviscerated the Federal Communications Commission's central controls, not the other way around.

Similar dynamics occur in international capital markets, whose awesome efficiency and liquidity dramatically limit the ability of central governments to run collective, inflationary experiments. The leaders of some Asian countries are not alone in having had to learn this lesson. In 1993, when an adverse reaction on Wall Street compelled the newly installed Clinton administration to abandon ambitious and expensive policy proposals, presidential adviser James Carville famously remarked that he would like to return in a second life as the bond market—the only place of real power in American politics.

These examples do not in and of themselves demonstrate the superiority of regional regulatory arrangements. They may illustrate that global capitalism and changing technologies mow down all such arrangements, at whatever level. The central point, though, is that attempts to trump complexity with political centralization often founder on the harsh reality that complexity is increasing very fast. Centralization is a catch-up game, and that creates opportunities for second thoughts about its benefits.

Of late, we have had quite a few second thoughts. We understand much better than we once did that centralized schemes create extraordinary costs and inefficiencies. They require far more information than even the largest bureaucracy can amass and digest. The need to regulate a vast array of different events (or producers or circumstances) with a uniform rule produces rigidities, inefficiencies, and unintended consequences. Large bureaucracies lack the flexibility to learn and to adjust to rapidly changing circumstances, thus creating additional rigidities. Politicians and interest groups manage to game even the best-designed system. The costs increase exponentially as the system becomes more centralized and complex.

This, in a nutshell, is the case for managing a complex system in small chunks. The case is well understood (if not always applied) with respect to property rights—a system of exclusive control within well-defined boundaries, combined with free exchange across the boundaries and remedies for infractions and intrusions. Millions of property owners possess more information than even the best-informed bureaucrat. They have better incentives to act on that information, since they bear the costs of their own mistakes. And they can bargain with their neighbors and procure gains from trade—as opposed to a political process that has at least one loser for every winner.

Federalism—in the sense of jurisdictional competition—follows the same logic and intuition. The state's police power to regulate for its citizens' health, safety, morals, and welfare corresponds to the property owner's exclusive control. The Commerce Clause invests Congress with the authority to protect free exchange across state boundaries and to prevent destructive competition in the form of predatory or protectionist state legislation. States will produce better government not when or because they are somehow more competent or responsive than federal bureaucrats but rather because fifty of them know more than one federal agency, especially about the circumstances that affect each of them in particular; because they are better able to tailor their output to their citizens' peculiar needs; and because they learn faster. Under conditions of jurisdictional competition, each state has to bear the costs of its own mistakes. As in the case of property rights, decentralization and competition help to manage complexity.

The rub of the complexity argument is not that complexity *will* induce centralization but that it *should*. No doubt, the New Deal faced an increasingly complex world. What is suspect, however, is the contention that the expansion of national authority was an inevitable result of that increased complexity—as distinct from rather more tangible interest group pressures. For a prominent example, the Agricultural Adjustment Act of *Wickard* fame was ostensibly enacted for the protection of small producers. In effect, though, the act "shifted wealth away from smaller, integrated farms in the East (including Ohio) and toward larger, specialized farms in the West," thus hastening the demise of family farmers. That result had nothing to do with increased complexity; rather, it flowed from the overrepresentation of Western interests in the Congress.[8] Similarly, the Fair Labor Standards Act sustained in *United States v. Darby* (1941) was ostensibly intended to cut off a pernicious "race to the bottom"; its principal effect was to redistribute income from those who lacked jobs to those who had them.[9] That result was not caused by complexity, either. It was caused by trade unions. Time and again, the New Deal's nationalist measures cut in favor of entrenched interests. At the same time, and notwithstanding its commitment to a nationally regulated economy, the New Deal Court endorsed experiments in the "laboratories of democracy"—so long as state regulation also cut in favor of collective action and interest group politics.[10]

Similar examples of interest group arrangements masquerading as complexity could be multiplied *ad nauseam et infinitum.* The proffered benefits of European integration—to mention but one modern example— could be had from an agreement to prohibit trade barriers (a sort of European equivalent of the Commerce Clause). That, however, would force the member states to compete. The envisioned union, in contrast, is not a competitive but a cooperative federalism. It is in essence a cartel arrangement *not* to compete—to compete, for instance, by dismantling elaborate social welfare and environmental protections. Perhaps, something can be said for a "federalism" that enables Germany to impose its extravagant regulatory standards on Spain and Greece. But one cannot mistake the arduous process of European integration for some iron law of centralization. It is an act of political will—an attempt to shield welfare state arrangements from international competition and democratic control.[11]

Put differently, political arrangements require a certain legitimacy, and the arguments that used to supply that legitimacy—"race to the bottom," "complexity"—no longer do the job. They can no longer mask the political gamesmanship, the rank redistribution, and the cartel arrangements that are the real basis of our nationalized politics. While there may be altars on which we would and should sacrifice federalism, the altar on which we in fact sacrificed it serves up mostly junk. The creed of "complexity" ensures that we can feed the five thousand interest groups who show up at the commons; it even produces additional baskets, which we feed to the virtual constituencies who show up in focus groups. But why should we accept this doctrine?

An increasingly complex American economy needs a common currency and monetary system, and it needs a central authority to prevent protectionist warfare among the states. The economy has always needed a national government capable of providing those common goods. In other words, it has always needed, and continues to need, the national government the Founders in fact created. Plenty of interest groups and politicians *want* a national government that provides much, much more, and maybe in a handful of cases they should have their wish. But such schemes require some justification other than the alleged functional needs of a complex economy. An integrated national economy *needs* a muscular federal government about as much as an increasingly complex global economy needs a United Nations with teeth.[12] Like a fish needs a bicycle.

* * * * *

Federalism's history has been the history of its demise. Some of the Founders may have wished for and encouraged this development. Others may have foreseen it and thought that not much could be done about it. In the course of two centuries, the Founders' design was overwhelmed by social and institutional changes that they did not and could not foresee.

But if the Founders failed to anticipate the democratic demands that would cut against federalism, they also failed to foresee the contemporary demands that cut in its favor. And whatever the Founders' expectations and hopes and fears, they endowed us with a federalism that happens to be uniquely suited to present circumstances. We do not have to invent fifty states. They *exist*—enough of them to permit effective competition and pretty good places to mobilize resistance to national schemes. We need not invent a Supreme Court to impose constraints. It *exists*, and it will respond to the gravitational pull of constitutional norms—even if those norms are less than perfectly clear and straight and even if the Court cannot always enforce them.

Above all, the Founders endowed us with an awareness of the central political problem—to govern, and yet to control government. They thought of government as a monopoly problem, and they endeavored to solve it by subjecting government itself to competition—the separation of powers, and federalism. And although much of the Founders' wisdom has been buried under the rubble of interest group politics and ideological cant, their federalism and the insights on which it rests are a powerful historical echo, not a bloodless theoretical choice.

America is a lucky country in many ways. This is one of them.

Notes

Chapter 1: Real Federalism: What It Is, Why It Matters

1. Federalism's tentative rediscovery by the Supreme Court and Congress has generated a burgeoning stream of scholarly comment, which is illustrated by numerous law review volumes and symposia dedicated to the subject. See, for example, *Michigan Law Review*, vol. 94, no. 2 (1995); *Case Western Reserve Law Review*, vol. 46, no. 3 (1996); *Georgia State University Law Review*, vol. 13, no. 4 (1997); *University of Minnesota Law Review*, vol. 82, no. 2 (1997); *Arizona Law Review*, vol. 38 (Fall 1996); and *Yale Law and Policy Review*, vol. 14 (March 1996). The introduction to this last volume is a splendid essay by Peter H. Schuck, which develops the theme of these first few pages ("Some Reflections on the Federalism Debate," pp. 1–22).

2. The precise figure for home-state residence was 61.8 percent in 1990. Mark C. Gordon, "Differing Paradigms, Similar Flaws: Constructing a New Federalism in Congress and the Court," *Yale Law and Policy Review*, vol. 14 (1996), p. 187, p. 210 n. 112 (citing Brookings Institution study).

3. Edward L. Rubin and Malcolm Feeley, "Federalism: Some Notes on a National Neurosis," *UCLA Law Review*, vol. 41 (1994), p. 903.

4. The classic modern formulation of federalism as jurisdictional competition is Charles Tiebout, "A Pure Theory of Local Expenditures," *Journal of Political Economy*, vol. 64 (1956), p. 416. Tiebout's groundbreaking article produced a flood of public finance and public choice literature. A useful, nontechnical over-

view is Ronald McKinnon and Thomas Nechyba, "Competition in Federal Systems" in John Ferejohn and Barry Weingast, eds., *The New Federalism: Can the States Be Trusted?* (Hoover Institution Press, 1997), p. 3. In recent years, economists and public choice scholars have turned their attention to the institutional prerequisites for a "market-preserving" federalism. See, e.g., Barry R. Weingast, "The Economic Role of Political Institutions: Market-Preserving Federalism and Economic Development," *Journal of Law, Economics, and Organization,* vol. 11 (1995), p. 1. Both articles just cited contain useful bibliographies.

5. McKinnon and Nechyba, "Competition in Federal Systems," p. 12 n. 8 and sources cited by the authors.

6. My nontechnical account largely follows the excellent discussion by Michael W. McConnell, "Federalism: Evaluating the Founders' Design," *University of Chicago Law Review,* vol. 54 (1987), p. 1484 and esp. pp. 1493–1507. An extended, very good discussion and defense of federalism as competition is Thomas R. Dye, *American Federalism: Competition among Governments* (Lexington Books, 1990). See also Jacques Leboeuf, "The Economics of Federalism and the Proper Scope of the Federal Commerce Power," *San Diego Law Review,* vol. 31 (1994), p. 556; and Ferejohn and Weingast, eds., *The New Federalism.* For more critical perspectives, see the Symposium on the Law and Economics of Federalism, *Minnesota Law Review,* vol. 82, no. 2 (1997).

7. The point has been made emphatically by William Van Alstyne, "Federalism, Congress, the States, and the Tenth Amendment: Adrift in the Cellophane Sea," *Duke Law Journal* (1987), p. 769.

8. Normative concerns tend to overwhelm the empirical analysis. Social scientists who dislike citizen choice in the first place are inclined to deny its existence (see, e.g., Rubin and Feeley, "National Neurosis," p. 918), whereas prochoice scholars argue that there is enough mobility to make state competition work (see, e.g., Dye, *American Federalism,* pp. 15–16). To my mind, it is preposterous to deny the force of jurisdictional choice; millions of refugees and (at a national level) of suburbanites attest to its existence. The real dispute concerns the prescription—that is, the question of whether one should favor or oppose rules and institutions that encourage low-cost choices among jurisdictions.

9. See Richard L. Revesz, "Rehabilitating Interstate Competition: Rethinking the Race to the Bottom Rationale for Federal Environmental Regulation," *New York University Law Review,* vol. 67 (1992), p. 1210. See Revesz, pp. 1210–11 for a brief discussion of the influence of the race-to-the-bottom argument on the New Deal and modern environmental regulation. Revesz's pathbreaking article has produced a flurry of criticism. The references can be found in Revesz's rejoinder, "The Race to the Bottom: A Response to Critics," *Minnesota Law Review,* vol. 82 (1997), p. 535.

10. See Schuck, "Some Reflections on the Federalism Debate," pp. 18–20.

11. For a mathematical demonstration, see James Buchanan and Gordon Tullock, *The Calculus of Consent* (University of Michigan Press, 1962), pp. 135–40.

Chapter 2: Federalism's Demise—and Renaissance?

1. The extent to which the dormant Commerce Clause prohibits state protectionist legislation has always been controversial and in recent years has sparked an intense debate on the Supreme Court and in the law reviews. Recent attempts to chart a path through this notoriously confused area of the law include Stanley E. Cox, "Garbage In, Garbage Out: Court Confusion about the Dormant Commerce Clause," *Oklahoma Law Review,* vol. 50 (1997), p. 155; and Michael A. Lawrence, "Toward a More Coherent Dormant Commerce Clause: A Proposed Unitary Framework," *Harvard Journal of Law and Public Policy,* vol. 21 (1998), p. 395.

2. *The Federalist Papers* No. 46 (New American Library, 1961) (Clinton Rossiter, ed.), p. 295. This background understanding in some sense defines the gulf that separates the modern from the original constitutional intuitions. For a prominent example, Chief Justice Marshall's opinion in *Gibbons* v. *Ogden,* 9 Wheat. 1 (1824), was decried at the time as extreme nationalism, and the New Deal Court characterized *Gibbons* as "describ[ing] the federal commerce power with a breadth never yet exceeded." *Wickard* v. *Filburn,* 317 U.S. 111, 120 (1942). But while some general statements in Marshall's opinion may suggest such an interpretation, his opinion also rattles off an "immense" mass of functions *not* surrendered to the federal government, including "[i]nspection laws, quarantine laws, health laws of every description, as well as laws for regulating the internal commerce of a State." *Gibbons,* 9 Wheat. at 203. There, one would think, goes most of the Environmental Protection Agency, the Food and Drug Administration, and the Occupational Safety and Health Administration. Even so, modern-day nationalists continue to read *Gibbons* as an endorsement of unlimited federal power and the pre–New Deal Court's insistence on limits as a temporary aberration. See, for example, Justice Souter's dissent in *United States* v. *Lopez,* 515 U.S. 549, 605–6 (1995). This reading—to my mind fantastic—is effectively rebutted by Justice Thomas's concurrence in *Lopez,* 515 U.S. at 598–600.

3. *The Federalist Papers* No. 45, p. 289.

4. To state the obvious alternative, federalism can be defended on the grounds that it enables citizens to vote and participate in government at close range. Participation may in turn enhance civic virtue. The most vociferous and sophisticated advocate of such a radical-democratic interpretation of the Constitution is Akhil Reed Amar, *The Bill of Rights* (Yale University Press, 1998). See also Akhil Reed Amar and Alan Hirsch, *For the People* (Free Press, 1998). But Amar's take on the

Founders has been questioned even by scholars who sympathize with his liberal-egalitarian intentions. See, e.g., Cass R. Sunstein, "Originalism for Liberals," *New Republic*, September 28, 1998, p. 31.

5. *The Federalist Papers* No. 51, p. 322.

6. *The Federalist Papers* No. 73, p. 444.

7. The Federalists suggested that the "auxiliary precautions" of federalism and the separation of powers would tend to protect against special interest legislation and still permit public-spirited laws. In a large, diverse federal republic, Madison wrote, "a coalition of a majority of the whole society could seldom take place on any other principles than those of justice and the general good." *The Federalist Papers* No. 51, p. 325. Modern political science is more skeptical about the possibility of constraining the legislative process. Logrolling and other mechanisms facilitate special-interest deals, while determined minorities may frustrate measures that are plainly in the public interest. The distance between the Federalists and modern theory is not quite so large, however. Most public choice theorists would concede that America's size and her fragmented political system do *something* to inhibit collectivist schemes—compared with, for example, the parliamentary (and sometimes unitary) systems of smaller countries. *They* have socialism; we do not. Conversely, the Federalists were quite attuned to the mischief of faction. Their optimistic pronouncements about the prospects of harnessing factionalism for public-regarding legislation to some extent reflect their desire to persuade a reluctant political establishment to ratify the work product of a runaway Constitutional Convention. Given that objective, what should they have written? That congressional legislation would be an uninterrupted flow of piggishness?

8. Rubin and Feeley, "Federalism: Some Notes on a National Neurosis," pp. 915–26, argue that citizen choice and state competition (among other features) flow from decentralization rather than federalism, the difference being that federalism protects the states' genuine (if partial) autonomy. This is simply not so. Real federalism permits choice and competition with respect to ends as well as means, whereas a unitary system will permit decentralized decisionmaking only to the extent that it promotes centrally determined values and objectives (if then). Denying this difference is like saying that we need no competition in the automobile industry, since even a monopolistic producer will allow its sales force some flexibility.

9. *The Federalist Papers* No. 45, p. 292. The scope of the federal government's "definite" powers—a matter of considerable contention even before the ratification—soon produced a long, hard-fought debate over the question of whether Congress possessed powers that are implied (but not stated) in the constitutional text. But neither that debate nor the inevitable lack of precision in marginal cases obscured the constitutional principle. In *Gibbons* v. *Ogden*, 9 Wheat. 1, 194–95 (1824), Chief Justice Marshall declared in reference to Congress's constitutional authority

to regulate interstate commerce that "[t]he enumeration presupposes something not enumerated."

10. *The Federalist Papers* No. 39, pp. 245–46.

11. Van Alstyne, "Federalism, Congress, the States, and the Tenth Amendment," p. 774. This logic explains why federal systems of government (such as Germany, Australia, and Canada) need and always have an independent supreme or constitutional court with the authority to adjudicate constitutional questions. Centralized systems (such as France or England) do not.

12. Georg Friedrich Wilhelm Hegel, *Philosophy of Right* (Oxford University Press, 1952) (T. M. Knox, trans.), p. 7. The paraphrase in the text is closer than the Knox translation to the original German ("Das Gesetz ist das Schiboleth an dem die falschen Brüder und Freunde des sogenannten Volkes sich abscheiden.").

13. The distinction is drawn explicitly in *E. C. Knight v. United States*, 156 U.S. 1, 12 (1895).

14. In more recent years, prominent scholars have defended the pre–New Deal Supreme Court's Commerce Clause as being actually quite closely tied to the text and structure of the Constitution and to federalism's purposes of citizen choice and state competition. The leading proponent of this revisionist view is Richard A. Epstein, whose article on "The Proper Scope of the Commerce Clause," *University of Virginia Law Review*, vol. 73 (1987), p. 1387, presents a spirited defense of the pre–New Deal Court Commerce Clause jurisprudence and even criticizes some of the leading cases as too accommodating of congressional power. To state my own view on pre–New Deal jurisprudence, on textual and other grounds, the Commerce Clause cases are more easily defended against the charge of laissez-faire activism than *Lochner v. New York* (1905) and its progeny—that is, cases in which the Supreme Court relied on an expansive, "substantive" interpretation of the Due Process Clause of the Fourteenth Amendment to strike down state (not federal) health and safety regulations. The Commerce Clause cases share with the substantive due process cases a preference for private orderings, suspicion of interest group politics, and confidence in the Supreme Court's competence and authority to defend constitutional boundaries against democratic attempts to circumvent them. But there is also a tension between the two lines of cases. In preventing the states from enacting social legislation, even if they were perfectly willing to live with the consequences, the *Lochner*-type cases betray a certain lack of confidence in federalism.

15. This "argument from changed conditions" has been standard fare among advocates of an expensive federal government. See Lynn A. Baker, "Federalism: The Argument from Article V," *Georgia State University Law Journal*, vol. 13 (1997), p. 923, p. 924, and sources cited therein. The argument played an important role in the Supreme Court's abandonment of its pre–New Deal Commerce Clause juris-

prudence. Professor Epstein, naturally, will have none of it. See "The Proper Scope of the Commerce Power," pp. 1452–54 ("[T]he point about economic interdependence mistakes the disease for the cure.").

16. *Hammer* v. *Dagenhart*, 274 U.S. 251, 273 (1918).

17. Richard L. Revesz, "Rehabilitating Interstate Competition: Rethinking the Race to the Bottom Rationale for Environmental Regulation," *New York University Law Review*, vol. 67 (1992), p. 1210; pp. 1244–47.

18. See, for example, Justice Holmes's celebrated dissent in *Hammer* v. *Dagenhart*, 247 U.S. 251, 277–81 (1918). After the New Deal revolution, Holmes's position in *Hammer* was elevated to a near-canonical status. It bears mention, though, that Holmes was less than consistent on the Court's authority to review Commerce Clause legislation. In antitrust cases, for example, he aggressively advocated the very restrictive doctrines he denounced in *Hammer*. See Holmes's dissent in *Northern Securities Co.* v. *United States*, 193 U.S. 193, 400–11 (1904).

19. 295 U.S. 495 (1935). The Schechter Brothers also challenged the act as an unconstitutional delegation of legislative authority. They prevailed on this claim, too.

20. *NLRB* v. *Jones & Laughlin Steel Corp.*, 301 U.S. 1 (1937) (sustaining National Labor Relations Act and abandoning the distinction between production and commerce); *Steward Machine Co.* v. *Davis*, 301 U.S. 548 (1937) (sustaining Social Security Act).

21. Justice Brandeis coined his famous phrase in just such a case: *New State Ice Co.* v. *Liebmann*, 285 U.S. 262, 311 (1932) (Brandeis, J., dissenting).

22. *United States* v. *Darby*, 312 U.S. 100 (1941), overturned both *Hammer* v. *Dagenhart* and the distinction between the regulation of "direct" and "indirect" effects on interstate commerce that had been in force as late as *Carter* v. *Carter Coal*, 298 U.S. 238 (1936). Summarizing the government's argument, the Supreme Court wrote:

> No State, acting alone, could require labor standards substantially higher than those obtaining in other States. . . . Employers with lower labor standards possess an unfair advantage in interstate competition, and only the national government can deal with the problem.

United States v. *Darby*, 312 U.S. at 102.

23. *United States* v. *Lopez*, 514 U.S. 549, 589 (1995) (Thomas, J., concurring) (emphasis in the original).

24. Herbert Wechsler, "The Political Safeguards of Federalism: The Role of the States in the Composition and Selection of the National Government," *Columbia Law Review*, vol. 54, p. 543 (1954). See also Jesse Choper, *Judicial Review and the National Political Process* (University of Chicago Press, 1980), pp. 175–84. Like

the race-to-the-bottom argument, process federalism assumed enormous influence despite a lack of intellectual coherence or plausibility. Barry Friedman, "Valuing Federalism," *Minnesota Law Review,* vol. 82 (1997), p. 317. Friedman calls the Supreme Court's heavy reliance on Choper and Wechsler "somewhat stunning given the many persuasive critiques of their position" (p. 325 n. 22). Friedman cites several of those critiques.

25. *Garcia v. San Antonio Metropolitan Transit Authority*, 469 U.S. 528, 552 (1985).

26. Wechsler, "The Political Safeguards of Federalism," p. 559. Despite disagreement about Wechsler's "process federalism," his view that the Supreme Court should exercise extreme deference in federalism cases was shared by all but a handful of constitutional scholars. For a modern, revisionist attempt to resurrect federalism as a central judicial value, see Steven G. Calabresi, "A Government of Limited and Enumerated Powers: In Defense of *United States v. Lopez,*" *Michigan Law Review,* vol. 94 (1995), p. 752.

27. *Garcia*, 469 U.S. at 556 (1985).

28. The origin of this combination of strict scrutiny in individual rights cases and deference on all else is a famous footnote in *Carolene Products v. United States*, 304 U.S. 144, 152 n. 4 (1938). The dual standard defines constitutional jurisprudence to this day.

29. See *Brown v. Board of Education*, 347 U.S. 403 (1954); *Engel v. Vitale*, 370 U.S. 421 (1962); *Miranda v. Arizona*, 384 U.S. 436 (1966); *New York Times v. Sullivan*, 376 U.S. 254 (1964); *Roe v. Wade*, 410 U.S. 113 (1973). Some of these judicial assertions of federal rights enjoyed broad public support; others remain fiercely contested. For present purposes, the legal or policy merits are beside the point, which is that federalism's fate hangs not only on the Supreme Court's willingness to restrain Congress but also on its willingness to restrain itself and the lower federal courts from inventing new federal rights.

30. *Lopez*, 514 U.S. 549 (1995); *Seminole Tribe of Florida v. Florida*, 517 U.S. 44 (1996).

31. Jesse H. Choper, "On the Difference in Importance between Supreme Court Doctrine and Actual Consequences: A Review of the Supreme Court's 1996–1997 Term," *Cardozo Law Review,* vol. 19 (1998), p. 2259; esp. p. 2259 and sources cited in nn. 1–5.

32. *Printz v. United States*, 117 S. Ct. 2365 (1997); *City of Boerne v. Flores*, 117 S. Ct. 2157 (1997). In a third federalism decision, *Idaho v. Coeur d'Alene Tribe of Idaho*, 117 S. Ct. 2028 (1997), the Supreme Court held that the Eleventh Amendment barred the Coeur d'Alene tribe from pursuing certain land claims against the state of Idaho in federal court.

33. See *Vacco v. Quill*, 117 S. Ct. 2293 (1997) and *Washington v. Glucksberg*,

117 S. Ct. 2302, 2303 (1997) (denying constitutional right to doctor-assisted suicide and holding that the "challenging task of crafting appropriate procedures for
safeguarding . . . liberty interests is entrusted to the 'laboratory of the States'"
(O'Connor, J., concurring) (quoting *Cruzan* v. *Director, Mo. Dept of Health*, 497 U.S.
261, 292 (1990) (O'Connor, J., concurring). See also *Reno* v. *Bossier Parish School
Board*, 117 S. Ct. 1491, 1498 (1997) (curtailing U.S. Department of Justice's
"preclearance" authority to deny approval of local election statutes under the Voting Rights Act and observing that opposite result would "increase further the serious federalism costs already implicated" by the act).

34. William W. Van Alstyne, "The Second Death of Federalism," *Michigan
Law Review*, vol. 83 (1985), p. 1709, p. 1724 n. 64.

35. I state the point with some emphasis so as to register my disagreement with
what one may call the "No Judicial Review for Anyone" school of thought. While
complaints about an "imperial judiciary" have considerable merit, advocates of
extreme judicial deference toward legislatures ought to be clear about the costs—
in this case, the costs to federalism.

36. Alexander M. Bickel, *The Supreme Court and the Idea of Progress*, 2d ed.
(Yale University Press, 1978), esp. pp. 11–42.

37. Robert G. McCloskey, *The American Supreme Court* (University of Chicago
Press, 1960), pp. 77–80.

38. Grover Norquist, "Republicans and Democrats," *The American Enterprise*,
January/February 1996, p. 24.

39. To put the point in the strongest, most visceral form, Justices Kennedy and
O'Connor (two critical votes among the Supreme Court's federalist Justices) are
loathed by Leave-Us-Alone activists, chiefly on account of their votes and opinions
in *Planned Parenthood*, 505 U.S. 833 (1992) (sustaining abortion rights) and *Romer*
v. *Evans*, 517 U.S. 620 (1996) (invalidating popular state referendum against homosexual rights). (Chapter 7 discusses both cases and their implications.) Some
conservative advocates have gone so far as to suggest that *Casey*, *Romer*, and similar
decisions deprive the American "regime" of its legitimacy. See, e.g., the symposium on "The End of Democracy? The Judicial Usurpation of Politics," *First Things*,
November 1996, p. 18. Strange as it may sound, though, even such hostility may
gradually give way to the pursuit of broader objectives. In its litigation campaign
for racial justice that culminated in *Brown*, the National Association for the Advancement of Colored People confronted unreconstructed racists on the Southern
courts and, on the Supreme Court, a former Klansman (Hugo Black) and a Chief
Justice (Earl Warren) who in an earlier career had interned American citizens on
account of their Japanese descent. Now as then, the pursuit of broader political
objectives by means of establishing constitutional norms presumes that even a hostile judiciary may be a better forum than hopelessly corrupt legislatures—plus a

confidence that the Supreme Court ultimately plays not to the existing but to what it believes to be the emerging social consensus.

Chapter 3: Enumerated Powers?

1. *United States* v. *Lopez*, 514 U.S. 549, 552 (1995).

2. "'[S]imply because Congress may conclude that a particular activity substantially affects interstate commerce does not necessarily make it so.'" *Lopez*, 514 U.S. at 557 n. 2 (quoting *Hodel* v. *Virginia Surface Mining & Reclamation Ass'n*, 452 U.S. 264, 311 (Rehnquist, J., concurring) (1989). See Deborah Jones Merritt, "Commerce!" *Michigan Law Review*, vol. 94 (1995), p. 674, p. 677 (*Lopez* embodies a "toughened rational basis standard"); and Richard A. Epstein, "Constitutional Faith and the Commerce Clause," *Notre Dame Law Review*, vol. 71 (1996), p. 167, p. 177 (*Lopez* moves "from rational basis (back) to intermediate scrutiny").

3. See *Lopez*, 514 U.S. at 605–7 (Souter, J., dissenting). A typical press reaction is Linda Greenhouse, "Focus on Federal Power," *New York Times*, May 24, 1995, p. A1. For legal commentary in the same genre see, e.g., Kathleen M. Sullivan, "Dueling Sovereignties: *United States Term Limits, Inc.* v. *Thornton*," *Harvard Law Review*, vol. 109, p. 78, p. 80 (discussing the Supreme Court's "dramatic antifederalist revival").

4. See Robert F. Nagel, "The Term Limits Dissent: What Nerve," *Arizona Law Review*, vol. 38 (1996), p. 843.

5. The majority arrives at the distinction between "substantial effects" and "simple effects" only after considerable splitting of hairs and wringing of hands. *Lopez*, 514 U.S. at 559–61. Amazingly, the majority then walks away from the distinction and fails to perform the analysis it would seem to suggest—that is, an examination of whether guns on school grounds "substantially affect" interstate commerce. Robert F. Nagel, "The Future of Federalism," *Case Western Law Review*, vol. 46 (1996), p. 643, pp. 646–47.

6. *Lopez*, 514 U.S. at 560–61. The purportedly noncommercial nature of the regulated conduct may also account for the difference between *Lopez* and *Perez* v. *United States*, 402 U.S. 146 (1971), which sustained a federal statute criminalizing wholly in-state loan-sharking. The thinness of the distinction is suggested by the fact that Mr. Lopez had carried his gun to school for the purpose of *selling* it. Probably sensing that this fact would further undermine an already questionable distinction, the *Lopez* Court conveniently neglected to mention it. It is mentioned in the appellate court's opinion in *United States* v. *Lopez*, 2 F.3d 1342, 1345 (5th Cir. 1993).

7. *Lopez*, 514 U.S. at 564–65. Justices Kennedy's and O'Connor's concurring opinion is equally schizophrenic: "In a sense any conduct in this interdependent

world of ours has an ultimate commercial origin or consequence, but we have not yet said the commerce power may reach so far." Id. at 580 (Kennedy, J., concurring).

8. *Lopez,* 514 U.S. at 567. The preceding analysis and assessment of *Lopez* is consistent with the general tenor of the legal commentary. See, e.g., Barry Friedman, "Valuing Federalism," *Minnesota Law Review,* vol. 82 (1997), p. 317, pp. 336–37 n. 77, and sources cited therein. For a substantially broader reading of *Lopez,* see Steven Calabresi, "A Government of Limited and Enumerated Powers," *Michigan Law Review,* vol. 94 (1996), p. 752. My account in the text below of the contrast between the majority opinion and Justice Thomas's concurrence is similar to Jesse H. Choper, "Did Last Term Reveal a Revolutionary States' Rights Movement within the Supreme Court?" *Case Western Reserve Law Review,* vol. 46 (1996), p. 663.

9. Id. at 586. As Justice Thomas observes, the modern, expansive interpretation of the constitutional language, which holds that the power to regulate "commerce" encompasses the power to regulate manufacture and agriculture, makes nonsense of the constitutional text. For what is one to make of a congressional power to regulate manufacture or agriculture "among the several states"?

10. Id. at 600 (emphasis in original).

11. Id. at 596–99. For a brief discussion of the exchange and its larger context, see chapter 2, n. 2.

12. *Lopez,* 514 U.S. at 601. Looking for an explanation in the footnote to this statement, one finds a few observations about the value of *stare decisis.* But if the Supreme Court must adhere even to demonstrably untenable precedents, one must wonder about the normative force of the original-intent arguments that form the substance of Justice Thomas's opinion. The problem is a general one for "textualist" or "originalist" scholars and judges. See Gary Lawson, "The Rise and Rise of the Administrative State," *Harvard Law Review,* vol. 107 (1994), p. 1231.

13. Epstein, "Constitutional Faith and the Commerce Clause," p. 191.

14. Epstein's seminal article on "The Proper Scope of the Commerce Clause," pp. 1454–55, ends in a mildly despairing reflection over the impossibility of a return to (pre-1937) constitutional norms ("We had our chance with the commerce clause, and we lost it."). So does Lawson's examination of "The Rise and Rise of the Administrative State," p. 1232.

15. See, e.g., *Cargill* v. *United States,* 116 S. Ct. 407 (1995) (Thomas, J., dissenting from denial of *certiorari*); *United States* v. *Robertson,* 115 S. Ct. 1732 (1995) (*per curiam*); *National Association of Home Builders* v. *Babbitt,* 130 F.3d 1041 (D.C. Cir. 1997), *cert. denied,* 118 S. Ct. 2340 (1998).

16. *National League of Cities* v. *Usery,* 426 U.S. 833, 840, 842 (1976).

17. *Garcia* v. *San Antonio Metropolitan Transit Authority,* 469 U.S. 528, 546 (1985).

18. The observation is Richard Epstein's. See his "Constitutional Faith and the Commerce Clause," pp. 179–80. The argument also applies, albeit less clearly, to education, another area *Lopez* marks out as "traditional." Conceivably, competition could induce states to let others provide an expensive education and then to beggar their neighbors for the products of that education. Experience, however, points to the opposite conclusion. Parents move into expensive suburban neighborhoods with high levels of public school spending. Most states spend lavishly on higher education (and attempt to internalize the benefits—for instance, by charging higher tuition rates to out-of-state students). A high demand and willingness to pay for education render an educational "race to the bottom" a remote possibility.

19. *Lopez*, 514 U.S. at 581 (Kennedy, J., concurring) (emphasis added).

20. Id. (Kennedy, J., concurring). Mr. Lopez's journey from state to federal prosecution is described in the majority opinion, 514 U.S. at 551.

21. 494 U.S. 872 (1990).

22. See *The Slaughterhouse Cases*, 111 U.S. 746 (1884) ("privileges and immunities" clause of the Fourteenth Amendment provides no protection against anticompetitive state and local regulation). Shifts in the Supreme Court's interpretation of the substantive, rights-granting provisions of the Fourteenth Amendment— "substantive due process" during the *Lochner* era, the incorporation of the Bill of Rights in the wake of the New Deal, the rediscovery of substantive due process as a protection of sexual and other "privacy" rights in the 1960s and 1970s—have affected federalism far more profoundly and pervasively than the Court's interpretation of the Enforcement Clause. Chapter 7 discusses some of those issues.

23. *The Civil Rights Cases*, 109 U.S. 3 (1883); *United States* v. *Harris*, 106 U.S. 629 (1883).

24. See, e.g., *Burton* v. *Wilmington Parking Authority*, 365 U.S. 715 (1961); *Reitman* v. *Mulkey*, 387 U.S. 369 (1967).

25. *Katzenbach* v. *Morgan*, 384 U.S. 641, 651 (1966).

26. Occasionally, the Supreme Court has considered it sufficient that Congress *could have* legislated under Section 5 even if it failed to do so explicitly, so long as the statute under consideration bears some relation to generally recognized Fourteenth Amendment purposes. See, e.g., *EEOC* v. *Wyoming*, 460 U.S. 226, 243 n. 18 (1983). But see *Pennhurst State Hospital* v. *Halderman*, 451 U.S. 1, 16 (1981) (courts should not quickly attribute an unstated intent to legislate under Section 5).

27. See the discussion of the case law in *City of Boerne* v. *Flores*, 117 S. Ct. 2157, 2163–64 (1997).

28. It also enforces the obvious proviso that Section 5 legislation must not violate other constitutional guarantees.

29. The paragraph in the text paraphrases Justice Brennan's famous "ratchet" footnote in *Katzenbach* v. *Morgan*, 384 U.S. 641, 651 n. 10 (1966).

30. A version of this argument appears in Judge Richard Posner's pre-*Flores* decision in *Sasnett* v. *Sullivan*, 91 F.3d 1018 (1997), vacated and remanded, 117 S. Ct. 2502 (1997).

31. Seven Justices endorsed the Section 5 analysis; Justices Souter and Breyer declined to address it. See *Flores*, 117 S. Ct. at 2159 (majority opinion); id. at 2176 (O'Connor, J., concurring); id. at 2185 (Souter, J., dissenting); id. at 2186 (Breyer, J., dissenting).

32. 117 S. Ct. at 2162 (1997).

33. Id. at 2164.

34. *Sasnett* v. *Sullivan*, 91 F.3d at 1020. Michael W. McConnell, "Institutions and Interpretation, A Critique of *City of Boerne* v. *Flores*," *Harvard Law Review*, vol. 111 (1997), p. 153, argues that the distinction between enforcement and rights-creation is actually too extreme and leaves out "the possibility of an intermediate, 'interpretive' role for the Congress" (p. 164). Not every new or different interpretation, McConnell argues, creates a new substantive right, and on close questions (such as the different interpretations of the Free Exercise Clause in *Smith* and RFRA), the Court should defer to Congress. I am inclined to agree with McConnell's conceptual distinction but not, for reasons below, with his inferences and conclusions.

35. Compare *Mobile* v. *Bolden*, 446 U.S. 55 (1980) with *City of Rome* v. *United States*, 446 U.S. 156 (1980). The example is Judge Posner's *Sasnett* v. *Sullivan*, 91 F.3d at 1020, 1022. For an even more dramatic example, Title VII of the Civil Rights Act—the most important federal antidiscrimination statute—provides not only a right to be free from intentional discrimination but also a prohibition against discrimination in the form of "disparate impact," which extends much beyond the rights guaranteed by the Fourteenth Amendment. *Washington* v. *Davis*, 426 U.S. 229 (1976). Read for all it is worth, *Flores* suggests that the disparate impact provisions of Title VII are unconstitutional. But the decision makes no mention at all of Title VII. As briefly discussed below, pp. 73–74, the courts are unlikely to extend the reasoning of *Flores* to Title VII.

36. *Flores*, 117 S. Ct. at 2159, 2164.

37. This may be the *Flores* majority's most questionable argument. It is true, as the majority asserts (*Flores*, 117 S. Ct. at 2168–69), that the congressional testimony on RFRA evidenced little deliberate persecution against religion. But so what? With respect to the rights of racial minorities, Congress has often exercised its Section 5 authority to remedy violations short of "deliberate persecution." Moreover, one can argue that the *Smith* regime, which forces religious groups to seek accommodations through the political process, puts small or unpopular religions at

a disadvantage and that RFRA is a perfectly proportionate remedy for the problem. This rationale is quite similar to the grounds on which the Supreme Court has traditionally sustained voting rights legislation. See *Sasnett v. Sullivan*, 91 F.3d at 1020. See also McConnell, "Institutions and Interpretation," pp. 165–67, 191.

38. *Flores*, 117 S. Ct. at 2170.

39. Id. at 2171.

40. *Flores*, 117 S. Ct. at 2162 (emphasis added). The *Flores* Court vacated and remanded a case involving the application of RFRA to federal bankruptcy laws. *Christians v. Crystal Evangelical Free Church*, 117 S. Ct. 2502 (1997). On remand, however, RFRA was sustained (to my mind correctly) as constitutional in its federal application. *Young v. Crystal Evangelical Free Church*, 141 F.3d 854 (8th Cir. 1998). But see *United States v. Sandia*, F. Supp. 2d (D. N.M. 1998) (*Flores* declared RFRA unconstitutional with respect to the federal government). Marci A. Hamilton, "*City of Boerne v. Flores:* A Landmark for Structural Analysis," *William and Mary Law Review*, vol. 39 (1998), p. 699, pp. 717–20, has argued that RFRA is invalid even as applied to federal law. The argument in the text rejects Hamilton's position and instead follows Ira C. Lupu, "Why Congress Was Wrong and the Court Was Right—Reflections on *City of Boerne v. Flores*," *William and Mary Law Review*, vol. 39 (1998), p. 793, p. 810 ("RFRA as applied to the federal government does not rest on Section 5 of the Fourteenth Amendment. Rather, it rests . . . on whatever power authorizes Congress to act in that context.") Lupu's position reflects the scholarly consensus, which in this instance happens to be right.

41. Michael W. McConnell, "Institutions and Interpretation," pp. 154–56 *et passim*. See also David Cole, "The Value of Seeing Things Differently: *Boerne v. Flores* and Congressional Enforcement of the Bill of Rights," *Supreme Court Review* (1997), p. 31. While their arguments differ in many respects, both Professor McConnell and Professor Cole argue for substantially more judicial deference than I would endorse. See, e.g., McConnell, p. 186 (*Flores* should have been decided under a "rational basis" standard of review). Moreover, I do not share Professor McConnell's view, pp. 192–94, that the balance between religious freedom and various government interests must not be left to the states. Provided the states abide by the minimum neutrality requirements of *Smith*, I have no problem with religious accommodation provisions that vary from state to state. These observations, however, do not affect the analysis in the text.

42. To state the obvious alternative, the Supreme Court could have held that RFRA's selective exemption for religious citizens violates the Establishment Clause (and, thus, the *Katzenbach* proviso that Section 5 statutes must not violate other provisions of the Constitution). Only one member of the *Flores* Court expressed this view, however. *Flores*, 117 S. Ct. at 2172 (Stevens, J., concurring).

43. Under RFRA, state prisons had to accommodate the dietary wishes of reli-

gious inmates. Why then should a private restaurant not have to show a "compelling need" for its failure to offer a choice of kosher or vegetarian food? Congress could and probably would enact a "private RFRA" under the Commerce Clause (as opposed to the Fourteenth Amendment) to avoid potential state action problems. See, e.g., *Heart of Atlanta Motel* v. *United States*, 379 U.S. 241 (1964); *Katzenbach* v. *McClung*, 379 U.S. 294 (1964) (both sustaining application of civil rights laws to private actors under the Commerce Clause). On this theory, though, Congress could also have passed the actual RFRA under the Commerce Clause. This defense was never raised in the RFRA litigation—most probably, because RFRA's defenders could not foresee that the Supreme Court would for the first time in memory invalidate a civil rights statute enacted under Section 5.

44. The most prominent—and, to date, uniformly unsuccessful—*Lopez* challenges outside the noncommercial crime context are *United States* v. *Olin Corp.*, 107 F.3d 1506 (11th Cir. 1997) (sustaining the Comprehensive Environmental Response, Compensation, and Liability Act against *Lopez* challenge); *National Association of Home Builders* v. *Babbitt*, 130 F.3d 1041 (D.C. Cir. 1997), *cert. denied*, 118 S. Ct. 2340 (1998) (sustaining Endangered Species Act application to local species against *Lopez* challenge); *Hoffman* v. *Hunt*, 126 F.3d 575 (4th Cir. 1997) (sustaining Freedom of Access to Clinics Act); *Brzonkala* v. *Virginia Polytechnic Institute et al.*, 132 F.3d 949 (4th Cir. 1997) (sustaining Violence against Women Act) (*case pending on rehearing en banc*). I discuss this last, particularly intriguing case below.

45. This record surpasses even the most pessimistic predictions of *Lopez*'s likely impact. See, e.g., Deborah Jones Merritt, "The Fuzzy Logic of Federalism," *Case Western Reserve Law Review*, vol. 46 (1996), p. 685, p. 693 (predicting that successful *Lopez* challenges would be rare); Suzanna Sherry, "The Barking Dog," *Case Western Law Review*, vol. 46 (1996), p. 877; Barry Friedman, "Valuing Federalism," *Minnesota Law Review*, vol. 82 (1997), p. 317, p. 338 (*Lopez* is unlikely to have even an *in terrorem* effect on Congress). For a sample of appellate decisions, see *United States* v. *Hawkins*, 104 F.3d 437 (D.C. Cir. 1997), *cert. denied*, 118 S. Ct. 126 (1997); *United States* v. *Orozco*, 98 F.3d 105 (3d Cir. 1997); *United States* v. *Zorrilla*, 93 F.3d 7 (1st Cir. 1996); *United States* v. *Rogers*, 89 F.3d 1326 (7th Cir. 1996), *cert. denied*, 117 S. Ct. 495 (1996) (all sustaining Drug Free School Zones Act against *Lopez* challenges). See also *United States* v. *Wright*, 117 F.3d 1265 (11th Cir. 1997); *United States* v. *Rybar*, 103 F.3d 273 (3d Cir. 1996), *cert. denied*, 118 S. Ct. 46 (1997); *United States* v. *Beuckelaere*, 91 F.3d 781 (6th Cir. 1996); *United States* v. *Kenney*, 91 F.3d 884 (7th Cir. 1996); *United States* v. *Kirk*, 105 F.3d 997 (5th Cir. 1997) (*en banc*), *cert. denied*, 118 S. Ct. 47 (1997) (all sustaining federal ban on possession of machine guns). And see *United States* v. *Bailey*, 115 F.3d 1222 (5th Cir. 1997), *cert. denied*, 118 S. Ct. 866 (1998), and

United States v. *Black*, 125 F.3d 454 (7th Cir. 1997), two among several appellate decisions sustaining the Child Support Recovery Act (or "deadbeat dad" law) against *Lopez* challenges.

46. *Fitzpatrick* v. *Bitzer*, 427 U.S. 445, 455 (1976).

47. The one instructive exception is that in rejecting the contention that Congress may legislate new rights under Section 5, the *Flores* majority relied on *Oregon* v. *Mitchell* (1970), which arose over a federal moratorium on the use of literacy tests and a federal provision lowering the voting age from twenty-one to eighteen in state and local elections. The closely divided Court sustained prohibition on *racially* discriminatory literacy requirements. It invalidated the prohibition against the equally, though not racially, discriminatory age requirements as an impermissible intrusion into state and local affairs. *Oregon* v. *Mitchell*, 400 U.S. 112, 126–27 (1970) (Black, J., announcing the judgment of the Court). The *Flores* majority's reliance on this precedent supports the analysis in the text.

48. Richard H. Fallon, Jr., "The Supreme Court—Foreword: Implementing the Constitution," *Harvard Law Review*, vol. 111 (1997), p. 56, p. 132 ("[M]any important questions remain whether congressional prohibitions against discrimination based on nonsuspect criteria, such as age, should now be upheld or invalidated") (footnote omitted). Age may not be a particularly good example. While divided panels of the Eighth and the Eleventh Circuit have found that the Age Discrimination in Employment Act (ADEA) was not a valid exercise of congressional power under the Fourteenth Amendment (see *Humenansky* v. *Regents of the University of Minnesota*, 152 F.3d 822 (8th Cir. 1998); *Kimel* v. *Florida Board of Regents*, 139 F.3d 1426 (11th Cir. 1998)), six other circuits have sustained the ADEA against challenges under *Flores* (and under *Seminole Tribe of Florida* v. *Florida*, 517 U.S. 44 (1996), discussed in chapter 5). See, e.g., *Scott* v. *University of Mississippi*, 148 F.3d 493 (5th Cir. 1998); *Coger* v. *Board of Regents of the State of Tennessee*, 154 F.3d 296 (6th Cir. 1998). Fallon's observation applies more forcefully to other nonsuspect legislative classifications. See chapter 5, pp. 73–74.

49. *Wilson-Jones* v. *Caviness*, 99 F.3d 203, 209 (6th Cir. 1996) (footnote and citations omitted; emphasis added). For a post-*Flores* decision articulating the same concern, see *Velasquez* v. *Frapwell*, 160 F. 3d 389, 391–92 (7th Cir. 1998) (Posner, C. J.).

50. A good analysis along these lines—which, alas, is guaranteed a short shelf life in this rapidly changing area of the law—is Note, "Section 5 and the Protection of Nonsuspect Classes after *City of Boerne* v. *Flores*," *Harvard Law Review*, vol. 111 (1998), p. 1542.

51. *Nihiser* v. *Ohio E.P.A.*, 979 F. Supp. 1168, 1173–74 (S.D. Ohio 1997). With remarkable bluntness, the court expressed its concern "that Congress could transfer the costs of any social program to the states by the simple and circular expedi-

ent of defining as discrimination the failure on the part of the state employer to provide benefits to members of special interest groups." Id. at 1175. See also *Pierce* v. *King*, 918 F. Supp. 932, 940 (E.D. N.C. 1996), *affirmed on other grounds*, 131 F.3d 136 (4th Cir. 1997), *judgment vacated and remanded*, 119 S. Ct. 33 (1998); and *Brown* v. *North Carolina Division of Motor Vehicles*, 987 F. Supp. 451 (E.D. N.C. 1997). But see, e.g., *Coolbaugh* v. *Louisiana*, 136 F.3d 430 (5th Cir. 1998), *cert. denied*, 119 S. Ct. 58 (1998) (ADA constitutes valid exercise of congressional power under Fourteenth Amendment). The Supreme Court has reserved the question: *Penn. Dept. of Corrections* v. *Yeskey*, 118 S. Ct. 1952, 1956 (1998) ("We do not address . . . whether application of the ADA to state prisons is a constitutional exercise of Congress' power under either the Commerce Clause . . . or § 5 of the Fourteenth Amendment.").

52. David B. Kopel and Glenn H. Reynolds, "Shirt-Pocket Federalism: *Lopez* and the Partial-Birth Abortion Ban" (http://i2i.org/CrimJust.htm), p. 18, argue that "the majority and concurring opinions in *Lopez* . . . [suggest] that the [proposed] Partial-Birth Abortion Act should be declared unconstitutional." The authors refrain from discussing the possible Section 5 basis for the proposed ban. Under *Flores*, however, no such basis exists, least of all with respect to private abortion providers. Roger Clegg, "The ENDA Big Government?" *Weekly Standard*, September 22, 1997, p. 16, has pointed to the lack of a Section 5 rationale for the proposed Employment Nondiscrimination Act.

53. *Sasnett* v. *Sullivan*, 91 F.3d at 1022 (citations omitted).

54. Congress cannot effectively use the Commerce Clause to impose such obligations on the states because the states enjoy something called "sovereign immunity." Congress can trump sovereign immunity under the Fourteenth Amendment but, since the Supreme Court's 1996 decision in *Seminole Tribe* v. *Florida*, 517 U.S. 44 (1996), not under its enumerated Article I powers. Chapter 5 discusses this doctrine and its complications and qualifications.

55. One federal district court has so held: *Brzonkala* v. *Virginia Polytechnic Institute*, 935 F. Supp. 779 (W.D. Va. 1996); *reversed on other grounds*, 132 F.3d 949 (4th Cir. 1997); *case pending on rehearing en banc.* In all other VAWA cases to date, courts have failed to reach the Section 5 question, ruling instead that VAWA's civil remedies provision is constitutional under the Commerce Clause.

56. Justice Kennedy cites the *Civil Rights Cases* and other Reconstruction Era precedents as evidence for the distinction, endorsed in *Flores*, between permissible, "corrective" (or enforcement) legislation and impermissible, "definitional" (that is, rights-creating) legislation. *Flores*, 117 S. Ct. at 2166. Justice Kennedy adds that "the specific holdings of these early cases [i.e., that Section 5 does not reach private conduct] might have been superseded or modified." One should not, however, make too much of this dictum because neither of the two cases Kennedy

cites in support, *Heart of Atlanta Motel, Inc.* v. *United States*, 379 U.S. 241 (1964) and *United States* v. *Guest*, 383 U.S. 745 (1966), is clearly a Fourteenth Amendment case.

57. *Brzonkala*, 132 F.3d at 969 (4th Cir. 1997) (quoting *United States* v. *Wright*, 117 F.3d 1265, 1269 (11th Cir. 1997) (Kravitch, J.)). See also *United States* v. *Wall*, 92 F.3d 1444, 1448 (6th Cir. 1996), *cert. denied*, 117 S. Ct. 690 (1997) ("courts have resisted urgings to extend *Lopez* beyond § 922(q)"); *United States* v. *Wilson*, 73 F.3d 675, 685 (7th Cir. 1995), *cert. denied*, 117 S. Ct. 47 (1996) (*Lopez* "reaffirmed, rather than overturned, the previous half century of Commerce Clause precedent").

58. *Brzonkala*, 132 F.3d at 997 (Luttig, J., dissenting). Judge Luttig expressed his "every hope" that the full Fourth Circuit and, failing that, the Supreme Court would reverse the panel decision.

59. I overlooked this point until Michael E. Rosman alerted me to it.

60. *United States* v. *Wilson*, 133 F.3d 251, 257–58 (4th Cir. 1997). The Court set aside the convictions on the grounds that the Clean Water Act, if interpreted as authorizing regulations that reached purely intrastate waters, would violate the Commerce Clause under *Lopez*.

Chapter 4: Federal Commandeering

1. *New York* v. *United States*, 505 U.S. 144 (1992); *Printz* v. *United States*, 117 S. Ct. 2365 (1997).

2. *FERC* v. *Mississippi*, 456 U.S. 742, 764 (1982) (O'Connor, concurring); *Hodel* v. *Virginia Surface Mining and Reclamation Ass'n*, 452 U.S. 264, 290 (1981) (O'Connor, concurring and dissenting).

3. A perfect example of this tendency, and in fact the origin of the characterization of the Tenth Amendment as the "truism that all is retained which has not been surrendered," is *United States* v. *Darby*, 312 U.S. 100, 124 (1941).

4. For a brief critique of the Tenth Amendment as a kind of supraconstitutional rule of construction, see Deborah Jones Merritt, "Three Faces of Federalism," *Vanderbilt Law Review*, vol. 47 (1994), p. 1563, pp. 1581–82. Scholars and judges committed to a "textual" interpretation of the Constitution should find it particularly difficult to defend this use of the Tenth Amendment.

5. 78 U.S. 113 (1870).

6. *Metcalf & Eddy* v. *Mitchell*, 269 U.S. 514, 521 (1926).

7. *Helvering* v. *Gerhardt*, 304 U.S. 405 (1938) (*Day* applies only to state judicial officers); *Graves* v. *People of State of New York*, 306 U.S. 466, 486 (1939) (federal government may tax salaries of state officers).

8. *Maryland* v. *Wirtz*, 392 U.S. 183 (1968) (sustaining Fair Labor Standards

Act as applied to state schools and hospitals); *National League of Cities* v. *Usery*, 426 U.S. 833 (1976) (invalidating application of Fair Labor Standards Act to certain state and local employees); *Garcia* v. *San Antonio Metropolitan Transit Authority*, 469 U.S. 528 (1985) (overruling *National League of Cities*).

9. *New York* v. *United States*, 505 U.S. 144, 175–76 (1992) (quoting *Hodel*, 452 U.S. at 288).

10. *Hodel*, 452 U.S. at 291–92 (characterizing a suggestion to the contrary as "a radical departure from long-established precedent").

11. See, e.g., *South Carolina* v. *Baker*, 486 U.S. 505 (1988) (state bond interest not immune from nondiscriminatory federal tax); *EEOC* v. *Wyoming*, 460 U.S. 226 (1983) (sustaining extension of Age Discrimination in Employment Act to state and local employees); *Transportation Union* v. *Long Island RR. Co.*, 455 U.S. 678 (1982) (Railway Labor Act applies to state railroads); *Fry* v. *United States*, 421 U.S. 542 (1975) (state employees subject to federal wage control law); and *New York* v. *United States*, 326 U.S. 572 (1946) (New York State not immune from nondiscriminatory federal excise tax).

12. *Hodel*, 452 U.S. at 287 n. 28 ("constitutional principles of federalism do not restrict congressional power to invade state autonomy when Congress legislates under § 5 of the Fourteenth Amendment") (citing *Fitzpatrick* v. *Bitzer*, 427 U.S. 445, 452–56 (1976). But chapter 5 will show that the Tenth Amendment is not altogether inapplicable in Fourteenth Amendment cases.

13. The most recent Supreme Court case on the question of commandeering under the Spending Clause, *South Dakota* v. *Dole*, 483 U.S. 203 (1987), sustained the withholding of federal highway funds for a state's failure to adopt the federal minimum drinking age. As discussed below, however, the Supreme Court's decision in *Printz* v. *United States* has cast some doubt on the continued validity of this precedent.

14. The leading cases are *Hodel* v. *Virginia Surface Mining & Reclamation Ass'n*, 452 U.S. 264 (1981) (sustaining Surface Mining Control and Reclamation Act against federalism challenge) and *FERC* v. *Mississippi*, 456 U.S. 742 (1982) (Public Utility Regulation Policies Act violates neither the Commerce Clause nor the Tenth Amendment). Further examples include *Arkansas* v. *Oklahoma*, 503 U.S. 91 (1992) (Clean Air Act); *Gade* v. *National Solid Wastes Management Ass'n*, 505 U.S. 88 (1992) (Occupational Health and Safety Act); *Department of Energy* v. *Ohio*, 503 U.S. 607 (Clean Water Act and Conservation and Recovery Act); *Kenaitze Indian Tribe* v. *Alaska*, 860 F.2d 312 (9th Cir. 1988), *cert. denied*, 491 U.S. 905 (1989) (Alaska National Interest Lands Conservation Act).

15. The decisions are *Acorn* v. *Edwards*, 81 F.3d 1387 (5th Cir. 1996), *cert. denied*, 117 S. Ct. 2532 (1997) (Lead Contamination Control Act); and *Board of Natural Resources* v. *Brown*, 992 F.2d 937 (9th Cir. 1993) (Forest Resources Act).

Congress promptly amended the latter statute so as to give the state the "choice" of regulating on its own or being regulated by the secretary of the interior.

16. There were additional, shorter dissents by Justice Souter and by Justice Breyer, joined by Justice Stevens. Following the practice of the *Printz* majority, I refer to Justice Stevens's principal dissent as "the dissent," unless otherwise indicated.

17. The majority opinion characterizes the impositions on local law enforcement officers as substantial. The dissent calls them "minimal" and stresses the important public purposes of the Brady Act. Nothing hangs on this dispute: in the end, the majority opinion simply says that even trivial impositions may be unconstitutional. *Printz*, 117 S. Ct. at 2383.

18. *Printz*, 117 S. Ct. at 2369–70 (emphasis added). Actually, there *is* constitutional text that speaks "to this precise question." The Militia Clause of Article I, Section 8, empowers Congress "to provide for calling forth the Militia *to execute the Laws of the Union*" (emphasis added). Although this power seems to have been intended chiefly for emergencies, such as to suppress insurrections and to repel invasions (see *The Federalist Papers* No. 29), the clause lists these purposes *separately* and in addition to the execution of federal laws. The clause can be read to mean that Congress may not dragoon state officers into federal law enforcement, short of calling forth the militia. But the explicit grant of authority to "commandeer" one way does not foreclose an implied authority to commandeer in some other fashion, which may be the reason why Justice Scalia's *Printz* opinion makes no mention of the Militia Clause.

19. My reading of *Printz* as a highly formalistic and doctrinaire opinion is largely (though not in all particulars) consistent with Evan H. Caminker, *"Printz*, State Sovereignty, and the Limits of Formalism," *Supreme Court Review* (1997), p. 199. Caminker's article—to my mind, the single best contribution to the already voluminous commentary on *Printz*—expresses severe doubts about the merits of Justice Scalia's analysis and, in the end, considers it untenable. I disagree with that assessment, but the disagreement does not affect the interpretation of the majority opinion.

20. *Printz*, 117 S. Ct. at 2389 (Stevens, J., dissenting). A countervailing historical argument is that the Founders' experience with the Articles of Confederation had led them to suspect that indirect federal legislation was not only ineffective but also obnoxious to the states. A federal government that can exert authority directly *and* through the states would reproduce resentment and disaffection, the effects of which the Constitution was meant to overcome. Justice Scalia does not, however, press this argument.

21. Saikrishna Bangalore Prakash, "Field Office Federalism," *Virginia Law Review*, vol. 79 (1993), p. 1957; pp. 1998–99. Prakash's careful historical analysis

concludes that the Founders did envision the federal commandeering of state executive (and judicial) officers.

22. "[W]e have never suggested that the failure of the early Congresses to address the scope of federal power in a particular area or to exercise a particular authority was an argument against its existence. That position, if correct, would undermine most of our post–New Deal Commerce Clause jurisprudence." 117 S. Ct. at 2391 (Stevens, J., dissenting).

23. Justice O'Connor noted the point, albeit with a different twist, in her opinion for the Court in *New York* v. *United States:*

> The Federal Government undertakes activities today that would have been unimaginable to the Framers in two senses; first, because the Framers would not have conceived that *any* government would conduct such activities; and second, because the Framers would not have believed that the *Federal* Government, rather than the States, would assume such responsibilities.

New York, 505 U.S. at 157 (italics in the original). The point is too obvious to escape either Justice Scalia or the dissenters in *Printz*. But neither side wants to make too much of it, because it shows that the modern Supreme Court's Constitution has little to do with the Founders' Constitution. The dissent wishes to suppress any suggestion to that effect; Justice Scalia, for his part, seeks to dispel any sense that he is about to mount a challenge to the New Deal. As a result, the combatants engage in historical shadowboxing. The match is interesting, but the punches do not connect.

24. *Printz*, 117 S. Ct. at 2367. From this assertion, Justice Scalia proceeds to the debatable inference that the paucity of "compelling examples" of federal commandeering evidences pervasive constitutional doubts about the practice.

25. See id. at 2397 (Stevens, J., dissenting; citing *Printz* at 2379).

26. Justice Scalia's list of constitutional provisions that illustrate the constitutional "structure" mentions the Tenth Amendment only at the end, and only as tautology. Id. at 2376–77. An additional footnote, id. at 2379 n. 13, explains the "structural" argument and again downplays the Tenth Amendment.

27. Id. at 2382.

28. *New York*, 505 U.S. at 167, implausibly argues that accountability suffers only when the states are being "commandeered" *but not* when the federal government browbeats them into a "partnership." *Lopez*, 514 U.S. at 576–77 (Kennedy, J., concurring) observes that "citizens must have some means of knowing which of the two governments to hold accountable for the failure to perform a given function" (or, one might add in a vain effort to correct the statist bias of the concurrence, for making a mess of their lives). But the concurrence first limits this concern to pro-

grams that interfere with "traditional," noncommercial state regulation and then segues into a discourse on the "sworn obligation" of the *political* branches to protect the "proper federal balance." There is no contest between that solemn exhortation and the politicians' incentives to diffuse responsibility.

29. The observation that the accountability argument transcends the commandeering context has become a standard theme of the legal commentary on *Printz*. For example, Vicki C. Jackson, "Federalism and the Uses and Limits of Law: *Printz and Principle?*" *Harvard Law Review*, vol. 111 (1998), p. 2180, pp. 2201–4, notes the difficulty of "connecting" the public accountability argument of *Printz* with its anticommandeering rule. Similarly, Roderick M. Hills, Jr., "The Political Economy of Cooperative Federalism: Why State Autonomy Makes Sense and 'Dual Sovereignty' Does Not," *Michigan Law Review*, vol. 96 (1998), p. 813, p. 826, observes that the accountability "argument seems to condemn not merely federal laws that commandeer state or local services but also even voluntary intergovernmental cooperation." Just so. Contrary to Hills (p. 826), however, that is not a "deeper conceptual difficulty" with the argument. It is the *point* of the argument, as expounded by Justice Scalia.

30. The example is taken from an actual case decided by the U.S. Court of Appeals for the District of Columbia. *Commonwealth of Virginia v. E.P.A.*, 108 F.3d 1397 (D.C. Cir. 1997), *decision modified on rehearing*, 116 F.3d 499 (1997). In this dispute over certain clean air regulations, the commonwealth prevailed on statutory grounds.

31. Mark C. Gordon, "Differing Paradigms, Similar Flaws: Constructing a New Federalism in Congress and the Court," *Yale Law and Policy Review*, vol. 14, p. 187, p. 212 (1996). The argument of the preceding two paragraphs is based on Gordon's analysis, pp. 211–12.

32. A concern over the congressional emasculation of the president's constitutional law enforcement powers has been a recurring theme of Justice Scalia's opinions. See, most notably, *Morrison v. Olson*, 487 U.S. 654, 697 (1988), where Justice Scalia, alone among all Justices, argued that the office of the independent counsel is unconstitutional. See also Justice Scalia's opinion for the Court in *Lujan v. Defenders of Wildlife*, 504 U.S. 555 (1992) (environmental law enforcement by private citizen attorneys general violates president's authority to ensure faithful execution of the laws). Caminker, "*Printz*, State Sovereignty, and the Limits of Formalism," p. 226, suggests that "one might view *Printz* . . . as an attempted end run around the Court's rejection of [Scalia's] extreme unitarian position in *Morrison v. Olson*" and notes, with justified amazement, that "it is astonishing to see a five-member majority so casually embrace this controversial principle, without so much as a whisper of reservation or qualification."

33. The dissent mentions the Clean Water Act, the Occupational Safety and

Health Act, and the Resource Conservation and Recovery Act. Scalia's cavalier response is a footnote to the effect that the states' "voluntary" participation in federal schemes "significantly reduces" the ability of Congress to emasculate the presidency. *Printz,* 117 S. Ct. at 2378 n. 12. The dissent, however, charges that the executive-power argument threatens heretofore constitutional federal schemes that are in no sense voluntary, such as programs that commandeer states alongside private parties. Justice Scalia says nothing to discourage that inference.

34. Justice Scalia's lone authority for the argument is an extremely clever and persuasive law review article coauthored by a former law clerk. *Printz,* 117 S. Ct. at 2379 (citing Gary Lawson and Patricia B. Granger, "The 'Proper' Scope of Federal Power: A Jurisdictional Interpretation of the Sweeping Clause," *Duke Law Journal,* vol. 43 (1993), p. 267).

35. In particular, Justice Thomas's suggestion that the Second Amendment right to bear arms may bar legislation such as the Brady Act, *Printz,* 117 S. Ct. at 2385–86 (Thomas, J., concurring), concerns at issue that were not before the Court. Its mention seems chiefly calculated to induce apoplexy among the politically correct.

36. Id. at 2392 n. 12; see also id. at 2395.

37. The language quoted in the text appears in id. at 2395 n. 18. Recall that *Flores* permits and implicitly encourages states to enact Religious Freedom Restoration Acts; Justice Stevens, alone among all Justices, would not permit even that much democracy. See chapter 3, n. 42. For further examples of Justice Stevens's hostility to state democracy, see his votes in *U.S. Term Limits* v. *Thornton,* 514 U.S. 779 (1995) and *Romer* v. *Evans,* 517 S. Ct. 620 (1996), both discussed in chapter 7.

38. Speaking of demagogy, "[b]y limiting the ability of the Federal Government to enlist state officials in the implementation of its programs," the dissent avers, "the Court creates incentives for the National Government to aggrandize itself." *Printz,* 117 S. Ct. at 2396; see also Justice Breyer's dissent, id. at 2404. Coming as it does from partisans of federal omnipotence, this argument is disingenuous. In any event, the rejoinder is blazingly obvious: the federal government would be reluctant to "aggrandize" itself were it made to bear political responsibility for the intrusions attendant to its schemes.

39. Jackson, "Federalism and the Uses and Limits of Law," p. 2255, notes the "tension" between the two cases and the underlying adjudicatory models.

40. *Printz,* 117 S. Ct. at 2376. Among the early targets is the federal Drivers Privacy Protection Act, which regulates the states' disclosure of data contained in drivers' records. The Fourth Circuit has declared the act unconstitutional: *Condon* v. *Reno,* 155 F. 3d 453 (4th Cir. 1998). Two other circuits have sustained the statute. *Oklahoma* v. *Reno,* 1998 WL 833627 (10th Cir. (Okla.)); *Travis* v. *Reno,* 1998 WL 871038 (7th Cir. (Wis.)),

41. For a partial list and an excellent analysis, see Jonathan H. Adler, "The Green Aspects of *Printz:* The Revival of Federalism and Its Implications for Environmental Law," *George Mason Law Review,* vol. 6 (1998), p. 573. For another list of a "handful" of statutes that are plainly unconstitutional under *Printz,* see Evan H. Caminker, "*Printz,* State Sovereignty, and the Limits of Formalism," *Supreme Court Review* (1997), p. 199, p. 200 n. 7.

42. *South Dakota* v. *Dole,* 483 U.S. 203 (1987). The most vulnerable federalism precedent is *Garcia,* which, after *Printz,* is probably a dead letter. See Caminker, "*Printz,* State Sovereignty, and the Limits of Formalism," pp. 244–46.

Chapter 5: From Collusive Nationalism to Noncooperation

1. AFDC was not understood to guarantee private entitlements until the Court, over three decades after the enactment of the statute, determined otherwise. *King* v. *Smith,* 392 U.S. 309 (1968); *Townsend* v. *Swank,* 404 U.S. 282 (1971); *Carleson* v. *Remillard,* 406 U.S. 598 (1972). Far and away the best discussion of the courts' role in welfare policy is R. Shep Melnick, *Between the Lines: Interpreting Welfare Rights* (Brookings Institution, 1994), esp. pp. 65–134.

2. See, for example, *United Steelworkers* v. *Weber,* 443 U.S. 193 (1979). In an earlier case, the Supreme Court read the Civil Rights Act to prohibit not only intentional racial discrimination but also otherwise legitimate, nondiscriminatory employment practices that have a "disparate impact" on minorities. *Griggs* v. *Duke Power Co.,* 401 U.S. 424 (1971).

3. Among the many available sources on this development is my own account: Michael S. Greve, *The Demise of Environmentalism in American Law* (AEI Press, 1996), esp. pp. 41–46 and 126–27. Still the best source of the policy consequences of environmental standing is R. Shep Melnick, *Regulation and the Courts: The Case of the Clean Air Act* (Brookings Institution, 1983).

4. *Maine* v. *Thibotout,* 448 U.S. 1 (1980). The Supreme Court appeared to limit the scope of *Thibotout* only a year later, when it held, in *Middlesex County Sewerage Authority* v. *National Seaclammers Ass'n,* 453 U.S. 1 (1981), that a comprehensive statutory scheme of nonjudicial remedies precludes private enforcement under § 1983. But *Seaclammers* has been followed only once since then. *Smith* v. *Robinson,* 468 U.S. 992 (1984).

5. Jerry L. Mashaw and Dylan S. Calsyn, "Block Grants, Entitlements, and Federalism: A Conceptual Map of Contested Terrain," *Yale Law and Policy Review,* vol. 14 (1996), p. 297, p. 304.

6. The distinction is far from airtight. Every judicial statement that "Congress may not enact *X*" can be rephrased as saying that "the federal courts will not enforce *X*" (which is actually more accurate: courts never really strike down laws

but merely refuse to enforce them). Still, the distinction captures the different political dynamics and underlying intuitions about the judiciary's role.

7. Occasionally, plain-meaning analysis has proregulatory results—for instance, when it precludes judicial exemptions from strict legislative requirements. See, e.g., *Environmental Defense Fund* v. *City of Chicago*, 511 U.S. 328 (1994). The Supreme Court's 1997–1998 term brought two interesting plain-meaning cases in this vein: *Oncale* v. *Sundowner Offshore Services*, 118 S. Ct. 998 (1998) (Title VII of the Civil Rights Act covers same-sex harassment); *Pennsylvania Dep't of Corrections* v. *Yeskey*, 118 S. Ct. 1952 (1998) (Americans with Disabilities Act applies to state prisons). But the tendency is in the direction indicated in the text. See William N. Eskridge, "Overriding Supreme Court Statutory Decisions," *Yale Law Journal*, vol. 101 (1991), p. 331, pp. 404–14 (contrasting the Supreme Court's "accommodationist pluralism" before 1986 with its "confrontational formalism" thereafter).

8. This assessment of *Lujan* v. *Defenders of Wildlife*, 504 U.S. 555 (1992) is Cass Sunstein's: "What's Standing after *Lujan?* Of Citizen Suits, 'Injuries' and Article III," *Michigan Law Review*, vol. 91 (1992), p. 163, p. 165. Other cases denying environmental standing include *Lujan* v. *National Wildlife Federation*, 497 U.S. 871 (1990) and *Steel Corp.* v. *Citizens for a Better Environment*, 118 S. Ct. 1003 (1998).

9. *Commonwealth of Virginia* v. *Browner*, 80 F.3d 869 (4th Cir. 1996), *cert. denied*, 117 S. Ct. 764 (1997). The commonwealth lost this particular battle.

10. See chapter 4, pp. 57–58. The majority opinion in *Defenders of Wildlife*, like that in *Printz*, was written by Justice Antonin Scalia.

11. *Chisholm* v. *Georgia*, 2 Dall. 419, 1 L.Ed. 440 (1793). The case, which rested on a cause of action under Georgia state law, was brought in federal court because the state was immune from such suits in its own courts.

12. *Seminole Tribe of Florida* v. *Florida*, 517 U.S. 44, 54 (1996) (quoting *Blatchford* v. *Native Village of Noatak*, 501 U.S. 775, 779 (1991)).

13. *Hans* v. *Louisiana*, 134 U.S. 1, 17 (1890) (quoting *Beers* v. *Arkansas*, 61 U.S. 527, 529 (1857)). The passage is quoted with approval in Chief Justice Rehnquist's majority opinion in *Seminole Tribe*, 517 U.S. at 69.

14. *Seminole Tribe*, 517 U.S. at 185 (Stevens, J., dissenting); at 185 (Souter, J., dissenting). Justice Stevens is quoting his own concurrence in *Pennsylvania* v. *Union Gas Co.*, 491 U.S. 1, 25 (1989). Still the most thorough judicial attack on the broad understanding of the Eleventh Amendment is Justice Brennan's dissent in *Atascadero State Hospital* v. *Scanlon*, 473 U.S. 234, 259–99 (1985). The Brennan-Stevens-Souter position is supported by the "great weight of contemporary scholarship." Vicki C. Jackson, "*Seminole Tribe*, the Eleventh Amendment, and the Potential Evisceration of *Ex Parte Young*," *New York University Law Review*, vol. 72 (1997),

p. 495, p. 500 and sources cited in id., n. 29. It is doubtful, however, that the revisionists will be heard after the *Seminole Tribe* exhortation to please shut up. For a thorough, learned, and instructive attempt at a revival, see James E. Pfander, "History and State Suability: An 'Explanatory' Account of the Eleventh Amendment," *Cornell Law Review*, vol. 83 (1998), p. 1269.

15. *Fitzpatrick* v. *Bitzer*, 427 U.S. 445 (1976). As shown later in this chapter, however, the Fourteenth Amendment trump seems to be diminishing in value.

16. The issue is somewhat more complicated than the sentence in the text suggests (see Jackson, "*Seminole Tribe*," pp. 503–4 and sources cited therein). Moreover, the Supreme Court's *Seminole Tribe* decision has raised doubts as to whether plaintiffs may assert federal rights against state defendants in state court where Eleventh Amendment immunity bars the pursuit of such cases in federal court—and, if so, whether the U.S. Supreme Court will then review state court judgments. State Supreme Courts have split on the question, and the U.S. Supreme Court has agreed to examine it. *Alden* v. *Maine*, 715 A.2d 172 (1998), *cert. granted*, 1998 WL 650942 (U.S. Me.).

17. *Ex parte Young*, 209 U.S. 123 (1908).

18. Henry Paul Monaghan, "The Sovereign Immunity 'Exception,'" *Harvard Law Review*, vol. 110 (1996), p. 102, p. 127. State officers are protected from lawsuits for damages under a doctrine of "qualified immunity."

19. Jackson, "*Seminole Tribe*," pp. 498–99.

20. Environmental lawsuits, for instance, are typically brought, as intended, to prod government agencies at all levels into tougher law enforcement.

21. *Seminole Tribe*, 517 U.S. at 183 (Souter, J., dissenting) (quoting *Garcia* v. *Metropolitan Transit Authority*, 469 U.S. 528, 552 (1986)).

22. Monaghan, "The Sovereign Immunity 'Exception,'" p. 130–31. The other way of reaching the result is to invoke the Indian Commerce Clause (thus distinguishing *Union Gas*) or to invalidate the statutory provision at issue on Tenth Amendment "commandeering" grounds. Id., pp. 116–21.

23. Recall Professor Robert Nagel's observation that even the humblest judicial challenge to nationalist preconceptions tends to prompt histrionics—which tells us a lot about the zeal with which the preconceptions are held and next to nothing about the scope of the challenge. Nagel, "The *Term Limits* Dissent: What Nerve," *Arizona Law Review*, vol. 38 (1996), p. 843.

24. I shall ignore the fourth, exceedingly technical "exception" mentioned earlier—that is, the option of pursuing in state court federal causes of action that cannot be pursued in federal courts owing to the states' Eleventh Amendment immunity. As suggested above (n. 16), however, the argument in the text also applies to this "exception."

25. See, e.g., *Atascadero State Hospital* v. *Scanlon*, 473 U.S. 234, 246–47 (1985)

(state did not waive sovereign immunity by receipt of federal funds under the Rehabilitation Act); *Pennhurst* v. *Halderman*, 451 U.S. 1 (1981) (mere acceptance of federal funds does not constitute waiver of sovereign immunity); *United States* v. *Nordic Village, Inc.*, 503 U.S. 30 (1992) (bankruptcy code does not establish unequivocal waiver of government's immunity from private claim for monetary relief).

26. Kit Kinports, "Implied Waiver after *Seminole Tribe*," *Minnesota Law Review*, vol. 82 (1998), p. 793, acknowledges this possibility but argues that Congress may still secure implied and express waivers of state immunity.

27. See Justice Souter's correct observation to this effect, *Seminole Tribe*, 517 U.S. at 180–81. The majority's "detailed remedial scheme" test is imported from the § 1983 cases briefly mentioned in n. 4 of this chapter. The underlying theory is that such schemes indicate a congressional intent to supplant other remedies, including judicial enforcement.

28. Jackson, "*Seminole Tribe*," p. 535 (footnote omitted). Jackson provides a thorough analysis of the subject matter covered in that and the preceding paragraphs. On a more optimistic note, John C. Jeffries, Jr., "In Praise of the Eleventh Amendment and Section 1983," *Virginia Law Review*, vol. 84 (1998), p. 47, argues that the Eleventh Amendment matters only in rare cases because individuals may always sue state officers. Monaghan, "The Sovereign Immunity 'Exception,' " p. 132, reaches the same conclusion.

29. *Seminole Tribe*, 517 U.S. at 65–66 (discussing *Fitzpatrick* v. *Bitzer*, 427 U.S. 445 (1976)). The argument in the text also applies to legislation under the Thirteenth and Fifteenth Amendments.

30. Professor Laurence Tribe, a principal champion of expansive civil rights, has berated the *Seminole Tribe* majority and especially Justice Scalia, a member of that majority, for its "remarkable" construction of the Eleventh Amendment. See Professor Tribe's response to Antonin Scalia, *A Matter of Interpretation* (Princeton University Press, 1997), pp. 78–79 n. 25. At or about the same time, Professor Tribe set his name to a brief arguing that the state of Texas was immune from damage claims under Title VI of the Civil Rights Act. The case, *Hopwood* v. *State of Texas*, was a white law school applicant's successful challenge to racial preferences in student admissions. 78 F.3d 932 (5th Cir. 1996), *cert. denied*, 518 S. Ct. 1033 (1996).

31. See *Reynolds* v. *Alabama Department of Transportation*, 4 F. Supp.2d 1092 (M.D. Ala. 1998) (state not immune from disparate impact suit under Title VII). The decision is probably wrong: barring proof of intentional institutional discrimination, *Flores* would appear to bar "disparate impact" lawsuits. Jesse Choper, "On the Difference in Importance between Supreme Court Doctrine and Actual Consequences: A Review of the Supreme Court's 1996–1997 Term," *Cardozo Law Review*, vol. 19 (1998), p. 2259, p. 2297. But the judicial designation of suspect classes and their treatment often follows perceived political dictates, and the legal

tests of *Flores* (such as "proportionality" and "remedial" purposes, see chapter 3, p. 37) are loose enough to accommodate those considerations.

32. More precisely, the decision pushes Congress to recast statutes as having been enacted pursuant to both the Commerce Clause *and* the Fourteenth Amendment. If Congress acted only under the Fourteenth Amendment, it could abrogate sovereign immunity but could no longer reach private conduct.

33. *Wilson-Jones* v. *Caviness*, 99 F.3d 203; *opinion amended on denial of rehearing*, 107 F.3d 358 (6th Cir. 1997). For further examples of the courts' tendency to preclude congressional, Fourteenth Amendment endruns around *Seminole Tribe*, see *Velasquez* v. *Frapwell*, 160 F.3d 389 (7th Cir. 1998) (states are immune from private suit under the Uniformed Services Employment and Reemployment Rights Act, which was enacted under the War Powers Clause and cannot also be viewed as enforcing the Fourteenth Amendment); *Schlossberg* v. *Maryland*, 119 F.3d 1140, 1149–50 (4th Cir. 1997) (Bankruptcy Reform Act abrogation of immunity cannot be upheld as exercise of Fourteenth Amendment power) and *Chavez* v. *Arte Publico Press*, 139 F.3d 504, 510–11 (5th Cir. 1998), opinion superseded, 157 F.3d 282 (5th Cir. 1998) (federal Copyright Act and Lanham Act do not abrogate sovereign immunity). See also *Condon* v. *Reno*, 155 F.3d 453 (4th Cir. 1998) (Drivers Privacy Protection Act cannot be viewed as Fourteenth Amendment legislation).

34. *Thomson* v. *Ohio State University Hospital*, 5 F. Supp.2d 574 (S.D. Ohio 1998) (Family Medical Leave Act is unenforceable in federal court against state defendants). But see *Biddlecome* v. *University of Texas*, 1997 WL 124220 (S.D. Tex. 1997); *Jolliffe* v. *Mitchell*, 986 F. Supp. 339 (W.D. Va. 1997) (both holding, without much analysis, that Family Medical Leave Act constitutes a valid exercise of Congress's power under the Fourteenth Amendment). *Thomson* is the correct decision.

35. In *Gregory* v. *Ashcroft*, a leading case, the Supreme Court established the link explicitly: "[I]nasmuch as this Court . . . has left primarily to the political processes the protection of the States against intrusive exercises of Congress' Commerce Clause powers, we must be absolutely certain that Congress intended such an exercise." *Gregory* v. *Ashcroft*, 501 U.S. 452, 464 (1991).

36. *Blatchford* v. *Native Village of Noatak*, 501 U.S. 775 (1991), held that Native Alaskans cannot sue the state for money damages for equal protection violations inflicted on a native village by an Alaska revenue-sharing statute, because the statute under which they sued did not contain a plain statement overriding Alaska's sovereign immunity. Compare *Alaska Pacific Fisheries* v. *United States*, 248 U.S. 78, 89 (1918) ("statutes passed for the benefit of Indian tribes . . . are to be liberally construed, doubtful expressions being resolved in favor of the Indians.").

37. *Chevron* v. *Natural Resources Defense Council, Inc.*, 467 U.S. 837 (1984). For a glaring failure to apply this presumption in a plain-statement case, see *Gregory* v. *Ashcroft*, 501 U.S. 452 (1991).

38. The decision concerning the Rehabilitation Act is *Atascadero State Hospi-*

tal v. *Scanlon*, 473 U.S. 234 (1985). The EHA decision is *Dellmuth* v. *Muth*, 491 U.S. 223 (1989). A good discussion of these decisions and the congressional responses and of the plain-statement rule in general is William N. Eskridge, Jr., *Dynamic Statutory Interpretation* (Harvard University Press, 1994), pp. 284–85.

39. See *Blanciak* v. *Allegheny Ludlum Corp.*, 77 F.3d 690 (3d Cir. 1996) (rejecting plaintiff's position that Age Discrimination in Employment Act abrogated state's immunity for discrimination by state employment referral services).

40. They do not symbolize anything to anyone, except perhaps to teachers of classes on federal courts.

41. 501 U.S. 452 (1991). The application of the plain-statement rule to the congressional invasion of "core state functions" arises not from the Eleventh but rather from the Tenth Amendment. But *Gregory* quoted liberally from earlier Eleventh Amendment cases, and the interpretive principle operates in the same manner. The Tenth Amendment, like the Eleventh, is trumped by the Fourteenth; like the Eleventh Amendment, however, the Tenth Amendment informs the judiciary's analysis of Fourteenth Amendment statutes. Note that this application of the plain-statement rule, unlike its application to sovereign immunity, leaves the plaintiff no escape into *Ex parte Young:* if the federal provision under which his claim arises does not apply, nothing is left to litigate.

42. Id. at 463. The Court reasoned that "the authority of the people of the States to determine the qualifications of their most important government officials" lies "at the heart of representative government."

43. William N. Eskridge, Jr., and Philip Frickey, "Quasi-Constitutional Law: Clear Statements Rules as Constitutional Lawmaking," *Vanderbilt Law Review*, vol. 45 (1992), p. 593, p. 634.

44. *Chisom* v. *Roemer*, 501 U.S. 380 (1991).

45. See generally R. Shep Melnick, "Federalism and the New Rights," *Yale Law and Policy Review*, vol. 14 (1996), p. 325. An instructive case is *Anderson* v. *Edwards*, 514 U.S. 143 (1995) (sustaining narrow interpretation of state obligations under AFDC).

46. See, for example, *Will* v. *Michigan Dep't of State Police*, 491 U.S. 58, 65 (1989) (refusing to recognize states as "persons" liable under 42 U.S.C. § 1983). See also *Suter* v. *Artist M*, 503 U.S. 347 (1992) and *Thompson* v. *Thompson*, 484 U.S. 174 (1988).

47. *Blessing* v. *Freestone*, 117 S. Ct. 1353 (1997).

Chapter 6: The Supreme Court's Federalism

1. Barry Friedman, "Valuing Federalism," *Minnesota Law Review*, vol. 82 (1997), p. 317, p. 341. Robert F. Nagel, "Real Revolution," *Georgia State University Law Review*, vol. 13 (1997), p. 985, p. 999, has pointed out that "every first

year law student knows the various ways the *Lopez* majority indicated that Congress can get around its ruling." Spending Clause legislation is one such means. Lynn A. Baker, "Conditional Federal Spending after *Lopez*," *Columbia Law Review*, vol. 95 (1995), p. 1911, argues for limits on the spending power in light of *Lopez*. Even under her approach, however, the scope of the Spending Clause exceeds Congress's power to regulate the states directly. Id., p. 1989. Similar considerations apply to conditional preemption: so long as Congress is free to threaten the states with a "choice" between a complete federal takeover of regulatory areas and a surrender to federal commandeering, the anticommandeering protection of *New York* and *Printz* is a meaningless formality. Roderick M. Hills, Jr., "The Political Economy of Cooperative Federalism," *Michigan Law Review*, vol. 96 (1998), p. 813, pp. 921–27, discusses the problem and proposes limits to conditional preemption.

2. Justice Thomas has articulated a coherent doctrine of enumerated powers; Justice Scalia and Chief Justice Rehnquist have not. But this difference is easily exaggerated. Scalia and Rehnquist will move toward a federalism of enumerated powers, provided that this is politically feasible. Conversely, and as noted in chapter 3, Justice Thomas's ringing endorsement of enumerated powers in *Lopez* does not advocate a prompt return to pre–New Deal jurisprudence but simply serves to remind the Court of how far it has strayed from the constitutional vision.

3. *South Dakota* v. *Dole*, 483 U.S. 203, 208 (1987) (citation omitted).

4. To pursue the institutional competence argument and analogy: if any institution is "competent" to decide questions of campaign finance, it is Congress. But Congress is *also* highly competent—and very much inclined—to write such laws so as to entrench incumbents. In light of those incentives, and in consideration of the First Amendment interests at stake, the Supreme Court has been loath to defer to Congress on campaign finance questions—and rightly so. See Lillian R. Bevier, "Money and Politics: A Perspective on the First Amendment and Campaign Finance Reform," *California Law Review*, vol. 73 (1985), p. 1045, p. 1089. The same considerations apply to enumerated powers questions. Congress certainly knows how to interpret the Commerce Clause so as to suit its purposes. Why then should the Court permit Congress to be the sole arbiter in these matters?

Chapter 7: Federalism's Constituency

1. Antonin Scalia, "Economic Affairs as Human Affairs," in *Scalia* v. *Epstein: Two Views on Judicial Activism* (Cato Institute, 1985), p. 6.

2. Alexander M. Bickel, *The Supreme Court and the Idea of Progress*, 2d ed. (Yale University Press, 1978). The notion of *Brown* as a hugely powerful symbol represents the scholarly consensus. A differing, sophisticated but to my mind unduly empiricist perspective is Gerald N. Rosenberg, *The Hollow Hope: Can Courts Bring about Social Change?* (University of Chicago Press, 1991), pp. 107–56.

3. Martin Shapiro, "The Supreme Court from Early Burger to Early Rehnquist," in Anthony King, ed., *The New American Political System*, 2d ed. (AEI Press, 1990), p. 47, p. 48.

4. Id., p. 51. The paragraph in the text partially summarizes pp. 48–53 of Shapiro's essay.

5. A spirited libertarian manifesto for such a program is Clint Bolick, *Grassroots Tyranny: The Limits of Federalism* (Cato Institute, 1993). For a more federalism-friendly approach, also from a libertarian perspective, see Richard Epstein, "The Proper Scope of the Commerce Clause," *Virginia Law Review*, vol. 73 (1987), p. 1387.

6. The phenomenon is readily explained: national impositions leave no exit and no choice and seem for that reason much harsher than comparable regulations in (some) states. Federal one-size-fits-all laws tend to produce resistance in states that, by reason of culture, economy, or geography, do not fit the national mold. And national legislation enables faraway "stakeholders" to meddle with the concerns of local citizens, as when federal legislators preserve Montana's natural resources for the benefit of backpackers from Brookline and Manhattan.

7. The best-known expression of these resentments is Robert H. Bork, *Slouching towards Gomorrah* (New York: Regan Books, 1997).

8. An instructive discussion of the Contract with America and its federalist aspects is John DiIulio, Jr., and Donald Kettl, *The Contract with America, Devolution, and the Administrative Realities of American Federalism* (Brookings Institution, 1995). The Unfunded Mandates Reform Act and welfare reform are further discussed below, pp. 120–23, 125–27.

9. *U.S. Term Limits* v. *Thornton*, 514 U.S. 779 (1995).

10. Robert F. Nagel, "The *Terms Limits* Dissent: What Nerve," *Arizona Law Review*, vol. 38 (1996), p. 843, p. 853.

11. Id. at 856–57 (footnote omitted).

12. Justice Kennedy supplied the critical fifth vote and wrote the majority opinion in *Term Limits*. On Justices O'Connor's and Justice Kennedy's statist federalism conception, see pp. 30–33 above. On their aversion to populist constituencies see, e.g., *Planned Parenthood* v. *Casey*, 505 U.S. 833 (1992) and *Romer* v. *Evans*, 517 U.S. 620 (1996). I discuss both cases below in this chapter.

13. The opening salvo was *City of Richmond* v. *J. A. Croson Co.*, 488 U.S. 469 (1989). The false step was *Metro Broadcasting, Inc.* v. *Federal Communications Comm'n*, 497 U.S. 547 (1990), which sustained racial preferences in the FCC's broadcast licensing process. *Metro Broadcasting* was effectively overruled in *Adarand Constructors* v. *Pena*, 515 U.S. 200 (1995).

14. One member of the federal bench has noted the tension. *Messer* v. *Meno*, 130 F.3d 130, 142–43 (5th Cir. 1997) (Garza, J., specially concurring).

15. *Hopwood* v. *State of Texas,* 78 F.3d 932 (5th Cir. 1996); *cert. denied,* 518 S. Ct. 1033 (1996).

16. *Los Angeles Times,* April 9, 1997, p. A1 (quoting the American Civil Liberties Union's Marc Rosenbaum, plaintiffs' counsel in the litigation against Proposition 209).

17. *Coalition for Economic Equity* v. *Wilson,* 122 F.3d 692 (9th Cir. 1997); *cert. denied,* 118 S. Ct. 397 (1997).

18. Compare the Court's trust in the electorate on matters of race and sex discrimination with its disapproval of popular initiatives concerning homosexual rights. See *Romer* v. *Evans,* 517 U.S. 620 (1996), reviewed below.

19. *Rosenberger* v. *Rector and Board of the University of Virginia,* 515 U.S. 819 (1995). Earlier decisions in the same vein include *Widmar* v. *Vincent,* 454 U.S. 263 (1981); *Witters* v. *Department of Washington Dep't of Services for the Blind,* 474 U.S. 481 (1986); *Board of Education of Westside Community Schools* v. *Mergens,* 496 U.S. 226 (1990); and *Lamb's Chapel* v. *Center Moriches Union Free School District,* 508 U.S. 384 (1993). In 1997 the Supreme Court actually overruled two of its most crabbed and restrictive decisions on public aid to religion: *Agostini* v. *Felton,* 117 S. Ct. 1997 (1997) (overruling *Aguilar* v. *Felton,* 473 U.S. 402 (1985) and *School District of Grand Rapids* v. *Ball,* 473 U.S. 373 (1985)).

20. See, e.g., *County of Allegheny* v. *ACLU,* 492 U.S. 573 (1989) and *Lee* v. *Weisman,* 505 U.S. 577, 636 (1992) (Scalia, J., dissenting) ("interior decorating is a rock-hard science compared" with Supreme Court precedents on the public display of religion).

21. Conversely, RFRA often proved useless in curbing petty bureaucratic tyranny against religious citizens, from injunctions against the invocation of a deity in high school commencement speeches to prohibitions on the public display of creches and menorahs. With or without RFRA, demands for the public accommodation of such practices often run afoul of the Supreme Court's interpretation of the Establishment Clause.

22. For an argument very similar to the paragraph in the text and from an identical perspective, see Roger Clegg, "*City of Boerne* v. *Flores:* An Overview," *Nexus,* vol. 2 (Fall 1997) ("[T]he Court has done its job. . . . [C]onservatives have more to fear from a Congress unchecked by the Constitution than from the Supreme Court."). For a conservative response that exemplifies the posture described in the text, see Robert P. George and Ramesh Ponnuru, "Courting Trouble," *National Review,* August 17, 1998, p. 33, p. 34 (attempt to reenact RFRA under the Commerce Clause "jettisons RFRA's strong point—its challenge to the courts—while implicitly going along with the post–New Deal loose view of the commerce clause (just when the courts are recovering the old one).").

23. Even before *Flores,* scholars who harbor no religious antipathies questioned

RFRA's constitutionality. See, e.g., John Harrison, "The Free Exercise Clause as a Rule about Rules," *Harvard Journal of Law and Public Policy*, vol. 15 (1992), p. 169; William W. Van Alstyne, "The Failure of the Religious Freedom Restoration Act under Section 5 of the Fourteenth Amendment," *Duke Law Journal*, vol. 46 (1996), p. 291; and Timothy E. Flanigan, "Carried About with Every Wind of Doctrine," *Public Interest Law Review* (1994), p. 75. Doubts about RFRA's constitutionality among scholars with Leave-Us-Alone ties and sympathies have contributed both to the waning enthusiasm for the statute and to the muted response to its invalidation.

24. It spurred them to push for the enactment of "little RFRAs" in various states.

25. *Jackson* v. *Benson*, 578 N.W.2d 602, 218 Wis.2d 835 (1998); *cert. denied,* 119 S. Ct. 466 (1998).

26. *Planned Parenthood* v. *Casey*, 505 U.S. 833, 851 (1992).

27. *Romer* v. *Evans*, 517 U.S. 620 (1996).

28. This is the central point of Justice Scalia's acerbic dissents. See *Romer,* 517 U.S. at 653 ("When the Court takes sides in the culture wars, it tends to be with the Knights rather than the villeins"); *Planned Parenthood*, 505 U.S. at 996–97 ("The Imperial Judiciary lives . . . leading a Volk who will be 'tested by following.'").

29. *Romer,* 517 U.S. at 640–44 (Scalia, J., dissenting) (criminal sodomy laws sustained in *Bowers* v. *Hardwick*, 478 U.S. 186 (1986), betray a possible "animus" much more clearly than Colorado referendum). Compare, on a related note, the Supreme Court's readiness to infer an "animus" in *Romer* with its reluctance to do so in the very similar case over Proposition 209.

30. *Equality Foundation* v. *City of Cincinnati*, 128 F.3d 289 (6th Cir. 1997); *cert. denied,* 119 S. Ct. 365 (1998).

31. *Casey*, 505 U.S. at 880 ("undue burden"); at 875 ("potential life"); at 879 (life and health of the mother exception). The mind boggles at the characterization of a viable, protein-based human creation as "*potential* life." But binding Supreme Court precedent now establishes that everyone has an inalienable right to define his own meaning of life. Id. at 851.

32. As of July 1998, partial-birth abortion bans have been struck down in eighteen states. In eight states, the laws have not been challenged and are in effect. Alabama's ban is being enforced only after viability; Virginia's ban is in effect, pending a judicial resolution. The National Abortion and Reproductive Rights Action League Foundation (NARAL) publishes updates on "Bans on So-Called 'Partial-Birth' Abortion and Other Abortion Procedures" at http://www.naral.org. This footnote and the accompanying text are based on information on the NARAL website. The characterization of abortion jurisprudence as a game of "gotcha" fol-

lows Judge Boggs's dissent from a Sixth Circuit decision invalidating Ohio's ban on partial-birth abortions. *Women's Medical Professional Corporation* v. *Voinovich*, 130 F.3d 187, 218–19 (Boggs, J., dissenting) (6th Cir. 1997), *cert. denied*, 118 S. Ct. 1347 (1998).

33. Under the mystery right of *Casey,* government is unconstitutional. (Only *I* can circumscribe the conduct that validates *my* meaning of life.) In a retreat from this position, *Romer* merely declared democracy unconstitutional.

34. *Vacco* v. *Quill*, 117 S. Ct. 2293 (1997); *Washington* v. *Glucksberg*, 117 S. Ct. 2302 (1997).

35. Bickel, *The Morality of Consent* (Yale University Press, 1975), pp. 27–29.

36. Ruth Bader Ginsburg, "Speaking in a Judicial Voice," *New York University Law Review,* vol. 67 (1992), p. 1185, pp. 1205–8. Justice Ginsburg's speech explicitly contrasts *Roe* with *Brown*. See also Jeffrey Rosen, "The Book of Ruth," *New Republic,* August 2, 1993, p. 19, p. 30.

37. *Casey*, 505 U.S. at 866–69 (opinion of O'Connor, Kennedy, and Souter, JJ.); at 994–96 (Scalia, J., dissenting).

38. Among legal scholars, a dogmatic faith in the Wechslerian premise that the courts should stay out of federalism cases, combined with the undeniable reality that the states will not protect themselves, has produced attempts to identify other informal, nonlegal forces that protect federalism. For example, and notably, Larry Kramer, "Understanding Federalism," *Vanderbilt Law Review,* vol. 47 (1994), p. 1485, has argued that the political parties (among other informal mechanisms) provide an effective federalism constraint. But the empirical validity of this claim is becoming increasingly doubtful, as party politics and electoral campaigns are becoming more and more nationalized. Moreover, even if Kramer is right, the dynamics of party politics protect only a "cooperative" federalism, not a federalism of enumerated powers. The same is true of other forces that allegedly enhance federalism. If they were effective, competitive federalism would not be in such a sorry state to begin with.

39. The Federalists' public assurances that the states would easily repel federal usurpations were calculated to dispel the anti-Federalists' dire warnings of an omnipotent, tyrannical federal government. Closer reading suggests that the Founders expected the states to play a less ambitious role: "The subtle message of the *The Federalist* is that the states will gradually decline." Jean Yarbrough, "Madison and Modern Federalism," in Robert A. Goldwin and William A. Schambra, eds., *How Federal Is the Constitution?* (AEI Press, 1987), p. 84, p. 87. The chief safeguard of the states' independence, Publius argued, lies in the citizens' natural affinity and attraction to their local governments—not in the Constitution, which actually contains very little to guarantee the states' independence. The Constitution does guarantee the states' representation at the federal level. But the effectiveness of this

safeguard, too, eventually depends on the citizens' affections, and those affections may gravitate from the states to the federal government in the event of "such manifest and irresistible proofs of a better administration as will overcome all the [citizens'] antecedent propensities." *The Federalist Papers* No. 46 (New American Library, 1961) (Clinton Rossiter, ed.), p. 295. Madison did not consider this a remote contingency: he commented at great length on the corrupt practices of state governments and on the difficulty of controlling the pernicious influence of faction at the state level. Similarly, Hamilton observed (*The Federalist Papers* No. 17 (p. 119)) that the people will be attracted to their local governments "unless the force of that principle should be destroyed by a much better administration of the [federal government]." Hamilton almost certainly expected the federal government to be much better administered, especially because and so long as he himself would do the administering.

40. James Q. Wilson, "The Rise of the Bureaucratic State," in Nathan Glazer and Irving Kristol, eds., *The American Commonwealth: 1976* (Basic Books, 1976), p. 91.

41. The New Deal Court cited this lack of resistance, erroneously, as evidence that New Deal nationalism did not really constitute a threat to state prerogatives. See *Steward Machine Co. v. Davis*, 301 U.S. 548 (1937).

42. Robert F. Nagel brought this point to my attention. See Nagel, "Federalism as a Fundamental Value: National League of Cities in Perspective," *Supreme Court Review* (1981), p. 81, pp. 100–108.

43. Roderick M. Hills, Jr., "The Political Economy of Cooperative Federalism: Why State Autonomy Makes Sense and 'Dual Federalism' Doesn't," *Michigan Law Review*, vol. 96 (1998), p. 813, p. 943, argues that this is the principal and most salutary effect of *Printz*.

44. An excellent account of this transaction is Jonathan H. Adler, "Clean Fuels, Dirty Air," in Michael S. Greve and Fred L. Smith, Jr., eds., *Environmental Politics: Public Costs, Private Rewards* (Praeger, 1992), p. 19.

45. Alex Daniels, "Tempest in a Tailpipe," *Governing Magazine*, vol. 8 (February 1995), p. 37. Two lawsuits challenging these and other regulatory programs under the 1990 Amendments revolved, predictably, around the commandeering of state resources. *Virginia v. Browner*, 80 F.3d 869 (4th Cir. 1996); *cert. denied*, 117 S. Ct. 764 (1997); *Missouri v. United States*, 109 F.3d 440 (8th Cir. 1997). Both lawsuits were unsuccessful, albeit in part for technical reasons.

46. In that sense, every federal law that precludes states from playing to their comparative advantages is an "unfunded mandate."

47. See, e.g., Walter Hellerstein, "Commerce Clause Restraints on State Tax Incentives," *University of Minnesota Law Review*, vol. 82 (1997), p. 413. In Congress, Rep. David Minge introduced a Distorting Subsidies Limitation Act (H.R.

3044, 105th Cong., 1st Sess.), which would impose an excise tax on "any person engaged in a trade or business who derives any benefit . . . from any targeted subsidy by any State or local governmental unit."

48. I exclude nonbusiness economic interests, especially labor unions, from the discussion because they consistently favor centralization, for reasons that should be obvious. Business warrants a more nuanced assessment.

49. On interest group choices of regulatory arenas, see Jonathan R. Macey, "Federal Deference to Local Regulators and the Economic Theory of Regulation: Toward a Public Choice Theory of Federalism," *Virginia Law Review*, vol. 76 (1990), p. 265.

50. Corporate chartering and credit card regulation are examples. See, respectively, Roberta Romano, *The Genius of American Corporate Law* (AEI Press, 1993); and Christopher C. DeMuth, "The Case against Credit Card Interest Rate Regulation," *Yale Journal on Regulation*, vol. 3 (1986), p. 201.

51. See George J. Benston, *The Separation of Commercial and Investment Banking: The Glass-Steagall Act Revisited and Reconsidered* (Oxford University Press, 1990).

52. Other developed nations view the idea as scandalous. Germany, for instance, requires a six-year education for certified computer technicians, with the predictable result of acute labor shortages and lagging innovation. William Dzordiak, "The German Status Quo," *Washington Post*, March 16, 1998, pp. A13–A14.

53. The reason that the Takings Clause of the Fifth Amendment—a seemingly firm constitutional constraint—can become a joke is that property owners must ordinarily bargain with the state (for instance, for construction or use permits). The constitutional right thus resembles a bargaining chip more than an *ex ante* restraint on government. Until roughly a decade ago, takings jurisprudence was extremely accommodating to government interests, which meant that the Fifth Amendment chip was worth next to nothing. Since then, however, the Supreme Court's takings decisions have become more favorable to property owners, thus improving their bargaining position. See, e.g., *Nollan* v. *California Coastal Commission*, 483 U.S. 825 (1987); *Lucas* v. *South Carolina Coastal Council*, 505 U.S. 1003 (1994); *Suitum* v. *Tahoe Regional Planning Authority*, 520 U.S. 725 (1997). A characteristically instructive analysis is Richard A. Epstein, *Bargaining with the State* (Princeton University Press, 1993), pp. 177–95.

54. For an analysis of the case, see Michael S. Greve, *The Demise of Environmentalism in American Law* (AEI Press, 1996), pp. 23–41, and (for the point in the text) the sources cited in id., p. 129.

55. See the overview by Edwin Chen, "A Closely Divided Congress Can't Get Traction on Legislation," *Los Angeles Times*, March 26, 1998, p. A5.

56. As recently as 1991, Congress overruled several Supreme Court decisions

on civil rights. Although Congress has since progressed from overruling the Court's civil rights decisions to ignoring them, a relapse is not out of the question. I examine the issue in chapter 8, pp. 128–29.

Chapter 8: The Court and Congress

1. The Gun Free School Zones Amendments Act added a jurisdictional predicate or nexus to interstate commerce that criminalizes the possession of a "firearm that has moved in or that otherwise affects interstate or foreign commerce." The Senate roll call vote to table this amendment was a lopsided twenty-seven to seventy-two. "Senate Votes Federal Gun-Free School Zones," *Human Events*, November 1, 1996, pp. 22–23. Among the backers of the amendment were such federalist stalwarts as Senators Abraham, Ashcroft, Gramm, Helms, Lott, McConnell, and Thurmond.

2. There are exceptions. The Fair Labor Standards Act, a New Deal statute, has remained a bone of constitutional contention to this day. But the general point stands.

3. For an analysis similar to (but less polemical than) the following paragraphs, see Ann Althouse, "Enforcing Federalism after *United States* v. *Lopez*," *Arizona Law Review*, vol. 38 (1996), p. 793, pp. 818–20.

4. Michael Fumento, "A Church Arson Epidemic? It's Smoke and Mirrors," *Wall Street Journal*, July 8, 1996, p. A8. See also Fumento, "Who's Fanning the Flames of Racism?" *Wall Street Journal*, June 16, 1997, p. A12. In a speech that provided the impetus for the consideration and, eventually, the unanimous enactment of the Church Arson Prevention Act of 1996 (18 U.S.C. § 247), President Clinton invoked his "vivid and painful memories of black churches being burned" during his Arkansas childhood. Those burnings, it turned out, never happened. "Arkansas Burning?" *Wall Street Journal*, June 21, 1996, p. A14.

5. See, e.g., David B. Kopel, "The Expanding Federal Police Power," in *Cato Handbook for Congress* (Cato Institute, 1996), pp. 197–204.

6. Congress could do so except for gun-wielding students with learning disabilities, who under federal law are entitled to special tutoring. See p. 128.

7. For example, the National Environmental Policy Act of 1970, the first federal statute of the modern environmental era, was originally intended as a wholly symbolic piece of legislation. With the assistance of the federal courts, it mutated into a comprehensive set of regulatory requirements. See Michael S. Greve, *The Demise of Environmentalism in American Law* (AEI Press, 1996), p. 126 and the sources cited therein.

8. Steven Calabresi, "A Government of Limited and Enumerated Powers: In Defense of *United States* v. *Lopez*," *Michigan Law Review*, vol. 94 (1995), p. 752,

p. 804, also argues that it is far too early to worry about judicial overreach in federalism cases.

9. The enactment of federal abortion restrictions under the Spending Clause would be a trickier proposition; a prohibition on abortions performed in interstate commerce would likely be constitutional. Neither of these suggestions, however, would reach all partial-birth abortions, and the proposed legislation does not contain a Spending Clause link or a jurisdictional predicate.

10. Obviously, the discussion here assumes that the Supreme Court addresses the (proposed) federal ban before an explicit ruling on the constitutionality of partial-birth abortion bans enacted by the states. The reverse sequence has already been discussed in chapter 7. Either way, judicial precedents and political calculations point to a federalist solution.

11. Confronted with a federal ban on partial-birth abortions, would Professor Laurence Tribe—a fierce defender of *Roe* and its progeny—have the gall to sing federalism's praises? Most likely, he would. As noted in chapter 5, n. 29, he is already on record for "states' rights" arguments on, of all things, civil rights questions.

12. The Defense of Marriage Act, Pub. L. No. 104-199, is codified at 1 U.S.C.A. 7, 28 U.S.C.A. 1738C. The observation in the text applies across ideological lines. President Clinton, a firm supporter of homosexual rights, was dismayed when insistent demands for the acceptance of homosexuals in the military derailed the ambitious program of his incoming first administration: Bob Woodward, *The Agenda* (Pocket Books, 1994), pp. 193–94. More recently, in 1998, Senator Lott found himself castigated for comparing homosexuality to kleptomania and alcoholism. See "Firestorm over Lott Remarks on Gays," *San Francisco Chronicle*, June 17, 1998, p. A1.

13. Congress has actually tried to deal with parental notification, one of the few areas of abortion regulation where the Supreme Court has left the states some latitude, in a manner quite similar to the Defense of Marriage Act. A proposed Child Custody Protection Act would criminalize the transport of a minor across state lines for the purposes of procuring an abortion. The explicit purpose of the bill is to protect the integrity of (widely varying) state regulations concerning parental consent. See T. R. Goldman, "Putting Teeth in Parental Consent Laws," *Legal Times*, May 25, 1998, p. 1.

14. See, e.g., Nelson Lund, "The Mandate Hoax of 1995," *National Review*, November 27, 1995, p. 52; and Daniel E. Troy, "The Unfunded Mandates Act of 1995," *Administrative Law Review*, vol. 49 (1997), p. 139, p. 143.

15. The Personal Responsibility Act permits official recognition that welfare problems in Utah are very different from those in New York City. For an account of the widely varying state responses to the act, see L. Jerome Gallagher et al., *One Year after Welfare Reform: A Description of State Temporary Assistance for Needy Families (TANF) Decisions as of October 1997* (Urban Institute, 1998).

16. Welfare rolls peaked in 1994 (before the enactment of the Personal Responsibility Act) and have steadily declined since then. A sophisticated analysis of the trend and its probable causes is Rebecca M. Blank, *What Goes Up Must Go Down? Explaining Recent Changes in Public Assistance Caseloads* (Joint Center on Poverty Research, October 1998).

17. Mark C. Gordon, "Differing Paradigms, Similar Flaws: Constructing a New Federalism in Congress and the Court," *Yale Law and Policy Review,* vol. 14 (1996), p. 187, pp. 214–15 (citing General Accounting Office studies).

18. For a description of the Reagan experience, see Gordon, "Differing Paradigms, Similar Flaws," pp. 193–94. The Democratic Leadership Council's Progressive Policy Institute has endorsed welfare swaps as a "progressive alternative" to half-hearted devolution but worries, with considerable justification, that such proposals will "prove difficult if not impossible" "so long as Congress and the President cannot resist the political pressure to intervene on any domestic concern that agitates focus group participants." Ed Kilgore and Kathleen Sylvester, "Blocking Devolution" (http://www.dlcppi.org/text/social (Policy Briefing February 16, 1995)). For the governors' continued demand for federal funding, see Garry Wills, "The War between the States . . . and Washington," *New York Times Magazine,* July 5, 1998, p. 26.

19. See T. R. Goldman, "Curbing Judges' Power over Prisons," *Legal Times,* November 24, 1997, p. 1.

20. See John J. DiIulio, "Questions for Crime-Buster Clinton," *Weekly Standard,* September 2, 1996, p. 24.

21. Most prison administrators welcome judicial oversight because it means fewer prisoners (on account of perceived constitutional prohibitions on overcrowding), much more money than any legislature would appropriate, and zero responsibility for policy outcomes.

22. The problem has arisen in several school districts under judicial supervision. With a graduate student's naiveté, I proposed a School Litigation Reform Act in 1983. Michael S. Greve, "Terminating School Desegregation Litigation," *Harvard Journal on Law and Public Policy,* vol. 7 (1983), p. 303. Since then, the conditions have become much more favorable. Even the National Association for the Advancement of Colored People has voiced doubts about the wisdom of elevating racial balancing over school quality, and a Democratic president is technically on record as supporting charter schools.

23. The Supreme Court has declined to hear two appellate decisions that sustained the PLRA: *Plyler* v. *Moore,* 100 F.3d 365 (4th Cir. 1996); *cert. denied,* 117 S. Ct. 2460 (1997); *Inmates of Suffolk County Jail* v. *Rufo,* 129 F.3d 649 (1st Cir. 1997); *cert. denied,* 118 S. Ct. 2366 (1998). Perhaps the safest indication that the Supreme Court will sustain the PLRA is that the notoriously intransigent Ninth

Circuit has struck it down. *Taylor* v. *U.S.* 143 F.3d 1178 (9th Cir. 1998) (Reinhard, J., opining that PLRA violates the separation of powers).

24. The Supreme Court's attempts to assist in the termination of judicial school district administration date back two decades. See *Pasadena City Board of Education* v. *Spangler*, 418 U.S. 717 (1974); *Freeman* v. *Pitts*, 503 U.S. 467 (1992); *Missouri* v. *Jenkins*, 515 U.S. 70 (1995). Despite these decisions, however, district courts have often failed to relinquish jurisdiction. A "school litigation reform act" along the lines suggested would send a much stronger signal than periodic Supreme Court exhortations. Depending on its wording, such an enactment might run up against the Supreme Court's decision in *Washington* v. *Seattle School District*, 458 U.S. 457 (1982), which invalidated a state referendum prohibiting local busing as a means of racial integration. But the absurd *Washington* decision was handed down by a narrow majority that has long ceased to exist. Among all the sitting ducks in the constitutional pond, *Washington* is one of the lamest.

25. R. Shep Melnick, "Federalism and the New Rights," *Yale Law and Policy Review*, vol. 14 (1996), p. 325, pp. 332–37. The article summarizes and updates Melnick's earlier book, R. Shep Melnick, *Between the Lines: Interpreting Welfare Rights* (Brookings Institution, 1994). Unless otherwise indicated, the following paragraphs are based on Melnick's penetrating analysis.

26. Mary Mannix et al., "Welfare Litigation Developments since the PRA," *Clearinghouse Review*, vol. 31 (January–February 1998), p. 435.

27. Melnick, "Federalism and the New Rights," pp. 342, 343, 346.

28. Such requirements, which are especially popular with states that wish to preserve relatively generous benefit levels without becoming welfare magnets, are said to interfere with the prospective welfare recipients' constitutional "right to interstate travel." *Shapiro* v. *Thompson*, 394 U.S. 618 (1969). *Shapiro*, a museum piece of the welfare rights era, is still good law. At this writing, however, the Supreme Court is reviewing an appellate decision that invalidated residency requirements. *Anderson* v. *Roe*, 134 F.3d 1400 (9th Cir. 1998).

29. Notably, the Personal Responsibility Act has eviscerated *Goldberg* v. *Kelly*, 397 U.S. 254 (1970), which held that statutory entitlements are a constitutional "property interest" whose denial must be preceded by due process hearings with the trappings of a criminal trial. As in statutory welfare rights cases, the Supreme Court subsequently retreated and limited *Goldberg* v. *Kelly*. The Personal Responsibility Act completes that development. Interpreting a "no-entitlement" provision virtually identical to the provision of the PRA, the D.C. Circuit has held that such provisions "reinforce" the conclusion that statutes conferring some measure of discretion on administrators do not create private property interests that trigger constitutional due process. *Washington Legal Clinic for the Homeless* v. *Barry*, 107 F.3d 32, 35–38 (D.C. Cir. 1997).

30. The Welfare Law Center (http://www.welfarelaw.org) publishes a periodic update on case developments, which confirms the pattern described in the text.

31. Jerry L. Mashaw and Dylan S. Calsyn, "Block Grants, Entitlements, and Federalism: A Conceptual Map of Contested Terrain," *Yale Law and Policy Review*, vol. 14 (1996), p. 297, pp. 305–6.

32. St. John Barrett, "The New Role of the Courts in Developing Public Welfare Law," *Duke Law Journal* (1970), p. 1, p. 8.

33. Melnick, *Between the Lines*, pp. 49–50.

34. The Religious Freedom Restoration Act, as noted, did little for the law-abiding members of mainstream religions, who are a core Republican constituency, and a lot for the incarcerated felon members of the church of the filet mignon, who are not. Similarly, the Equal Access Act, which prohibits the viewpoint-based exclusion of student groups from school facilities, was originally intended by its conservative supporters as a means of ensuring equal treatment for religious students. It did have that effect. In an effort to attract broad political support, however, the act was worded so broadly as to prohibit practically any viewpoint-based discrimination against student activities, with the result that school districts have been compelled to recognize groups with an explicitly sexual focus and orientation. Whatever the merits of this regime, it is at variance with the intent of its conservative sponsors.

35. Eskridge, "Overriding Supreme Court Statutory Decisions," *Yale Law Review*, vol. 101 (1991), p. 331. While factors such as the increased size of the congressional staff and the proliferation of interest groups partially account for the increased frequency of overrides, id., pp. 338–41, ideology seems to have played an independent role. As Eskridge concedes, his research method misses many statutory overrides (see Melnick, *Between the Lines*, p. 331 n. 13). But no apparent reason suggests that the undercount biases Eskridge's general results.

36. The judicial decision, *Commonwealth of Virginia v. Riley*, 106 F.3d 559 (4th Cir. 1997), was superseded by the 1997 Amendments to the Individuals with Disabilities Education Act, Pub. L. No. 105-17, § 612, 111 Stat. 37, 60, 28 U.S.C. § 1412. See *Amos v. Maryland Department of Public Safety*, 126 F.3d 589, 603 n. 8 (4th Cir. 1997); *vacated*, 118 S. Ct. 2339 (1998).

37. The Civil Rights Act reversed a dozen Supreme Court decisions. The most important among them were *Patterson v. McLean Credit Union*, 491 U.S. 164 (1989); *Martin v. Wilks*, 490 U.S. 754 (1989); and *Wards Cove Packing Co. v. Atonio*, 490 U.S. 642 (1989).

38. *Adarand Constructors v. Peña*, 515 U.S. 200 (1995) (federal race-based programs must be narrowly tailored to redress past discrimination). The voting rights cases are *Shaw v. Reno*, 509 U.S. 630 (1993); *Miller v. Johnson*, 515 U.S. 900 (1995); *Shaw v. Hunt*, 517 U.S. 899 (1996); and *Bush v. Vera*, 517 U.S. 952 (1996).

39. An arguable exception to this pattern is the reenactment of race-based contracting set-asides in federal transportation bills. Virtually identical provisions have already been declared unconstitutional (effectively so in the Supreme Court's *Adarand* decision and explicitly so in subsequent judicial decisions, see *Adarand Constructors* v. *Peña*, 965 F. Supp. 1556 (D. Colo. 1997); *In re Sherbrooke Sodding*, 17 F. Supp. 2d 1026 (D. Minn. 1998). But transportation set-asides constitute only a small fraction of the race-conscious federal programs that are highly suspect after *Adarand*. Moreover, the set-asides were reenacted without any accompanying attempt to create statutory language or legislative findings that would protect the program from legal challenges. This course of action does not signal a congressional will to confront or circumvent the courts. Rather, it signals a legislative desire to have judges do the dirty work of dismantling affirmative action.

40. *Gwaltney* v. *Chesapeake Bay Foundation*, 484 U.S. 49 (1984), was overturned in the Clean Air Act Amendments of 1990, § 707(g), 104 Stat. 2399, 2683 (1990).

41. *Lujan* v. *Defenders of Wildlife*, 504 U.S. 555 (1992). Cass Sunstein, "What's Standing after *Lujan*? Of Citizen Suits, 'Injuries,' and Article III," *Michigan Law Review*, vol. 91 (1992), p. 163, explains the scope of *Lujan* (p. 165) and proposes legislative remedies (p. 231).

42. See Eskridge, "Overriding Supreme Court Statutory Interpretation Decisions," p. 410 ("[F]ormalism substantially raises the costs of passing statutes. If statutes are costly to write and rewrite, fewer of them will exist.").

43. See, e.g., id., pp. 409–14.

Chapter 9: Federalism's Possibilities

1. Nor should anyone remember those measures. Despite the Reagan administration's firm federalist sentiments, the 1980s witnessed an "accumulation of new [federal] requirements roughly comparable to the record-setting pact of the 1970s." Timothy J. Conlan, "And the Beat Goes On: Intergovernmental Mandates and Preemption in an Era of Deregulation," *Publius*, vol. 21 (1991), p. 44.

2. Martin Shapiro, "The Supreme Court from Early Burger to Early Rehnquist," in Anthony King, ed., *The New American Political System*, 2d ed. (AEI Press, 1990), p. 47, pp. 49–53.

3. Alexis de Tocqueville, *Democracy in America* (J. P. Mayer, ed.) (Anchor Books, 1969), pp. 668–702.

4. Charles Murray, *What It Means to Be a Libertarian: A Personal Interpretation* (Broadway Books, 1997), pp. 144–62. This and the following paragraph in the text are based on Murray's splendid exposition.

5. In point of fact, the Supreme Court's precedents are much less restrictive.

They allow for local rent controls, *Pennell* v. *City of San Jose*, 485 U.S. 1 (1988), and for local controls on the "secondary effects" of sexual enterprises, *City of Renton* v. *Playtime Theatres*, 475 U.S. 41 (1986). But these precedents are odious to advocates of expansive rights (libertarians in the first instance, liberal civil libertarians in the second), and they do not affect the general point.

6. Clint Bolick, *Grassroots Tyranny: The Limits of Federalism* (Cato Institute, 1993), argues for an extraordinarily expansive understanding of federal rights under the Fourteenth Amendment.

7. I owe this example to Peter Schuck, "Some Reflections on the Federalism Debate," *Yale Law and Policy Review*, vol. 14 (1996), p. 1, pp. 17–19.

8. See Jim Chen, *"Filburn*'s Forgotten Footnote—Of Farm Team Federalism and Its Fate," *Minnesota Law Review*, vol. 82 (1997), p. 249. The quotation in the text appears in id., p. 300. Chen's view of the Agricultural Adjustment Act is more charitable than my own. He ascribes the *enactment* to the closure of foreign markets and portrays only the distributional *consequences* as an unintended result of Western overrepresentation. But Western interests were overrepresented at the time of enactment, a fact that suggests that the distributional consequences were anything but unintended.

9. William W. Van Alstyne, "The Second Death of Federalism," *Michigan Law Review*, vol. 83 (1985), p. 1709, p. 1709 and n. 3.

10. Justice Brandeis coined his famous phrase in the course of defending local price controls in a competitive market. *New State Ice Co.* v. *Liebman*, 285 U.S. 262, 311 (1932). Among the forms of regulation with which we need *not* experiment, price controls in competitive markets rank at the very top. They are never efficient.

11. Even the European voters, accustomed as they are to less-than-transparent politics and cozy welfare state protections, have understood this quite well. In Germany and Denmark, among other countries, the political class had to make inordinate efforts to bully a normally compliant populace into Europe's even more centralized, even less transparent future.

12. The comparison and the phrase are Richard Epstein's: "Constitutional Faith and the Commerce Clause," *Notre Dame Law Review*, vol. 71 (1996), p. 167, p. 190.

Index

About the Author

Michael S. Greve is a cofounder and, since 1989, the executive director of the Center for Individual Rights, a public interest law firm in Washington, D.C. He has taught political science at Hunter College, John Jay College, and Cornell University.

Mr. Greve's numerous articles on environmental law and policy have appeared in law reviews, scholarly journals, and newspapers. He is the author of *The Demise of Environmentalism in American Law* (AEI Press, 1996) and is coeditor, with Fred L. Smith, of *Environmental Politics: Public Costs, Private Rewards* (Praeger, 1992).

Mr. Greve is an adjunct scholar of the American Enterprise Institute and chairman of the Competitive Enterprise Institute. He received his M.A. and Ph.D. from Cornell University.